D0759728

CALLIMACHUS
III

LCL 550

CALLIMACHUS

MISCELLANEOUS EPICS
AND ELEGIES

OTHER FRAGMENTS

TESTIMONIA

EDITED AND TRANSLATED BY

DEE L. CLAYMAN

HARVARD UNIVERSITY PRESS
CAMBRIDGE, MASSACHUSETTS
LONDON, ENGLAND
2022

First published 2022

LOEB CLASSICAL LIBRARY® is a registered trademark
of the President and Fellows of Harvard College

Library of Congress Control Number 2022904856
CIP data available from the Library of Congress

ISBN 978-0-674-99749-3

*Composed in ZephGreek and ZephText by
Technologies 'N Typography, Merrimac, Massachusetts.
Printed on acid-free paper and bound by
Maple Press, York, Pennsylvania*

CONTENTS

MISCELLANEOUS EPICS
AND ELEGIES

INTRODUCTION

Pfeiffer himself grouped these poems together and entitled this section *Minor Epics and Elegies*. The title is not appropriate, because only one is written in dactylic hexameters (*Var.* 378–79), and we cannot judge the length or the significance of the others. Several are court poems, written for queens (*Var.* 392 for Arsinoe; *Var.* 383, 387–88 for Berenice II) and an influential minister (*Var.* 384 for Sosibius). More likely, the title refers to the paucity of fragments in every case except *The Victory of Sosibius* (*Var.* 384) and to the sparse testimonia that tell us little of the poems' contents.

TITLES, CONTENTS, AND DATES

The *Galatea* (*Var.* 378–79), which is the only "epic," tells the story of the Nereid Galatea, with whom the Cyclops Polyphemus was famously in love (Theoc. *Id.* 11; Call. *Epig.* 46). Her son Galates was the eponymous mythological leader of the Gauls. Since the historical Gauls made an aborted invasion of Greece in 279/8 BC that Callimachus describes in his *Hymn to Delos* (*Hymn* 4.171–87), the poem may have been an epic celebration of the victory that was claimed in the *Hymn* for Ptolemy Philadelphus.

The contents of the elegiac *Grapheion* are unknown.

The word means "Archive," and the only fragment (*Var.* 380) seems to be about the iambic poet Archilochus, suggesting that it may have included other literary caricatures.

There are no surviving fragments of Callimachus' *Ibis* (*Var.* 381–82), which is known only indirectly through comments in the scholia to Ovid's *Ibis*, which it apparently inspired. These suggest in turn that it contained veiled curses on one or more of Callimachus' unnamed enemies.

In this group Pfeiffer also placed fragments of elegies complimenting the poet's royal patrons, including two epinician poems celebrating victories at the Panhellenic games. Callimachus did editorial work on the fifth-century giants of this genre, Simonides, Pindar, and Bacchylides, and also compiled a chronology of the games (*Fr. Doct.* 403). An elegy on a Nemean victory of Berenice II (*Var.* 383) is now known to be part of Book 3 of the *Aetia* (*Aet.* 54–60j), almost certainly its opening *aition*. Additional fragments of it were published by Meillier in 1976 and again by Parsons the subsequent year. Since Berenice came to Egypt to be married in 246 BC, the poem must have been written after that date. The other *epinicion* is *The Victory of Sosibius* (*Var.* 384–384a), who was likely the minister of that name who became prominent in the reign of Ptolemy Euergetes and dominant in the court of his successor, Philopater.[1] The identity of the honorand suggests a date of composition around 240 BC, toward the end of Callimachus' life.

The Victory of Sosibius (*Var.* 384), which is extant in about sixty lines with substantial gaps between sections of

---

[1] On which Sosibius Callimachus intended to honor, see Fuhrer 1992, 144–49.

continuous verse, was originally about twice as long. It does not focus on one particular victory, but like Pindar's *Nemean* 10 (Pind. *Nem.* 10.25–31) it surveys an entire career, including victories in chariot racing at the Isthmian (1–15) and Nemean games (16–34), enlivened by a few words in praise of his nursling from the Nile himself (27–34). Two other victories are also celebrated, one as a youth in the men's wrestling at the Panathenaic games (35–39) and another in the *diaulos* (a footrace) at the Ptolemaea or Basilaea (39–41). These are recounted by the honorand himself, who also describes two dedications he made to mark the occasions: statues of the Charites in the temple of Hera at Argos (44–46) and a gift to Zeus Casius in Pelusium (47–50). The latter includes a quotation from the statue's dedicatory epigram (50). Finally, the character of Sosibius is praised by the poet in terms familiar from encomia (53–58). The poem's language and contents have several points in common with Pindar's *Odes* and with epinician epigrams.

With the victory poems, Pfeiffer grouped three other elegiac fragments containing references to the Ptolemies. In *Var.* 387, only "before," "star" and "Berenice" can be read securely, suggesting that it relates to the "Coma Berenices," though exactly how is not clear, since the "Coma" itself is a constellation of faint stars that cannot be distinguished by the naked eye. *Var.* 388 contains the names of Berenice and Magas, the father of Berenice II, who is called "king," and also the word "marriage." Magas was Berenice's father, a half brother of Ptolemy Philadelphus who was made governor of Cyrene by his stepfather, Ptolemy Soter, and only later declared himself king. The date of his death is uncertain, but it preceded Berenice's marriage to Ptolemy Euergetes in 246 BC, which he had originally arranged.[2] It is notable that Callimachus names her birthfather here. Later she became an honorary "sister" of her husband, and official documents as well as Callimachus' poems speak of her parents as Arsinoe II and Ptolemy II.[3] *Var.* 388 also contains an elaborate compliment to Berenice expressed as a series of *adynata* (9–11).

Var. 392 is the first verse of a poem for the wedding of Arsinoe, likely Arsinoe II. It is addressed to a stranger, which suggests a sympotic setting. The marriage, her third and his second, took place between 276 and 273/4[4] BC and was controversial because the couple were full siblings. The subject required delicate handling, and Callimachus must have treated it deftly because his career at court continued uninterrupted. It was likely written to mark the occasion.

CONSTITUTION AND HISTORY OF THE TEXT

These texts were brought together by Pfeiffer in volume 1 of his *Callimachus* in 1949 based on affinities of meter and contents. Fragments of *The Victory of Sosibius* (*Var.* 384) and the other elegies on Berenice were found in *P.Oxy.* 1793 (1st c. AD, ed. Grenfell), purchased in 1919 at the

---

[2] After his death the arrangement was briefly undone by his wife, Apame. For Berenice's lurid Cyrenean backstory, see Clayman 2014, 30–41.

[3] One example of many is the Canopus decree (*OGIS* 56). In the "Coma," the poet, addressing Berenice, speaks of "the ox-piercer of your mother Arsinoe" (*Aet.* 110.45); and in the "Victoria Berenices," she is "bride, sacred offspring of the sibling gods" (*Aet.* 54.2), i.e., of Arsinoe II and Ptolemy II.

[4] Carney 2013, 70.

site of Oxyrhynchus and published in 1922. This text is supplemented by *P.Oxy.* 2258 fr. 2 (7th c. AD, with scholia), which overlaps it in part and supplies the latter portions of the extant text. It was supplied to Pfeiffer by its editor, Edgar Lobel, before its formal publication in 1952, and Pfeiffer refers to it initially as "*P.Oxy. ined.*" Here, the opening lines of "Sosibius" immediately follow the end of the "Coma Berenices" (110–110f) minus its epilogue (112),[5] while in *P.Oxy.* 1793 the "Sosibius" is preceded by the elegy for Berenice and Magas (388).

CATALOG OF PAPYRI

The list of relevant papyri below follows the numbering and order of Mertens-Pack[3], the online database of the Center de documentation de papyrologie littéraire (CEDOPAL) at the Université de Liège, which provides additional information and bibliography.[6] Each entry begins with the inventory number assigned by Mertens-Pack[3], followed by the series name in standard abbreviations, the number in Pfeiffer, its estimated date, and the verses in the *Var.* that it supplies.

> 00186.000: *P.Oxy.* 2258 (+ *P.Oxy.* 30, pp. 91–92; *SH* 290–91). Pap. 37 Pf. 6th–7th c. AD. *Var.* 384.1–42 and schol.
>
> 00234.000: *P.Oxy.* 1793. Pap. 4 Pf. 1st c. AD. *Var.* 384.6–391.

---

5 This suggests that the "Coma," which concludes Book 4 of the *Aetia*, also circulated independently.

6 Additional information about the papyri can also be found in Pfeiffer vol. 2, ix–xxvi; *SH* 89–122; Lehnus 2011, 23–38; Asper 2004, 537–39.

BIBLIOGRAPHY

Barbantani, Silvia. "Receiving the Komos: Ancient and Modern Receptions of the Victory Ode." *Bulletin of the Institute of Classical Studies* Suppl. 112 (2012): 37–55.

Fuhrer, Therese. *Die Auseinandersetzung mit den Chorlyrikern in den Epinikien des Kallimachos.* Basel: Reinhardt, 1992.

Stephens, Susan. "Celebrating the Games." In *Callimachus Revisited*, edited by J. J. H. Klooster, M. Annette Harder, et al., 351–67. Groningen: Peeters, 2019.

CARMINA EPICA
ET ELEGIACA VARIA

ΓΑΛΑΤΕΙΑ

378 Ath. 7.284c

Θεόκριτος . . . ἐν τῇ ἐπιγραφομένῃ Βερενίκῃ τὸν λεύκον ὀνομαζόμενον ἰχθῦν ἱερὸν καλεῖ . . . Καλλίμαχος δ᾽ ἐν Γαλατείᾳ τὸν χρύσοφρυν,

> ἢ μᾶλλον χρύσειον ἐν ὀφρύσιν ἱερὸν ἰχθύν
> ἢ πέρκας ὅσα τ᾽ ἄλλα φέρει βυθὸς ἄσπετος
> ἅλμης

379 Schol. ad Dionys. Per. 74

Γαλάτης ῥόος· οἱ ἐν τῇ Ἀσίᾳ Γαλάται τῶν ἐν τῇ Εὐρώπῃ ἄποικοί εἰσιν . . . περὶ ὧν φησι καὶ Καλλίμαχος,

> οὓς Βρέννος ἀφ᾽ ἑσπερίοιο θαλάσσης
> ἤγαγεν Ἑλλήνων ἐπ᾽ ἀνάστασιν

MISCELLANEOUS EPICS
AND ELEGIES

GALATEIA

378 Athenaeus, *The Learned Banqueters*

Theocritus, in his *Berenice* calls the white fish sacred . . .
Callimachus in his *Galateia* calls it the gilt-head,

> or rather a sacred fish with gold on its brows
> or perch, or others the endless depth of the sea bears

379 Scholia to Dionysius Periegetes

A Galatian stream: the Gauls in Asia, some of whom are
settlers in Europe . . . about whom Callimachus says,

> [The Galatians] whom Brennus[1] led from the west-
> ern sea to the destruction of the Greeks[2]

---

[1] Leader of the Gauls during their invasion of Greece in 279/8
BC. They were defeated in an attack against Delphi (Paus.
10.22.12–23.14).   [2] *Hymn* 4.171–87.

ΓΡΑΦΕΙΟΝ

380 *Anon. Ambros. de re metrica* (Schoell and Studemund 1886, p. 224)

εἵλκυσε δὲ δριμύν τε χόλον κυνὸς ὀξύ τε κέντρον
σφηκός, ἀπ᾽ ἀμφοτέρων δ᾽ ἰὸν ἔχει στομάτων.[1]

[1] στομάτων codd.: στόματος Schneider, Pfeiffer

ΙΒΙΣ

381 Schol. B ad Ov. *Ib*. 315

Dareus secundus, primi Darei filius . . . iuravit quod cives suos veneno sicut primus non interficeret. Postquam vero fuit in regno, non veneno, sed ponens eos in arca plena calido cinere interficiebat, ut Callimachus dicit contra suum Ibin.

382 Schol. B ad Ov. *Ib*. 449

Callimachus scribit de ibide, quod purgat se rostro proiciens aquam per posteriora.

VICTORIA BERENIKES

383 Pf. = *Aet.* 54

GRAPHEION

380 Anonymous metrician

> He sucked up the fierce anger of the dog and the
>   sharp sting
> of the wasp; he has the poison from both mouths.[1]

[1] A characterization of an iambic poet, probably Archilochus,
on whom, see Introduction to the *Iambi*.

IBIS

381 Scholia to Ovid, *Ibis*

Darius the Second, son of Darius the First . . . swore that
he would not kill his own citizens by poison like his father
did. But afterward it happened in the kingdom that he
killed them not by poison, but by putting them in a chest
full of hot ashes, as Callimachus says against his own Ibis.

382 Scholia to Ovid, *Ibis*

Callimachus writes about the ibis that it cleans itself by
projecting water from its beak through its hindquarters.

THE VICTORY OF BERENICE

383 Pf. = *Aet.* 54

ΣΩΣΙΒΙΟΥ ΝΙΚΗ

Titulus in Schol. ad Lyc. *Alex.* 522.

384 1–15, *P.Oxy.* 2258 fr. 2 verso, 9–22; 6–13, *P.Oxy.* 1793
col. VI, 1–8; 16–34, *P.Oxy.* 2258 fr. 2 recto, 1–19; 23–30,
P.Oxy. 1793 col. VII, 1–8; 36–43, *P.Oxy.* 1793 col. VIII,
1–8; 44–52, *P.Oxy.* 1793 col. IX, 1–9; 50, Schol. ad Ar. *Av.*
598a (p. 99 Holwerda); 53–61, *P.Oxy.* 1793 col. X, 1–9.

Κ̣α̣ὶ̣ [   ]. [ ]λ̣[
   σπεί̣σ̣ωμεν¹   ] ετελειο[
. .σε. .ουπι[   ] τ νο̣ν̣[
   ᾧ τὸ μὲν ἐξ Ἐφύρης ἅρμα, σελι̣ νοφόρον
5 νεῖον ἀπ' οὖ̣ν̣ ̣μέμβλ̣.ωκεν· ἔ̣τι χνόον
   ἄξονος Ἀσβύστης ἵππος ἔναυλον ἔχει.
  σημερινὸν δ' ὡσεί περ ἐμὸν περὶ χεῖλος ἀΐσσει
   τοῦτ' ἔπος ἠδείῃ λεχθὲν ἐπ' ἀγγελίῃ·
  "δαῖμον ὃς ἀμφοτέρωθεν ἁλιζώνοιο κάθησαι
10 στείνεος, ἀρχαίοις ὅρκιε Σισυφίδαις,
  ἐν π[ο]δὶ ληγούσης Πελοπηΐδος ἱερὸν ἰσθμόν,
   τῇ μὲν Κρωμνίτην τῇ δὲ Λέχαιον ἔχ̣ων,
  ἔνθα ποδῶν ἵνα χειρὸς ἵνα κρίσις ὀξέο[ς ἵππου
   ἰθυτάτη, χρυσὸν δ' εὐδικίη παραθεῖ,
15 χρυσὸν ὃν ἀνθρώποι[σ]ι καλὸν κακὸν ἔτραφ[ε] μ̣]
   ὑ̣[ρ̣μ̣η̣]ξ . . ."²

[Desunt fere 4 vv.]

THE VICTORY OF SOSIBIUS

384 Oxyrhynchus papyri

And . . .

Let us pour a libation . . . for whom the chariot carrying the celery [crown][1] [5] came back lately from Ephyra.[2] The Asbystian[3] horse still has the dusty roar of the axle (in its ears), and as if it were today, this word, which was spoken at the time of the sweet announcement, darts about my lip: "O Lord who sits on both sides [10] of the salty strait,[4] invoked by the ancient sons of Sisyphus,[5] the sacred isthmus at the extremity of the Peloponnese, having Cromna on one side and Lechaeum on the other,[6] where the judgment of feet, of hand, and of fiery horse is most fair, and righteousness outruns gold—[15] gold a beautiful evil for men which the ant produces . . ."[7]

[About 4 verses missing]

[1] Victors at the Isthmian games were awarded crowns of celery (Diod. Sic. 16.79.3–4). [2] An ancient name for Corinth (Paus. 2.1.1). [3] The Asbystae were a nomadic people whom the Greeks encountered in Libya, renowned for their skills driving four-horse chariots (Hdt. 4.170). [4] Poseidon, who presides over the Isthmus of Corinth (Paus. 2.1.6). [5] The mythical founder of Corinth (Apollod. *Bibl.* 1.9.3). [6] The ancient harbors of Corinth (Paus. 2.2.3). [7] On the questionable value of gold and its ant miners, see *Iamb* 12 (*Ia.* 202.58–59, 64).

---

[1] Suppl. Lobel et Schol. [2] Fin. leg. Maas

```
                    ] [
                ]οιαγεν[
      ]ν ξ[            ]ε . ν· [
   ] οθε [           ] μ' ἀγων [
20  ]λας δ[ ]....σε [   ] ται
      ]υσεν, ἐπ' αὐτίκ[α δ' ἄλ]λα³ σέλινα
   τοῖς ἀπὸ Πειρήνης ἤγαγεν Ἀ[ργο]λικά,
   ὄφρα κε Σωσίβιόν τις Ἀλεξάνδρου τε πύθηται
   γῆν⁴ ἐπὶ καὶ ναίων Κίνυφι διστεφέα
25 ἀμφοτέρῳ παρὰ παιδί,⁵ κασιγνήτῳ τε Λεάρχου
   καὶ τὸ Μυριναῖον τῷ γάλα θησαμένῳ,
   θηλύτατον καὶ Νεῖλο[ς ἄ]γων ἐνιαύσιον ὕδωρ
   ὧδ' εἴπ[ῃ]· "καλά μοι θρεπτὸς ἔτεισε γέρα
   ...[...οὐ] γάρ πώ τις ἐπ[ὶ] πτόλιν ἤγαγ' ἄεθλον
30     ] . ταφίων τῶνδε πανηγυρίων
      κ]αὶ πουλύς, ὃν οὐδ' ὅθεν ο῀ι̇δεν ὁδεύω
   θνητὸ ͜ς ἀνήρ, ἐνὶ γοῦν τῷδ' ἔα λιτότερος
   κε[ίνω]ν, οὓς ἀμογητὶ διὰ σφυρὰ λευκὰ γυναικῶν
   κ[αὶ πα]ῖς⁶ ἀβρέκτῳ γούνατι πεζὸς ἔβη . . ."
```

[Desunt fere 8 vv.]

```
35 "— καὶ παρ' Ἀθηναίοις γὰρ ἐπὶ στέγος ἱερὸν ἧνται,
   κάλπιδες, οὐ κόσμου σύμβολον, ἀλλὰ πάλης⁷—
```

---

³ Suppl. Loeb   ⁴ γῆν Housman: την pap.

⁵ ἀμφοτέρῳ παρὰ παιδί corr. Hunt: -τερωπαραπαιδε *P.Oxy.* 1793: -τεροι]σπαραπ[αισι *P.Oxy.* 2258: -τερωπαραπαιδος Schol.   ⁶ Suppl. Hunt   ⁷ πάλης Schol. ad Pind.: πάτης *P.Oxy.* 1793

[21] And at once he added another, an Argive[8] celery [crown],[9] to those he brought from Peirene,[10] so that an Alexandrian and someone living on the banks of the river Cinyps[11] might learn that Sosibius was twice-crowned [25] beside the two children, the brother of Learchus[12] and the one who sucked the milk of Myrina,[13] so the Nile may say as it brings its nourishing annual flood, "A lovely gift of honor has my child paid back, for never has anyone brought to the city a double prize [30] from these funerary games . . . and huge though I am, and no mortal man knows from where I come, in this one respect I am more paltry than those which the white ankles of women cross without effort and a child crosses on foot without wetting their knees . . ."

[About 8 verses missing]

[35] ". . . and in Athens urns sit under a sacred roof, not as an ornament, but a token of wrestling, when unafraid

---

[8] Argos took control of the Nemean games at the end of the fifth century, and the games were located there after 271 BC. For the connection between Argos, Nemea, Ptolemaic self-fashioning, and the "Victoria Berenices," see Clayman 2014, 145–47.

[9] Callimachus tells how Heracles crowned himself with celery after slaying the Nemean lion (*Aet.* 54i).   [10] A fountain at Corinth (Paus. 2.3.2).   [11] A river in Libya (Hdt. 4.175).

[12] Melicertes, who died leaping into the sea with his mother, Ino, while escaping the anger of his father, Athamas (*Aet.* 91–92a). The Isthmian games were founded in his honor.

[13] Opheltes, whose death is commemorated by the Nemean games. He was the foster son of Hypsipyle, daughter of Myrina (Paus. 2.15.2–3).

ἄνδρας ὅτ᾽ οὐ δείσαντες ἐδώκαμεν ἡδὺ βοῆσαι
  νηὸν ἔπι Γλαυκῆς κῶμον ἄγοντι χορῷ
Ἀρχιλόχου νικαῖον ἐφύμνιον· ἐκ δὲ διαύλου,
40   Λαγείδη, παρὰ σοὶ πρῶτον ἀεθλοφορεῖν
εἱλάμεθα, Πτολεμ[αῖ]ε, τεῇ π[. . .]ρ ἡνίκ᾽ ἐλεγχ[. .
  . . .]†τετις ελαιη†[. . . . .]ου κονίῃ
. . . . . .]ῳ βασιλ[. . . . .]αχθει[. . . ”

[Desunt fere 13 vv.]

“ἀμφοτέρων ὁ ξεῖνος ἐπήβολος· οὐκέτι γυμνάς
45   παῖδας ἐν Ἡραίῳ στήσομεν Εὐρυνόμης.”
ὡς φαμένῳ δώσει τις ἀνὴρ ὁμόφωνον ἀοιδήν.
  τοῦτο μὲν ἐξ ἄλλων ἔκλυον ἱρὸν ἐγώ,
κεῖνό γε μὴν ἴδον αὐτός, ὃ πὰρ ποδὶ κάτθετο Νείλου
  νειατίῳ, Κασίην εἰς ἐπίκωμος ἅλα·
50   “Κυπρόθε Σιδόνιο‚ς[8] μ‚ε κατήγαγεν ἐνθάδε γα‚ῦλ‚ος”
  . .]‚ ωεκκε[. . . . .]ωσαθεων
[23 litt.   ]φν[

[Desunt fere 13 vv.]

καὶ τὸν ἐφ᾽ οὗ νίκαισιν ἀείδομεν, ἄρθμια δήμῳ
  εἰδότα καὶ μικρῶν[9] οὐκ ἐπιληθόμενον,
55   παύριστον τό κεν ἀνδρὶ παρ᾽ ἀφνειῷ τις ἴδοιτο
  ᾧτινι μὴ κρε[ί]σσων ᾖ νόος[10] εὐτυχίης·

---

[8] Κυπρόθε Σιδόνιο‚ς Schol. ad Ar.: κυπροθενειδονδιο *P.Oxy.*
1793   [9] καὶ μικρῶν G. Murray et Lobel: τὸν μικρῶν Hunt
ειδοταουκεπιμικρων *P.Oxy.* 1793   [10] ᾖ νόος coni. Hunt:
ητινοσς *P.Oxy.* 1793

of the men[14] we gave the chorus that accompanied the cortège to the temple of Glauce,[15] the chance to sing something sweet, the victory song of Archilochus.[16] And in the *diaulos*,[17] [40] O Ptolemy son of Lagus,[18] we first chose to carry off the prize near you when . . ."

[About 13 verses missing]

"The stranger, winner of both [prizes]. No more will he set up nude [45] statues of the children of Eurynome[19] in the temple of Hera."[20] After saying this someone will sing in unison with him. I heard from others about this holy offering, but I myself saw the one that he dedicated at the lowest foot of the Nile in a procession to the Casian Sea.[21] [50] "A Sidonian[22] merchant ship brought me from Cyprus . . ."

[About 13 verses missing]

We sing of him for his victories, who in his character is united with the people, nor does he forget the lowly, [55] something one sees rarely in a rich man, whose mind is not mightier than his good fortune. Neither will I praise

[14] Sosibius apparently competed as a youth in the men's wrestling contest.   [15] An epithet of Athena referring either to her birth in the sea or to the color of her eyes (Theoc. *Id*. 28.1).

[16] Sung also at Olympia (Pind. *Ol*. 9.1).   [17] A footrace of two laps around the stadium (Pind. *Pyth*. 10.9; Paus. 5.17.6).

[18] Ptolemy I Soter, for whom the Ptolemaea were established by Philadelphus circa 280 BC (*Syll*.[3] 390).   [19] Mother of the Graces (Hes. *Theog*. 907–9).   [20] Presumably, the Heraeon at Argos in celebration of Sosibius' victory at Nemea.

[21] To the temple of Zeus Casius near Pelusium (Strabo 1.2.31; Ach. Tat. 3.6).   [22] Phoenician.

οὔτε τὸν αἰνήσω τόσον ἄξ[ι]ος οὔτε λάθωμαι
  —δείδια γὰρ δήμου γλῶσσαν ἐπ' ἀμφοτέροις—,
μ.[..]ομενωιδ[.]πησιν[.].οὐδέπ[οτ' ἐ]σθλὸν ἔρεξεν
60   ερ[...]ψ[ε]υδὴς α[..].καπ[.........
[35 litt.   ]ν

384a Hephaestion 15 (p. 52 Consbruch)

  ἱερά, νῦν δὲ Διοσκουρίδεω γενεή

384b (vol. 1, pp. 311–15 Pf.) Schol. ad 1–32; P.Oxy. 2258
fr. 2 verso + fr. 2 recto

384.1 in marg. infer.

].κρειοντ( )· γέγραπται ἡ ἐλεγεία εἰς . . . Σωσιβίου
τοῦ Διοσκουρίδου ηνικ( ) γεγονοτ [ ] [οὗτο]ς ὁ Σωσί-
βιος λογογράφος ἦν Πτολεμαί[ο]υ, καὶ διὰ τιμῆς
αὐτὸν εἶχεν. τούτου ο.[ ] ... φ. εἰς αὐτόν. ποιητικὸ(ν)
δὲ τὸ ἀπὸ συνδέσμου ἄρχεσθ(αι)· Ἀλκμάν· "κ(αὶ) δ'
αὖ μετ[ ]"

384.2 in marg. sin.

...[..]να..σπείσωμεν

him as much as he is worthy, nor may I forget him; for I fear the tongue of the people in both cases . . . not ever has he said anything good [60] . . . than false . . .

384a Hephaestion

. . . sacred, but now the family of Dioscorides[1]

[1] Father of Sosibius (Schol.).

384b Oxyrhynchus papyrus (scholia)

384.1 (lower margin)

The elegy was written about Sosibius the son of Dioscurides when he lived . . . this Sosibius was a court official of Ptolemy[1] and he held him in honor . . . for him. The poem begins with a conjunction; [an example is in] Alcman, "and again with . . ."

[1] Ptolemy III Euergetes.

384.2 (left margin)

. . . let us pour a libation

384.4 in marg. sin.

ᾧ· ᾧτινι, τῷ Σωσιβίῳ

in marg. infer.

ᾧ τὸ μὲν ἐξ Ἐ]φύρης· ᾧτινι, τῷ Σωσιβίῳ· Ἐφύρα δὲ
ἡ Κόρινθ(ος). σεληνοφ[όρ]ον δὲ ἔφη τὸ ἅρ[μα διὰ τὸ
φορεῖν σ]τέφανον·[1] οἱ γὰρ νικ(ῶν)τες τὰ Ἴσθμια σε-
λίνῳ στέφονται

[1] Sugg. Pfeiffer

384.5 in marg. sin.

νεῖον· νεωστί
μέμβλ(ωκεν)· ἀφῖκται· ἄρτι ἐλήλυθεν

384.5–6 in marg. infer.

ἔτι χνόον [ ] τρι[γ]μόν· τοῦτον δέ, φ(ησί), τὸν τριγ-
μὸν ἔχει ὁ Κυρηνα[ϊ]κὸς ἵππος το [ ]διάφοροι δὲ καὶ
ἀγωνιστικοὶ οἱ Κυρηναϊκ[οὶ] ἵπποι. Ἀσβύται.[

384.7–10 in marg. dext.

[ ] .. [ ] ματτ[ ]ενε τοσπε[ ]οσεστιν. ιονε[(οἷον?) [
[]ματος ὁ μέλλων [

384.4 (left margin)

(*h*)*ōi*: (*h*)*ōitini* (for whom), for Sosibius

(lower margin)

for whom the [chariot] from Ephyra: for whom, for Sosibius. Ephyra is Corinth. He says the chariot was celery-bearing because it carried the crown. Those who were victorious at the Isthmian games were crowned with celery.

384.5 (left margin)

neion: just now.
memblōken: it arrived; just now it came.

384.5–6 (lower margin)

still dusty . . . creaking: he says this, the Cyrenean horse has the creaking [chariot] . . . excellent and fit for the contest, Cyrenean horses. The Asbystai . . .

384.7–10 (right margin)

. . . the one about to . . .

384.9–12 in marg. sin.

ἀλιζώνοιο· ἀλίζωνον εἶπ(ε) τὴν Κόρινθον διὰ τὸ δυσὶ
θαλάσσαις διεζῶσθαι, τῇ τε πρὸς τῷ Λεχαίῳ καὶ τῇ
ἐν τ̣[αῖς] Κεγχρεαῖ̣[ς. στεῖ]νος δὲ [εἶπε τὸν] ['Ι]σθμόν·
οἱ μὲν οὖν $\overline{\lambda\beta}$ [σ]ταδίων φ[ασὶ] τὸ μ̣ε̣ταξὺ δυεῖν

384.12 in marg. dext.

οὗτοι τόποι τῆς Κορίνθ(ου)· κ̣(αὶ) λ[ ]αφ(ων) κα̣ι̣
σπονδ(ῶν) Κρωμνι.[ ] Λέχαιο[ν] καλεῖται

384.14–15 in marg. dext.

χρυ[σὸν] δ' εὐδικίη παραθ(εῖ)· κα̣.. τὸ δικη .[] φ(ησὶν)
ἐκεῖ δικάζουσι κ[προσλα....[

384.15–23 in marg. infer.

[τοῖς ἔπι δῆθε̣(εν)· ἐν τούτοις []

384.20–22 in marg. dext.

φυλλα̣[ ] ο̣ι̣ουο.̣.[α[ ]..........[ ].. σαντας· [τοῖς
'Ι<σ>θμιονικ... ἐπήγαγε τὰ Νεμεακά·

384.21 in marg. infer.

] φ(ησὶ) λούεσθαι ἵππον νικήσ[αν]τ̣α τοὺς προειρημέ-
νους ἀγῶνας

384.9–12 (left margin)

sea-girt: he said that Corinth is sea-girt because it is surrounded by two seas, on one side [is] Lechaeus . . . and on the other is Cechraea. He says the Isthmus is narrow. They say there are thirty-two stadia between the two.

384.12 (right margin)

These are places in Corinth. And . . . and drink-offerings at Cromna. It is called Lechaeus.

384.14–15 (right margin)

he compares righteous and gold: . . . the just . . . he says there they pass judgment . . .

384.15–23 (lower margin)

. . . A circumlocution; in these . . .

384.20–22 (right margin)

. . . leaf (pelting?) . . . he gained Isthmian and Nemean victories.

384.21 (lower margin)

. . . he says that the horse that won the aforementioned contests was bathed.

384.22 in marg. infer.

]τοῖς ἀπὸ Πειρήνης ἤγαγ(εν) Ἀ[ργο]λικ(ά)· ἀπὸ Κο-
ρίνθου κ(αὶ) Ἰσθμ[ο]ῦ· ἡ φ[ὰ]ρ Πειρήνη κρήνη ἐν Κο-
ρίνθῳ []...ν.κ... ἀγῶνά φ(ησιν) ἐπακολουθηκ[έ]ναι
τὰ Ν[έ]μεα εἰς ἃ καὶ [ἐ]πίνικος γέγραπται [ ] τὸν
Νεμεακὸν ἀγῶνα δηλοῖ.

384.23–24 in marg. infer.

ὄφρα κε Σωσίβιόν τις· ἵνα κ(αὶ) τῆς τοῦ Σωσιβί[ου]
νίκης ἀκούσωσιν κ(αὶ) οἱ πόρρω οἰκοῦντες ἐπὶ τῷ
Κίνυφι, μὴ μόνον οἱ ἐν Ἀλεξανδρ[ε]ίᾳ. Κίν[υψ] .νος
τῆς αρ.εως ὁρίζ(ων) τὴν Καρχη[δ]ονίων χώραν· ἐστὶ
δὲ κ(αὶ) πόλις.[ ] διστεφέα διὰ τὸ δὶς νικῆσαι τὸν
Σωσίβιον.

in marg. dext.

ἵνα οὖν αὐτ[ὸν] καὶ Ἀλεξανδρεῖς καὶ Λίβυες ἀκούσω-
σιν διστεφέᾳ. Κίνυψ ποταμὸς τῆς Λιβύη[ς]

384.25–26 in marg. dext.

ἀμφοτέρῳ παρὰ παιδί· τὸν Μελικέρτην λέγ(ει) καὶ τὸν
Ἀρχέμορον· ἐπὶ μὲν γὰρ τῷ Μελικέρτῃ τίθεται τὰ
Ἴσθμια, ἐπὶ δὲ τῷ Ἀρχεμόρῳ τὰ Νέμεα.

super

⟨κασιγνήτῳ τε Λεάρχου⟩· τῷ Μελικέρτῃ

384.22 (lower margin)

He brought Argolic [victories] from Peirene: from Corinth
and the Isthmus. Peirene is a fountain in Corinth . . . he
says that the contest followed the Nemea for which the
victory ode was written . . . he means the Nemean contest.

384.23–24 (lower margin)

so that someone [might hear of] Sosibius: so that even
those that were living at a distance by the Cinyps might
hear of the contest of Sosibius, not only the ones in Alex-
andria. Cinyps . . . marks the boundary of the Carthaginian
land. It is also a city . . . Sosibius is twice-crowned because
he won two victories.

(right margin)

So that both the Alexandrians and the Libyans might hear
that he was twice-crowned. The river Cinyps of Libya . . .

384.25–26 (right margin)

beside both children: he speaks of Melicertes and Arche-
morus. The Isthmian games are held for Melicertes, the
Nemeans for Archemorus.

(above)

brother of Learchus: Melicertes.

in marg. infer.

καὶ τὸ Μυριναῖον· τ [ ] [Μυ]ριναῖ[ον] γάλα τὸ τῆς Ὑψι-
πύλης· καὶ γὰρ κ(α)τ(ὰ) Εὐριπίδ(ην) τροφὸς ἦν τοῦ
Ἀρχεμόρου[ ] Λήμν[ῳ] Μύρινα καὶ Ἡφαίστεια· ἀπὸ
τῆς Ὑψιπύλης οὖν τὸ τ(ῆς) Ὑψιπύλ(ης) .[ ] .ι. . .ν τὸ
τῆς Ὑ. γάλα καλεῖται Μυριναῖον

384.30 supra lineam

. . .τῶν περιοδικῶν

in marg. dext.

ἐπιτάφιοι ΄[ ] .ν.ι περιοδικ[οί

in marg. sin. litt. vestigia

384.31 in marg. dext.

οὐδ᾽ ὅθεν οἶδ(εν)· ρρζ[ ]ε οὐδὲ .[ ].πο.[

384.32 in marg. sin.

[ἐ]νὶ γοῦν τῶδ᾽ ἔα λι[τότ(ερος)· τούτω μόνω ε. .λ. .το-
μην

384.33 κ .[. . .] νους ἀμόγητι

384.34 κ[αὶ πα]ῖς

(lower margin)

and the Myrinean: the Myrinean milk of Hypsipyle; she
was the nurse of Archemorus according to Euripides . . .
on Lemnos Myrina and Hephaestaea . . . ; from Hypsipyle
therefore . . . the milk is called Myrinean.

384.30 (above the line)

of the recurrent

(right margin)

the funeral games: . . . recurrent

384.31 (right margin)

and one does not know from where: . . .

384.32 (left margin)

and in this one respect, more paltry: in this alone . . .

384.33 without effort

384.34 and the child

ELEGIARUM FRAGMENTA
INCERTAE SEDIS

385 1–3, *P.Oxy.* 1793 col. I, 1–3

$$]\ldots\xi\hat{v}v$$
$$\lambda\ldots\tau\ldots[$$
$$].[.]\tau$$

. . . .

386 1–2, *P.Oxy.* 1793 col. II, 1–2

$$]\eta\ \pi\rho\grave{\iota}v\ \check{a}v\alpha\xi\,.[\ldots]\,.\iota v\alpha\tau\,..[$$
$$]\tau\rho v\ldots.[\ldots].\,.[$$

. . . .

387 1–4, *P.Oxy.* 1794 col. III, 1–4

$$]\ldots\kappa\alpha\ldots\acute{\omega}\ldots\acute{\epsilon}\,[\ldots]\grave{}\,[.]\acute{a}\mu\epsilon\nu\alpha\iota$$
$$]\ldots\mu\iota\varsigma\ \kappa\lambda\epsilon\acute{\iota}\ldots\pi\rho\grave{\iota}v\ \grave{a}\sigma\tau\acute{\epsilon}[\rho\iota\ \tau]\hat{\omega}\ \text{B}\epsilon\rho\epsilon\nu\acute{\iota}\kappa\eta\varsigma$$
$$]\ldots\acute{\iota}\delta\alpha\ \beta ov[.]\,.\mu\,\acute{.}\pi[.\,.]\epsilon\,.[\ldots]v\cdot$$
$$]\ldots[.]\tau\alpha.\alpha\ldots[\ldots]\,.\epsilon\theta\acute{\eta}\sigma\epsilon\iota v$$

. . . .

388 1–5, *P.Oxy.* 1793 col. IV, 1–5; 6–11, col. V, 1–6 + fr. 1

$$]\acute{\iota}\delta\iota ov\ \pi o\lambda\acute{v}\pi\alpha\lambda\tau ov\ \acute{v}\pi\grave{\epsilon}\rho\,.\alpha\lambda\,.\alpha\sigma ov\ \gamma\acute{\alpha}\mu o\varsigma\ \eta\tau\ldots$$
$$]\,.\tau\eta\iota\kappa\alpha o\mu\eta v\ \epsilon\grave{v}\ldots\sigma\ldots\epsilon\iota\rho\iota\tau\iota\alpha\iota$$
$$]\,.v\eta\ \beta\alpha\sigma\iota\lambda\hat{\eta}\alpha\ \sigma\grave{\epsilon}\ldots\pi\rho\,.[.]\ \delta'\ \grave{a}\kappa\rho\omega[\ldots\ldots\ldots]$$
$$]\,.\,.\ \pi\acute{\alpha}v\tau\omega v\ \pi\acute{\alpha}[v]\tau\alpha\ \tau\epsilon\lambda\epsilon\iota\acute{o}\tau\alpha\tau\epsilon$$

ELEGIAC FRAGMENTS
OF UNCERTAIN PLACEMENT

385 Oxyrhynchus papyrus

. . .

386 Oxyrhynchus papyrus

formerly the leader . . .

387 Oxyrhynchus papyrus

. . . before by the star of Berenice . . .

388 Oxyrhynchus papyrus

. . . much-brandished above . . . marriage . . . the king . . .

5   ]ου μετ[..].νου..[   ]χιϲτον

. . . .

..]μμα μὲν αἰδ[.].αυταπ...[....]ια
τόϲϲα Μάγαν βαϲιλῆα τ..εν λ......[...]...[
τό]ϲϲα τὸν ἐν μη.[.].τευ.[......]υνναν ἔτι,
Φωκαέων μέχριϲ κε μέϙη .μέγαϲ ε.ἰν ἁλὶ μύδροϲ,

10   ἄχ]ρι τέκῃ Παλλὰ[ϲ κῇ γάμοϲ] Ἀρ[τ]έμιδι,
....]ϲ ἀεὶ πανάριϲτ[α μέ]νειν α[....] Βερενίκῃ

. . . .

389 *P.Oxy.* 1793 fr. 2

[
τα[
ζ[

. . . . . .

389a *P.Oxy.* 1793 fr. 3

]ουσα κ.[
]γέπω[

. . . .

390 *P.Oxy.* 1793 fr. 4

]..βόεϲ ἔντ[
]΅ρ.[

. . . .

at the height . . . [O] most accomplished of all in every
respect . . . as many as . . . king Magas[1] . . . so many . . . as
long as the great anvil of the Phocians stays in the sea,[2]
[10] until Pallas gives birth and Artemis marries always
will all good things remain for Berenice.

[1] Father of Berenice II and king of Cyrene. He was the half
brother of Ptolemy II Philadelphus, whom their father had ap-
pointed governor of the Cyrenaica. See Clayman 2014, 30–32.
[2] Cf. Hdt. 1.165.

389, **389a**, **390**, **391** Oxyrhynchus papyrus (unintelligi-
ble fragments)

391 *P.Oxy.* 1793 fr. 5

]σμενε...[
].εχν.[
. . . . .

IN ARSINOES NUPTIAS?

392 Schol. ad Pind. *Nem.* 11.1a

καταβολὰν ἱερῶν ἀγώνων· . . . τὴν καταβολὴν τουτ-
έστι τὴν ἀρχὴν καὶ τὸν θεμέλιον τῶν ἱερῶν ἀγώνων
. . . ὅτι δὲ καταβολὰς ἔλεγον τὰς ἀρχὰς οὑτινοσοῦν
ἔπους, Καλλίμαχός φησιν· "Ἀρσινόης—ἀείδειν." μετ-
ῆκται δὲ ἡ λέξις ἀπὸ τῶν τὰς οἰκίας κατασκευαζόν-
των καὶ βαλλόντων τοὺς θεμελίους.

Ἀρσινόης ὦ ξεῖνε γάμον καταβάλλομ᾽ ἀείδειν

ON THE MARRIAGE OF ARSINOE?

392 Scholia to Pindar, *Nemean Odes*

the beginning of the sacred contests: . . . the beginning, that is to say, the start and the foundation of the sacred contests . . . Callimachus says that they call the beginnings of any poem the foundations: "O stranger, I begin to sing . . ." the word is a metaphor taken from building and casting the foundations.

O stranger, I begin to sing of the marriage of Arsinoe[1]

[1] Arsinoe II, wife and sister of Ptolemy II Philadelphus. The marriage took place some time between 276 and 273 BC. See Fraser 1972 vol. 2, 367n228; Carney 2013, 70.

SCHOLARLY FRAGMENTS

INTRODUCTION

Pfeiffer collected Callimachus' prose under the heading
Fragmenta grammatica (Grammatical Fragments), but
the title is misleading. These are fragments, many of
them just titles, of a variety of scholarly works in roughly
four categories: bibliography, paradoxography, etiology,
and onomastics.[1] For greater clarity this section has been
retitled *Fragmenta docta* (Scholarly Fragments).

Of greatest interest is Callimachus' work on bibliogra-
phy, a field he likely invented.[2] The three titles in this
group are called *Pinakes* (Indexes). The *Index and Regis-
ter of the Dramatic Poets in Order From the Beginning*
(*Fr. Doct.* 454–56) is based on Aristotle's *Didascaliae*, a
record of performances with information about the dates
and results of the tragic and comic festivals in Athens. The
Index of the Glosses and Writings of Democritus, of which
there are no fragments, was perhaps similar to the collec-
tion attributed to Callimachus' older contemporary Phile-

---

[1] Nita Krevans, "Callimachus' Philology." In *Brill's Compan-
ion to Callimachus*, ed. Benjamin Acosta-Hughes, Luigi Lehnus,
and Susan Stephens (Leiden: Brill, 2011), 120. There are also a
few titles that cannot be categorized at all: *Hypomnemata* (Com-
mentaries?) (*Fr. Doct.* 461–64), *Peri logadōn* (*Fr. Doct.* 412), and
Mouseion (*Fr. Doct.* 412).

[2] Blum 1991, 244.

tas of Cos.[3] It may have been a subdivision of Callimachus' bibliographical masterwork, the *Index of All Those Pre-eminent in Literature and of Their Writings in 120 Books* (*Fr. Doct.* 429–53). This general index was organized by genre, including both poetry and prose. Within the subdivisions authors were listed alphabetically with short biographies, and line totals were added for each title and/or incipit (*Fr. Doct.* 433–34). It appears that Callimachus himself provided titles for some of the works, and he sometimes expresses uncertainty about attributions (*Fr. Doct.* 437, 442, 444–47, 449). Some believe that this *Pinax* was in fact a catalog of the great Library of Alexandria, but it is better characterized as a kind of encyclopedia of Greek literature.[4]

Another of Callimachus' prose works relating to literature is *Against Praxiphanes* (*Fr. Doct.* 460). This refers to Praxiphanes of Mytilene, a noted Peripatetic identified by the Scholia Florentina as one of the Telchines, Callimachus' mythic critics in the Prologue to the *Aetia*. Though there are good reasons to doubt this,[5] the work contains praise for the poetry of Aratus,[6] so it appears to have been a literary discussion in prose complementing the programmatic passages in his poetry.

Paradoxography is another field in which Callima-

---

[3] Philetas was the author of *Ataktoi Glossai*, comments on rare words including Homeric hapax legomena. See P. Bing, "The Unruly Tongue: Philetas of Cos as Scholar and Poet," *CP* 98 (2003): 330–48.

[4] Blum (1991, 239) calls it "a national bibliography."

[5] Cameron 1995, 376–77, and Lefkowitz 2012, 119–20.

[6] Aratus of Soli, also praised in *Epig.* 27.

chus was apparently a pioneer. His *Collection of Marvels throughout the World by Location* is represented by forty-four fragments preserved by Antigonus of Carystus, who quoted Callimachus directly in his own book of marvels, the *Mirabilia* (*Fr. Doct.* 407). Here Callimachus provides information about natural wonders that he found in written sources, usually fourth-century historians and ethnographers.[7] He cites his sources carefully, and briefly describes each apparently unnatural phenomenon without trying to explain it. As with the *Pinakes*, Callimachus had Peripatetic predecessors in this genre,[8] but it was he who set the standards followed by his successors.

Thanks to Antigonus, there are ample fragments from Callimachus' *Marvels*, but we know little of his other works in prose. Among the etiological works, only a single fragment remains of his *On Contests* (*Fr. Doct.* 403), one of *Barbarian Customs* (*Fr. Doct.* 405), and one bare title: *Foundations of Islands and Cities and Their Changes of Name* (*Fr. Doct.* 412a). In each case, Callimachus benefitted from the efforts of predecessors: Duris of Samos (*On Contests*), Hellanicus (*Barbarian Customs*), and Timaeus (*Foundations*), among others.

The fourth category, onomastics or nomenclature, is wider and includes *On Winds* (*Fr. Doct.* 404), *On Birds* (*Fr. Doct.* 414–428), *On Rivers of the Inhabited World* (*Fr. Doct.* 457–59), *On Nymphs* (*Fr. Doct.* 413), *Names of the Months by Tribes and Cities* (*Fr. Doct.* 412), and, again, *Foundations of Islands and Cities and Their Changes of*

---

[7] Including Pseudo-Aristotle, Ctesias, Lycus, Eudoxus, Theopompus, Theophrastus, and Timaeus.

[8] On Peripatetic influence, see Fraser 1972 vol. 1, 454, 770–71.

Name (*Fr. Doct.* 412). There is little information about how these works were organized or what sources Callimachus consulted. His interest in subjects like these spills over into his poetry, and the *Aetia* shows how such a wealth of material expanded his worldview and enriched his poetic language.

THE AFTERLIFE OF CALLIMACHUS' PROSE

Though not as well known to modern readers as his poetry, Callimachus' prose was influential in its own right, especially the *Pinakes*, which became a standard reference tool that was consulted for centuries on bibliographical questions such as attribution and authenticity. In the first century BC, Dionysius of Halicarnassus complains that neither Callimachus nor the *Pinakes* prepared at the Library in Pergamum give sufficient information about the orator Dinarchus (*Fr. Doct.* 447), and Athenaeus (2nd–3rd c. AD) cites Callimachus several times on questions of attribution (*Fr. Doct.* 437, 440). Since it is unlikely that either had a complete copy of the *Pinakes*, sections of it must have been available to scholars far from Alexandria, and once the Library's collection was dispersed, it became an authority on what had been lost.

Paradoxography continued to attract interest after Callimachus, though the tendency of authors to incorporate information from earlier sources without attribution makes it difficult to trace his influence. Two better known Greek paradoxographers are Antigonus of Carystus (3rd c. BC), who rearranged and occasionally complained about Callimachus's material, and Phlego of Tralles, who lived under Hadrian and had more lurid tastes. Varro and Cicero (both 2nd–1st c. BC) wrote learned works in Latin that might have owed something to Callimachus.

HISTORY AND CONSTITUTION
OF THE TEXT

There are no papyrus sources for Callimachus' prose, and the fragments remain almost unchanged from the time when Bentley collected them for publication in Graevius' edition of 1697. He collected them from a number of ancient sources, especially Athenaeus, who provides extracts of the *Wonders*; the scholia on Aristophanes' *Birds*, which cite Callimachus' *On Birds*; and the *Suda* (13th c. AD), a prime source for Callimachus' prose titles generally, and especially for the *Pinakes*. Pfeiffer produced the canonical modern text on which the present edition is based.

BIBLIOGRAPHY

Blum, Rudolf. *Kallimachus: The Alexandrian Library and the Origins of Bibliography*. Translated by H. H. Wellisch. Madison, WI: University of Wisconsin Press, 1991.

Giannini, Alessandro. *Paradoxographorum Graecorum Reliquiae*. Classici greci e latini. Sez. Testi e commenti, III. Milan: Istituto editoriale italiano, 1966.

Krevans, Nita. "Callimachus and the Pedestrian Muse." In *Callimachus II*, edited by M. Annette Harder et al., 173–83. Leuven: Peeters, 2004.

———. "Callimachus' Philology." In *Brill's Companion to Callimachus*, edited by Susan Stephens and Benjamin Acosta-Hughes, 118–33. Leiden: Brill, 2011.

Kwapisz, Jan, and Katarzyna Pietruczuk. "Your Own Personal Library of Alexandria: Callimachus' Scholarly Works and Their Readers." In *Callimachus Revisited: New Perspectives in Callimachean Scholarship*, edited by J. J. H. Klooster et al., 221–47. Leuven: Peeters, 2019.

Pfeiffer, Rudolf. *History of Classical Scholarship. From the Beginnings to the End of the Hellenistic Age*. Oxford: Oxford University Press, 1968. *Pinakes*, 127–34; other prose, 134–39.

FRAGMENTA DOCTA

ΠΕΡΙ ΑΓΩΝΩΝ

403 Harpocration s.v. Ἄκτια

. . . Ἄκτια ἀγὼν παλαιὸς ἦν ὡς δῆλον ποιεῖ Καλλίμαχος ἐν τῷ Περὶ ἀγώνων.

ΠΕΡΙ ΑΝΕΜΩΝ

404 Ach. Tat. *Isagog. in Arat.* (p. 68.18 Maass)

καὶ τοὺς μὲν ἐκ νεφῶν λέγουσιν εἶναι ἀνέμους καὶ καλεῖσθαι ἐκνεφίας, τοὺς δὲ ἀπὸ γῆς φερομένους ἀπογείους, . . . παρὰ Ἀριστοτέλει ἐν τῷ Περὶ ἀνέμων καὶ παρὰ Καλλιμάχῳ ὥστε καὶ ἀπὸ τόπων τινὰς λέγεσθαι, οἷον Καικίαν τὸν ἀπὸ Καΐκου τοῦ ποταμοῦ πνέοντα καὶ Σκείρωνα τὸν ἀπὸ τῶν Σκειρωνίδων πετρῶν.

SCHOLARLY FRAGMENTS

ON CONTESTS

403 Harpocration, *Lexicon of the Ten Orators*

. . . Actia was an ancient contest, as Callimachus makes clear in *On Contests*.

ON WINDS

404 Achilles Tatius, *Introduction to Aratus*

They say that winds that come from clouds are called *eknephiai* (from clouds) and the ones borne from the earth are called *apogeioi* (from the earth) . . . and some are named from places by Aristotle in *On Winds* and by Callimachus such as the Caecean wind blowing from the river Caïcus[1] and the Sceiron blowing from the Sceironian rocks.[2]

---

[1] The Caïcus flows from Mysia in Pitane (Plin. *HN* 5.121).

[2] The Sceironian rocks were a cliff on the Isthmus of Corinth, where the robber Sceiron murdered passersby by forcing them to wash his feet and then throwing them over the precipice, where they were eaten by a giant sea turtle (Paus. 1.44.8; Diod. Sic. 4.59.4; *Hec.* 59–60).

ΒΑΡΒΑΡΙΚΑ ΝΟΜΙΜΑ

405 Phot. *Lex.* s.v. Φασηλιτῶν θῦμα

Φασηλιτῶν θῦμα· ἐπὶ τῶν εὐτελῶν καὶ ἀναίμων τίθε-
ται· Φασηλίτας γὰρ τάριχον τῷ Κυλάβρᾳ θύειν φησὶ
Καλλίμαχος ἐν Βαρβαρικοῖς νομίμοις.

ΕΘΝΙΚΑΙ ΟΝΟΜΑΣΙΑΙ

406 Ath. 7.329a

Καλλίμαχος δ᾽ ἐν Ἐθνικαῖς Ὀνομασίαις γράφει οὕ-
τως· "ἐγκρασίχολος ἐρίτιμος Χαλκηδόνιοι. τριχίδια,
χαλκίς, ἴκταρ, ἀθερίνη." ἐν ἄλλῳ δὲ μέρει καταλέγων
ἰχθύων ὀνομασίας φησίν· "ὄζαινα, ὀσμύλιον Θούριοι·
ἴωπες, ἐρίτιμοι Ἀθηναῖοι."

ΘΑΤΜΑΤΩΝ ΤΩΝ ΕΙΣ ΑΠΑΣΑΝ ΤΗΝ
ΓΗΝ ΚΑΤΑ ΤΟΠΟΥΣ ΟΝΤΩΝ
ΣΤΝΑΓΩΓΗ

Titulus in *Suda* (v. test. 1).

407 Antig. Car. 129–73 (cod. Palat. Gr. 398)

(I) 129. Πεποίηται δέ τινα καὶ ὁ Κυρηναῖος Καλλίμα-
χος ἐκλογὴν τῶν παραδόξων, ἧς ἀναγράφομεν ὅσα
ποτὲ ἡμῖν ἐφαίνετο εἶναι ἀκοῆς ἄξια. φησὶν Εὔδοξον[1]

---

[1] Fr. 347 Lasserre 1966

BARBARIAN CUSTOMS

405 Photius, *Lexicon*

The Sacrifice at Phaselis: it is an expression applied to offerings that are meager and bloodless. Callimachus says in *Barbarian Customs* that the people of Phaselis[1] sacrifice pickled meat to Cylabra.[2]

[1] A town on the south coast of Bithynia (Strabo 14.3.9).
[2] A shepherd who had a hero cult in Lycia (Ath. 7.297e–98a).

NATIONAL NAMES

406 Athenaeus, *The Learned Banqueters*

Callimachus in *National Names* writes as follows: "anchovy (the Chalcedonians call it *eritimos*), pilchardlets, sardine, brisling, sand-smelt." In another part he lists names of fish and says, "*ozaina* (the Thurians call it *osmulion*); and *iōpes* (the Athenians call them *eritimoi*)."

COLLECTION OF MARVELS THROUGHOUT THE WORLD BY LOCATION

407 Antigonus of Carystus, *Mirabilia*[1]

(I) 129. Callimachus of Cyrene made a selection of paradoxes from which we record whichever at some time seemed to us to be worthy of acclaim. He says that Eu-

[1] Arabic numerals refer to the text of the *Mirabilia*; Roman numerals were assigned to each subfragment by Pfeiffer.

ἱστορεῖν, ὅτι ἐν τῇ κατὰ Ἱερὸν ὄρος θαλάττῃ τῆς Θρᾴκης ἐπιπολάζει κατά τινας χρόνους ἄσφαλτος, ἡ δὲ κατὰ Χελιδονίας ὅτι ἐπὶ πολὺν τόπον ἔχει γλυκείας πηγάς.

(II) 130. Θεόφραστον[1] δὲ τὴν περὶ τὰς Αἰόλου νήσους ἀναζεῖν οὕτως ἐπὶ δύο πλέθρων τὸ μῆκος, ὥστε μὴ δυνατὸν εἶναι διὰ τὴν θερμασίαν ἐμβαίνειν εἰς ταύτην.

[1] Fr. 196A Sharples vol. 3.1, 1998

(III) 131. Ἐκ δὲ τῆς κατὰ Δημόνησον τὴν Καλχηδονίων τοὺς κολυμβητὰς ἀναφέρειν εἰς δύο ὀργυιὰς χαλκόν, ἐξ οὗ καὶ τοὺς ἐν Φενεῷ τοὺς ὑπὸ Ἡρακλέους ἀνατεθέντας ἀνδριάντας εἰργάσθαι.

(IV) 132. Μεγασθένην[1] δὲ τὸν τὰ Ἰνδικὰ γεγραφότα ἱστορεῖν ἐν τῇ κατὰ τὴν Ἰνδικὴν θαλάττῃ δένδρεα φύεσθαι.

[1] BNJ 715 F 25

doxus[2] wrote that bitumin floats for some time in the Thracian sea below Mt. Hieron[3] and that the sea below Chelidonia[4] has fountains of sweet water in many places.

[2] Eudoxus of Cnidus (4th c. BC), astronomer and mathematician.   [3] Mountain in southeastern Thrace, now called Ganos.
[4] Chelidonia, a promontory in Cilicia (Livy 33.20.2).

(II) 130. [Callimachus says that] Theophrastus[1] [writes that] the sea around the islands of Aeolus[2] boils along the length of its two sides so that it is not possible to land on it on account of the heat.

[1] Theophrastus (4th c. BC), Peripatetic philosopher and successor of Aristotle as head of that school.   [2] Group of volcanic islands off the northwestern coast of Sicily.

(III) 131. [He says that Theophrastus writes[1] that] from the Calydonian sea opposite Demonesus[2] divers brought up bronze from a depth of two fathoms from which were fashioned statues of Heracles in Pheneus.[3]

[1] Perhaps in his *On Metals* (Pf.)   [2] An island near Chalcedon (Steph. Byz. δ 64 Billerbeck).   [3] A plain in northeastern Arcadia (Paus. 8.14.3).

(IV) 132. [He says that] Megasthenes,[1] who wrote the *Indica*, says that in the sea opposite India trees grow.

[1] Historian (4th c. BC) who traveled to India and wrote an account of it in four books; he stayed at the court of Chandragupta.

(V) 133. Περὶ δὲ τῶν ποταμῶν καὶ κρηνῶν Λύκον[1] μέν φησιν λέγειν, ὅτι ὁ μὲν Καμικὸς θαλάττης †ῥεούσης ῥεῖ†, ὁ δὲ †Κάπαιος καὶ Κριμισὸς ὅτι τὰ μὲν ἐπιπολῆς τῶν ὑδάτων εἰσὶ ψυχροί, τὰ δὲ κάτω θερμοί, τὸν δ' Ἱμέραν ἐκ μιᾶς πηγῆς σχιζόμενον τὸ μὲν ἁλυκὸν τῶν ῥείθρων ἔχειν, τὸ δὲ πότιμον.

[1] BNJ 570 F 9

(VI) 134. Τίμαιον[1] δὲ τῶν ἐν Ἰταλίᾳ ποταμῶν ἱστορεῖν Κρᾶθιν ξανθίζειν τὰς τρίχας.

[1] BNJ 566 F 46

(VII) 135. Πολύκριτον[1] δὲ καταγεγραφέναι τὸν μὲν ἐν Σόλοις οὐ ψευδῶς ὠνομάσθαι Λίπαριν, ἀλλ' οὕτως ἀπολιπαίνειν ⟨τοὺς λουομένους⟩ ὥστε μὴ προσδεῖσθαι ἀλείμματος, τὸν δὲ ἐν Παμφυλίᾳ Μούαβιν [?] ἀπολιθοῦν, ἐάν τις ἐμβάλῃ στοιβὴν ἢ πλίνθον.

[1] BNJ 128 F 11a

(V) 133. In *On Rivers and Springs* he asserts that Lycus[1] says of the Camicus,[2] which flows from the sea, and the Crimisus that these are cool at the top of the water and warm below and that the Himera[3] is divided from one source into two channels, one salty and the other potable.

[1] Lycus of Rhegium, also called Butheras (4th–3rd c. BC).
[2] The text is corrupt here, and three names of rivers can be read: Camicus, Capaeus, and Crimisus. On the Camicus in Sicily, see Duris of Samos (*BNJ* 76 F 59).   [3] Himera, a river and a city in Sicily (*BNJ* 76 F 59). On the river Himera, see Vitr. *De arch.* 8.3.7.

(VI) 134. [He says that] Timaeus[1] observes that of the rivers in Italy the Crathis[2] turns hair yellow.

[1] Greek historian (4th–3rd c. BC), who was first to organize the chronology of events by Olympiads.   [2] On the unusual power of the Crathis, Eur. *Tro.* 224–29. Pliny says it could turn sheep and cattle white (*HN* 31.9–10).

(VII) 135. [He says that] Polycritus[1] writes that the river Liparis in Soli[2] is not named falsely, but it is so oily that there is no need for grease, and the river Muabis in Pamphylia[3] turns to stone if anyone throws branches or a brick into it.

[1] Or perhaps Polyclitus of Larisa (historian, 4th c. BC).
[2] A town in Cilicia near the river Liparis (Vitr. *De arch.* 8.3.8).   [3] Pamphylia, coastal area in southern Asia Minor between Lycia and Cilicia.

(VIII) 136. Περὶ δὲ τὴν τῶν Ἀγριέων[1] Θρᾳκῶν χώραν φησὶν ποταμὸν προσαγορευόμενον Πόντον καταφέρειν λίθους ἀνθρακώδεις, τούτους δὲ κάεσθαι μέν, πᾶν δὲ τοὐναντίον πάσχειν τοῖς ἐκ τῶν ξύλων ἀνθρακευομένοις· ὑπὸ μὲν γὰρ τῶν ῥιπίδων πνευματιζομένους σβέννυσθαι, τῷ δὲ ὕδατι ῥαινομένους βέλτιον κάεσθαι, τὴν δ' ὀσμὴν αὐτῶν οὐδὲν ὑπομένειν ἑρπετόν.

[1] *BNJ* 115 F 268a

(IX) 137. Τὴν δ' ἐν Λούσοις κρήνην, καθάπερ παρὰ τοῖς Λαμψακηνοῖς, ἔχειν ἐν ἑαυτῇ μῦς ὁμοίους τοῖς κατοικιδίοις· ἱστορεῖν δὲ ταῦτα Θεόπομπον.[1]

[1] *BNJ* 115 F 269

(X) 138. Εὔδοξον[1] δὲ τὴν ἐν Ἅλῳ Ὀφιοῦσσαν τὸν ἀλφὸν παύειν.

[1] Fr. 355 Lasserre 1966

(XI) 139. Λύκον δὲ τὸν Ῥηγῖνον[1] λέγειν, τὴν μὲν ἐν τῇ Σικανῶν χώρᾳ φέρειν ὄξος, ᾧπερ ἐπὶ τῶν ἐδεσμάτων χρῶνται, τὴν δὲ ἐν Μυτιστράτῳ οἷον ἐλαίῳ ῥεῖν· τοῦτο δ' ἔν τε τοῖς λύχνοις κάεσθαι καὶ δύνασθαι φύ-

[1] *BNJ* 570 F 9

(VIII) 136. In the land of the Agrieis[1] of Thrace he says that the river that is called Pontus brings down carbonized rocks and that when these are burned everything is affected in the opposite way from those carbonized by wood. When these are fanned by bellows they are extinguished and when sprinkled with water they burn better and no creeping thing can stand the smell.

[1] A Paeonian tribe.

(IX) 137. [He says that] a spring in Lusi[1] just like the one at Lampsacus has mice in it like house mice and that Theopompus writes about these matters.

[1] City in Arcadia (Paus. 8.18.8); on the mice, see Plin. *HN* 31.10.

(X) 138. [He says that] Eudoxus[1] wrote that the white Ophiussa[2] in Halus[3] ceased to flow.

[1] Astronomer and mathematician (4th c. BC).   [2] "Snake Island," but here it seems to be a river.   [3] A city in Achaea or Thessaly. On various places called Halus, see Strabo 9.5.8.

(XI) 139. [He says that] Lycus of Rhegium says that [a river] in the land of the Sicanians[1] carries vinegar, which they use with food and that similarly one flows in Mytistratus[2] with oil. This is burned in lamps and is able to heal

[1] The Sicilians (Paus. 5.25.6).   [2] Town in Sicily three times besieged by the Romans (Diod. Sic. 23.9.1).

CALLIMACHUS

ματα καὶ ψώραν ἰᾶσθαι, προσαγορευόμενον Μυτι-
στράτιον. πλησίον δὲ εἶναι τὴν ἀπὸ μὲν Ἀρκτούρου
μέχρι Πλειάδος ἀναβάλλουσαν οὐδενὸς χεῖρον τῶν
ἄλλων ὑδάτων, ἀπὸ δὲ Πλειάδος μέχρι πρὸς Ἀρκτοῦ-
ρον τῆς μὲν ἡμέρας καπνὸν ἀναφέρουσαν καὶ πνέου-
σαν θερμόν, ἐν δὲ τῇ νυκτὶ φλογὸς πληρουμένην.

(XII) 140. Ἀρέθουσαν δὲ τὴν ἐν Συρακούσαις, (ὥσπερ
οἱ λοιποί φασιν καὶ Πίνδαρος), τὴν πηγὴν ἔχειν ἐκ
τοῦ κατὰ τὴν Ἠλείαν Ἀλφειοῦ, διὸ καὶ ταῖς Ὀλυμπι-
καῖς ἡμέραις, ὅταν ἐν τῷ ποταμῷ ἀποπλύνωσιν τῶν
θυμάτων τὰς κοιλίας, οὐ καθαρὰν εἶναι τὴν ἐν τῇ Σι-
κελίᾳ κρήνην, ἀλλὰ ῥεῖν ὄνθῳ. φησὶν δὲ καὶ φιάλην
ποτ' εἰς τὸν Ἀλφειὸν ἐμβληθεῖσαν ἐν ἐκείνῃ φανῆναι.
(τοῦτο δ' ἱστορεῖ καὶ Τίμαιος.)

(XIII) 141. Θεόπομπον[1] δέ φησιν γράφειν τῆς μὲν ἐν
Κίγχρωψιν τοῖς Θρᾳξὶν τὸν ἀπογευσάμενον τελευτᾶν
εὐθύς.

[1] BNJ 115 F 270a

(XIV) 142. Ἐν Σκοτούσσῃ δ' εἶναι κρηνίδιον οὐ μόνον
ἀνθρώπων ἕλκη, ἀλλὰ καὶ βοσκημάτων ὑγιάζειν δυ-
νάμενον· κἂν ξύλον δὲ σχίσας ἢ θραύσας ἐμβάλῃς
συμφύειν.[1]

[1] BNJ 115 F 271a

52

tumors and mange. It is called mytistratian. When the rising of Arcturus[3] to the Pleiades is near, it is not inferior to other bodies of water, but from the Pleiades to Arcturus it brings up smoke and breathes out heat by day, and at night it is full of flame.

[3] The time of the heliacal rising of the star Arcturus in spring.

(XII) 140. [He says that] the Arethusa in Syracuse (as the rest say, even Pindar)[1] has its source from the Alpheus[2] in Elis. Therefore even on Olympic days, when they wash the innards from the sacrifices in the river, the spring in Sicily is not clean, but it flows with dung. He says that a bowl once thrown into the Alpheus is not visible in it. (Timaeus wrote this.)

[1] Pind. *Nem.* 1.1.
[2] River in northwestern Arcadia (Paus. 5.7.1).

(XIII) 141. [He says that] Theopompus[1] writes that among the Cinchropes in Thrace [there is a river] and anyone who tastes it, dies at once.

[1] Theopompus of Chios (4th c. BC), historian.

(XIV) 142. In Scotussa[1] is a little spring able to heal wounds of men and also of cattle. And if you toss in wood that you have split or shattered, it grows together.

[1] Town in Macedonia (Plin. *HN* 31.14).

(XV) 143. Ἐκ δὲ τῆς περὶ Χαονίαν, ὅταν ἀφεψηθῇ τὸ ὕδωρ, ἅλας γίνεσθαι.[1]

[1] BNJ 115 F 272

(XVI) 144. Τῶν δ᾽ ἐν Ἄμμωνι κρηνῶν λέγειν Ἀριστοτέλη[1] ὅτι τὴν μὲν Ἡλίου γε νομιζομένην μέσων μὲν νυκτῶν καὶ μεσημβρίας γίγνεσθαι θερμήν, ἕωθεν δὲ καὶ δείλης καθαπερεὶ κρύσταλλον, ἡ δ᾽ ἄλλη διότι ἀναβαίνοντος μὲν ἡλίου πιδύει, ἐπὶ δυσμαῖς δ᾽ ἰόντος ἵσταται.

[1] Fr. 531 Rose 1886[2]

(XVII) 145. Κτησίαν[1] δὲ τὴν ἐν Αἰθιοπίᾳ τὸ μὲν ὕδωρ ἔχειν ἐρυθρόν, ὡσανεὶ κιννάβαρι, τοὺς δ᾽ ἀπ᾽ αὐτῆς πιόντας παράφρονας γίνεσθαι. (τοῦτο δ᾽ ἱστορεῖ καὶ Φίλων ὁ τὰ Αἰθιοπικὰ συγγραψάμενος.)

[1] F11a Lenfant 2004

(XVIII) 146. Τὴν δ᾽ ἐν τοῖς Ἰνδικοῖς κρήνην Σίλαν οὐδὲ τὸ κουφότατον τῶν βληθέντων ἐᾶν ἐπιμένειν, ἀλλὰ πάντα καθέλκειν.

(XIX) 147. Εὔδοξον[1] δ᾽ ἱστορεῖν τὴν μὲν ἐν Καλχηδόνι κροκοδείλους ἐν αὐτῇ ‹ἔχειν› μικρούς, ὁμοίους τοῖς ἐν Αἰγύπτῳ.

[1] Fr. 331 Lasserre 1966

(XV) 143. [He says that] water from the river near Chaonia[1] becomes salt when it is boiled down.

[1] Region in northwestern Epirus. On harvesting the salt, see Plin. *HN* 31.39.

(XVI) 144. [He says that] Aristotle says of the springs in Ammon,[1] that the one named from Helios becomes hot at midnight and at noon, and at dawn and early afternoon, like ice. And another gushes at sunrise and at sunset is still.

[1] Site of the oracle of Zeus Ammon in Siwah, Egypt (Hdt. 1.46).

(XVII) 145. [He says that] Ctesias[1] [says that] there is a spring in Ethiopia that has red water as if it were cinnabar, and that those who drink from it become deranged. (Philon,[2] who wrote the *Aethiopica*, wrote about this.)

[1] Physician and historian (5th–4th c. BC) who served at the court of Artaxerxes II of Persia. Author of histories of Persia, India, and other works.   [2] Historian (2nd c. AD).

(XVIII) 146. [He[1] says that] the Sila, a spring in India, does not carry downstream the lightest of things that are tossed into it, but everything sinks.

[1] Ctesias F47α Lenfant 2004.

(XIX) 147. [He says that] Eudoxus wrote about a spring in Chalcedon[1] that has small crocodiles in it just like the ones in Egypt.

[1] Greek city at the mouth of the Pontus, a colony of Megara (Thuc. 4.75.2).

(XX) 148. Περὶ δὲ τὴν Ἀθαμανίαν ἱερὸν εἶναι Νυμ-
φῶν, ἐν ᾧ τὴν κρήνην τὸ μὲν ὕδωρ ἔχειν ἄφατον ὡς
ψυχρόν, ὃ δ᾽ ἂν ὑπερθῇς αὐτοῦ θερμαίνειν· ἐὰν δέ τις
φρύγανον ἢ ἄλλο τι τῶν τοιούτων προσενέγκῃ, μετὰ
φλογὸς καίεσθαι.[1]

[1] Fr. 351 Lasserre 1966

(XXI) 149. Κατὰ δὲ τὴν Ἀραβίαν ἐν πόλει Λευκοθέᾳ
Ἀμώμητόν[1] φησιν γράφειν, τὸν πραγματευθέντα τὸν
ἐκ Μέμφεως Ἀνάπλουν, εἰς τὴν καλουμένην Ἴσιδος
κρήνην ἄν τις οἴνου ἐπιχέῃ κοτύλην, διότι γίγνεται τὸ
ποτὸν εὔκρατον.

[1] BNJ 645 F 1a

(XXII) 150. Περὶ δὲ λιμνῶν Κτησίαν[1] μὲν ἱστορεῖν λέ-
γει τῶν ἐν Ἰνδοῖς λιμνῶν τὴν μὲν τὰ εἰς αὐτὴν ἀφιέ-
μενα κάτω οὐ δέχεσθαι, καθάπερ τὴν ἐν Σικελίᾳ καὶ
Μήδοις, πλὴν χρυσίον καὶ σίδηρον καὶ χαλκὸν, καὶ
ἄν τι ἐμπέσῃ πλάγιον, ὀρθὸν ἐκβάλλειν, ἰᾶσθαι δὲ
τὴν καλουμένην λεύκην· τῇ δ᾽ ἑτέρᾳ κατὰ τὰς εὐδια-
ζούσας ἡμέρας ἐπιπολάζειν ἔλαιον.

[1] F45sa Lenfant 2004

(XXIII) 151. Ξενόφιλον[1] δὲ ἐν μὲν τῇ πλησίον Ἰόππης
(sc. λίμνῃ) οὐ μόνον ἐπινήχεσθαι πᾶν βάρος, ἀλλὰ

[1] BNJ 767

(XX) 148. [He says that] the spring near Athamania[1] is sacred to the Nymphs and in it is amazing water that is cold, but becomes hot when someone crosses over it. And if some dry wood, or anything similar is brought to it, it kindles with flame.

[1] In southeastern Epirus between Mt. Pindus and the river Arachthus (Strabo 9.5.14).

(XXI) 149. [He says that] in the city of Leucothea below Arabia, Amometus,[1] who wrote *Sailing up from Memphis*, says if anyone pours a cup of wine into the spring called "of Isis," the drink becomes tempered.

[1] Historian (3rd–4th c. BC; cf. Plin. *HN* 6.55).

(XXII) 150. He says in *On Marshes* that Ctesias writes of the marshes in India there is one that does not accept things that are thrown down into it as in Sicily and Media,[1] except gold and iron and bronze, and if something crooked falls in, it is cast out straight, and that it heals the [disease] called "white"; and in another on lucky days olive oil floats to the surface.

[1] Kingdom in northwestern Iran (Diod. Sic. 10.27).

(XXIII) 151. [He says that] Xenophilus[1] writes that the marsh near Joppa[2] not only causes heavy nausea through-

[1] Xenophilus (3rd c. BC), historian of Lydia.
[2] Ancient Jaffa (Joseph. *BJ* 1.2.50).

καὶ παρὰ τρίτον ἔτος φέρειν ὑγρὰν ἄσφαλτον· ὅταν
δὲ γίγνηται τοῦτο, παρὰ τοῖς ἐντὸς τριάκοντα στα-
δίων οἰκοῦσιν ἰοῦσθαι χαλκώματα.

(XXIV) 152. Τὴν δὲ ἐν τοῖς Σαρμάταις λίμνην Ἡρα-
κλείδην[1] γράφειν, ὅτι οὐδὲν τῶν ὀρνέων ὑπεραίρειν, τὸ
δὲ προσελθὸν ὑπὸ τῆς ὀσμῆς τελευτᾶν·

[1] Fr. 128a Wehrli 1969

(XXV) 153. Ἐκ δὲ τῆς ἐν Ζακύνθῳ λίμνης φησὶν Εὔ-
δοξον[1] ἱστορεῖν, ὅτι ἀναφέρεται πίσσα, καίτοι παρ-
εχούσης αὐτῆς ἰχθῦς· ὅ τι δ' ἂν ἐμβάλῃς εἰς ταύτην,
ἐπὶ θαλάττης φαίνεσθαι τεττάρων ὄντων ἀνὰ μέσον
σταδίων.

[1] Fr. 368 Lasserre 1966

(XXVI) 154. Λύκον[1] δὲ περὶ τὴν ἐν Μύλαις τῆς Σικε-
λίας δένδρα φύεσθαι, διὰ μέσης δ' αὐτῆς ἀναθεῖν
ὕδωρ τὸ μὲν ψυχρόν, τὸ δὲ τοὐναντίον.

[1] BNJ 570 F 10

(XXVII) 155. Φανίαν[1] δὲ τὴν τῶν† Πυράκων[2] λίμνην
ὅταν ἀναξηρανθῇ κάεσθαι.

[1] FHG vol. 2, p. 301, fr. 38   [2] Πυράκων codd.: Συράκων
Bentley

out, but for three years it carries damp asphalt. Whenever this happens bronze vessels become rusty for those dwelling within thirty stades.[3]

3 About 600 feet.

(XXIV) 152. [He says that] Heraclides[1] writes that no birds fly over a swamp in the land of the Sarmatians[2] and if they approach it they die from the smell.

1 Heraclides Ponticus (4th c. BC), philosopher and student of Plato.   2 Iranian peoples occupying the western part of Scythia (Plin. HN 2.12).

(XXV) 153. [He says that] Eudoxus writes of a swamp in Zacynthus[1] that carries pitch, and yet it produces fish. And whatever you cast into it appears four stadia out in the middle of the sea.

1 Island west of the Peloponnese (Paus. 8.24.3).

(XXVI) 154. [He says that] Lycus [says that] trees grow around the marsh in Mylae[1] in Sicily, and in the middle of it water shoots up, both cold and the opposite.

1 City in Sicily belonging to Messina (Thuc. 3.90.2).

(XXVII) 155. [He says that] Phanias[1] writes that the marsh of the Pyraci catches fire whenever it dries up.

1 Phanias of Eresus (4th c. BC), Peripatetic philosopher and student of Aristotle.

(XXVIII) 156. Καὶ τὴν Ἀσκανίαν πότιμον οὖσαν τὸ προσενεχθὲν αὐτῇ πλύνειν ἄνευ ῥύμματος, ἐὰν ἐαθῇ δ' ἐν αὐτῇ πλείω χρόνον, διαπίπτειν αὐτόματον.

(XXIX) 157. Περὶ δὲ τῆς ἐν Κιτίῳ φάσκειν Νικαγόραν[1] ὅτι ἀνιμηθείσης ἐπ' ὀλίγον τῆς γῆς (?) ἅλες εὑρίσκονται.

[1] FHG vol. 2, p. 332, fr. 5

(XXX) 158. Περὶ δὲ τῶν† αὐτῶν ὑδάτων Θεόφραστόν[1] φησι τὸ καλούμενον Στυγὸς ὕδωρ λέγειν, ὅτι ἐστὶν ἐν Φενεῷ, στάζει δ' ἔκ τινος πετριδίου· τοὺς δὲ βουλομένους αὐτοῦ ὑδρεύεσθαι σπόγγοις πρὸς ξύλοις δεδεμένοις λαμβάνειν, διακόπτειν δὲ πάντα τὰ ἀγγεῖα πλὴν τῶν κερατίνων, τὸν δὲ ἀπογευσάμενον τελευτᾶν.

[1] Fr. 213A–B Sharples vol. 3.1, 1998

(XXXI) 159. Ἐν δὲ τῇ Λεοντίνων ἱστορεῖν Λύκον[1] τοὺς ὀνομαζομένους <Δέλλους> ἀναζεῖν μὲν ὡς θερμότατον τῶν ἑψομένων, τὰς δὲ πηγὰς ἔχειν ψυχράς. τῶν δὲ πλησιαζόντων αὐτοῖς τὸ μὲν τῶν ὀρνίθων γένος ἀποθνήσκειν εὐθύς, τοὺς δὲ ἀνθρώπους μετὰ τρίτην ἡμέραν.

[1] BNJ 570 F 11a

(XXVIII) 156. [He says that] the river Ascanias[1] is drinkable because rain comes into it without sediment, and if it is held in it for a long time, it slips away of its own accord.

[1] A town in Phrygia was named for the river (Hom. *Il.* 2.862–63).

(XXIX) 157. [He says that] Nicagoras[1] asserted about a spring in Citium[2] that when the earth has been drawn out a little, salt is found.

[1] Nicagoras of Cyprus. He wrote on the source of the Nile (Schol. ad Ap. Rhod. 2.269).   [2] City in Cyprus (Strabo 14.6.3). On salt from Citium, produced by the evaporation of lake water, see Plin. *HN* 31.39.

(XXX) 158. About the same waters he says that Theophrastus says the water called Styx (which is in Pheneus),[1] drips from some rock. That those wishing to draw water from it take hold of sponges tied to wooden posts; it breaks all the vessels except those made of horn and it kills anyone tasting it.

[1] On the Styx near Pheneus (in Arcadia), see Strabo 8.8.4.

(XXXI) 159. [He says that] Lycus[1] says in the Leontinian plain[2] the [rivers] called Delli bubble up so that they are hottest of the boiling waters, but they also have cold springs. Of those who come near them the race of birds perishes immediately, but men after the third day.

[1] Lycus of Rhegium, also called Butheras (4th–3rd c. BC), historian.   [2] Leontini, a city in Sicily (Polyb. 7.6).

(XXXII) 160. Ὅμοιον δὲ τούτῳ καὶ τὸ περὶ τὸν Κώων χυτρῖνον γίνεσθαι· καὶ γὰρ ἐκεῖνον ἀτμὸν μὲν ἐκβάλλειν καὶ ποιεῖν ἔμφασιν τοῦ ζεῖν, τὰ δὲ καθειμένα καθ᾽ ὑπερβολὴν ψύχειν.

(XXXIII) 161. Εἶναι δὲ παρὰ τοῖς Κῴοις καὶ ἄλλο τι ῥευμάτιον, ὃ πάντας τοὺς ὀχετοὺς ὅθεν διαρρεῖ λίθους πεποίηκεν. τοῦτο δὲ καὶ Εὔδοξος[1] καὶ Καλλίμαχος παραλείπουσιν, ὅτι ἐκ τοῦδε τοῦ ὕδατος οἱ Κῷοι λίθους λατομήσαντες ᾠκοδόμησαν τὸ θέατρον· οὕτως ἰσχυρῶς ἀπολιθοῦται πᾶν γένος.

[1] Fr. 363 Lasserre 1966

(XXXIV) 162. Λέγειν δὲ τὸν Εὔδοξον[1] καὶ περὶ τῶν ἐν τῇ Πυθοπόλει φρεάτων, ὅτι παραπλήσιόν τι τῷ Νείλῳ πάσχουσιν· τοῦ μὲν γὰρ θέρους ὑπὲρ τὰ χείλη πληροῦσθαι, τοῦ δὲ χειμῶνος οὕτως ἐκλείπειν ὥστε μηδὲ βάψαι ῥᾴδιον εἶναι.

[1] Fr. 333 Lasserre 1966

(XXXV) 163. Καὶ περὶ τοῦ κατὰ τὴν Κρήτην ὑδατίου, οὗ οἱ ὑπερκαθίζοντες, ὅταν ὑετὸς ᾖ, διατελοῦσιν ἄβροχοι, παραδεδόσθαι δὲ τοῖς Κρησίν, ἀπ᾽ ἐκείνου λούσασθαι τὴν Εὐρώπην ἀπὸ τῆς τοῦ Διὸς μίξεως.[1]

[1] Fr. 866 Lasserre 1966

(XXXII) 160. [He says that] near Cos[1] there is a geyser like this one, and that it casts up steam and creates an appearance of boiling, but things that are let down [into the water] become excessively cool.

[1] Aegean island off the coast of Turkey (Arist. *Pol.* 5.1304b).

(XXXIII) 161. [He says that] in the territory of the Coans there is also another small river which made all the channels from which it flows through the rocks. Eudoxus and Callimachus omitted that the Coans built a theater after quarrying the rocks from this water. From this the whole race is strongly petrified.

(XXXIV) 162. [He says that] Eudoxus[1] says concerning the reservoirs in Pythopolis,[2] that they are affected in the same way as the Nile. They are full beyond their banks when it is hot, and in winter they are empty so that it is not easy to draw water.

[1] Eudoxus of Cnidus (4th c. BC), astronomer and mathematician. Student of Plato.   [2] Antioch on the Maeander in Anatolia.

(XXXV) 163. [He says] about the stream in Crete where those who sit by it stay dry in a rainstorm, that it was granted to the Cretans that Europa be washed in it after having sex with Zeus.

CALLIMACHUS

(XXXVI) 164. Ἐν δὲ Λυγκήσταις Θεόπομπον[1] φάσκειν
τι εἶναι ὕδωρ ὀξύ, τοὺς δὲ ἐκ τούτου πίνοντας ὥσπερ
ἐπὶ τῶν οἴνων ἀλλοιοῦσθαι (καὶ τοῦθ᾿ ὑπὸ πλειόνων
μαρτυρεῖται).

[1] *BNJ* 115 F 278b

(XXXVII) 165. Τὸ δ᾿ ἐκ τῆς πέτρας Ἀρμενίων ἐκπί-
πτον Κτησίαν[1] ἱστορεῖν ὅτι συμβάλλει ἰχθῦς μέλα-
νας, ὧν τὸν ἀπογευσάμενον τελευτᾶν.

[1] F61b Lenfant 2004

(XXXVIII) 166. Περὶ δὲ πυρὸς Κτησίαν[1] φησὶν ἱστο-
ρεῖν, ὅτι περὶ τὴν τῶν Φασηλιτῶν χώραν ἐπὶ τοῦ τῆς
Χιμαίρας ὄρους ἔστιν τὸ καλούμενον ἀθάνατον πῦρ·
τοῦτο δέ, ἐὰν μὲν εἰς ὕδωρ ἐμβάλῃς, καίεσθαι βέλ-
τιον, ἐὰν δὲ φορυτὸν ἐπιβαλὼν πήξῃ τις, σβέννυσθαι.

[1] F45ea Lenfant 2004

(XXXIX) 168. . . . Περὶ δὲ λίθων τὸν αὐτὸν τοῦτον
λέγειν τὸν παρὰ τοῖς Βοττιαίοις ἐν Θρᾴκῃ γινόμενον,
ὅταν ὁ ἥλιος προσβάλλῃ, πῦρ ἐξ αὐτοῦ ἐκθυμιᾶσθαι·
†ἐκεῖνος δ᾿ ἵνα παρέχῃ, γνοὺς μὲν τὴν τῶν ἀνθράκων
χροιὰν διαμένοντας ἀφθάρτους, κἂν σβέσας τί πάλιν
ἐπικεχειρήκασιν†, τὴν αὐτὴν ἐνέργειαν συντελεῖν.

(XXXVI) 164. In the river Lyncestis[1] [he says that] Theo-
pompus[2] pronounced that some water is bitter, that those
who drink from it become changed as if they were drink-
ing wine (and many testify to this).

[1] Plin. *HN* 2.106.   [2] Theopompus (4th c. BC), historian
and rhetorician.

(XXXVII) 165. [He says that] Ctesias writes that water
falling from a rock in Armenia carries black fish which kill
anyone tasting them.

(XXXVIII) 166. He says that Ctesias wrote in *On Fire* that
in the land of the Phaselites on Mt. Chimera,[1] is the so-
called eternal fire. This, if you cast water on it, burns even
more, and if someone throws kindling on it, it is quenched.

[1] Plin. *HN* 2.110.

(XXXIX) 168. . . . [in] *On Rocks* he says the same thing is
the case among the Bottiaei[1] in Thrace, whenever the sun
strikes [it], smoky fire pours from it. That one . . . in order
to provide continually pure [sacrifices] . . . after noting the
appearance of the coals . . . if after quenching it they make
another attempt to complete the same operation.

[1] A Thracian people who migrated to Macedonia from Crete
(Strabo 7.11).

(XL) 169. Περὶ δὲ φυτῶν τῆς ἀκάνθης εἶδος Ἀριστοτέλην[1] φάσκειν περὶ τὴν Ἐρύθην ἀνευρίσκεσθαι διαποίκιλον τὴν χρόαν, ἐξ οὗ πλῆκτρα γίνεσθαι.

[1] Fr. 269 Rose 1886[2]

(XLI) 170. Περὶ δὲ Θεσπρωτοὺς ἐκ τῆς γῆς ἄνθρακας ὀρύττεσθαι δυναμένους κάεσθαι Θεόπομπόν[1] φησιν καταγράφειν.

[1] BNJ 115 F 273

(XLII) 171. Φανίαν[1] δὲ κατά τινας τόπους τῆς Λέσβου καὶ περὶ τῶν Νεανδριέων τὰς βώλους πρὸς τὰς τῶν ὄψεων †καθηγήσεις γίνεσθαι χρησίμας, καὶ εἰς ὕδωρ ἐμβληθείσας οὔτε καταδύνειν οὔτε κατατήκεσθαι. (ὑπὸ τοῦτο τὸ γένος πίπτοι ἂν καὶ ἐν Πιτάνῃ πλίνθος ἡ λεγομένη ἐπιπλεῖν.)

[1] FHG vol. 2, p. 301, fr. 28

(XLIII) 172. Περὶ δὲ τῶν ζῴων Λύκον[1] μὲν ἐν τῇ Διομηδείᾳ τῇ νήσῳ φησὶν ἱστορεῖν, τοὺς ἐρωδιοὺς ὑπὸ μὲν τῶν Ἑλλήνων, ὅταν παραβάλλῃ τις εἰς τοὺς τόπους, οὐ μόνον ψαυομένους ὑπομένειν, ἀλλὰ καὶ προσπετομένους εἰς τοὺς κόλπους ἐνδύνειν καὶ σαίνειν φιλοφρόνως. λέγεσθαι δέ τι τοιοῦτον ὑπὸ τῶν ἐγχωρίων, ὡς τῶν τοῦ Διομήδους ἑταίρων εἰς τὴν τῶν ὀρνέων τούτων φύσιν μετασχηματισθέντων.

[1] BNJ 570 F 6

(XL) 169. [He says that] Aristotle in *On Plants* said of the appearance of the thistle that the variegated color was found around Erytha,[1] from which a spear point or a pick was made.

[1] Also spelled Erytheia, an island off southern Spain near Gades (Plin. *HN* 4.36).

(XLI) 170. He says that Theopompus wrote that coals dug from the earth around Thesprotia[1] are able to be kindled.

[1] Area in Epirus in northwestern Greece.

(XLII) 171. [He says that] Phanias says opposite some places in Lesbos and near the territory of the Neandrioi[1] there are clods of earth useful for healing vision, and after being thrown into water they neither sink nor melt away. (Under this category might fall the brick in Pitane[2] which is said to float.)

[1] Neandria, a Greek city in western Anatolia (*Suda* ν 105).
[2] Aeolian settlement in southern Asia Minor.

(XLIII) 172. He says that Lycus[1] writes in *On Animals* that on the island of Diomedes[2] whenever one of the Greeks approaches the place the herons not only stand still if touched, but even fly toward them, attempting to enter the folds of their garments and to fawn in a friendly way. [He says that] the inhabitants say that the nature of the companions of Diomedes was transformed into the the nature of these birds.

[1] Lycus of Rhegium, also called Butheras (4th–3rd c. BC), historian.   [2] Three islands in the Adriatic are associated with the hero (Strabo 5.1.9).

(XLIV) 173. Τοὺς δὲ περὶ τὸν Ἀδρίαν ἐνοικοῦντας
Ἐνετοὺς Θεόπομπον[1] φάσκειν κατὰ τὸν σπόρου και-
ρὸν τοῖς κολοιοῖς ἀποστέλλειν δῶρα, ταῦτα δ' εἶναι
ψαιστὰ καὶ μάζας. προθέντας δὲ τοὺς ταῦτα κομίζον-
τας ἀποχωρεῖν, τῶν δὲ ὀρνέων τὸ μὲν πλῆθος ἐπὶ τοῖς
ὁρίοις μένειν τῆς χώρας συνηθροισμένον, δύο δ' ἢ
τρεῖς προσπτάντας καὶ καταμαθόντας ἀφίπτασθαι
πάλιν καθαπερεί τινας πρέσβεις ἢ κατασκόπους. ἐὰν
μὲν οὖν τὸ πλῆ[

[1] BNJ 115 F 274a

408 Steph. Byz. κ 207 Billerbeck s.v. Κραννών

Κραννών· πόλις τῆς Θεσσαλίας . . . ἔστι καὶ ἄλλη
πόλις Ἀθαμανίας ἀπὸ Κράννωνος τοῦ Πελασγοῦ. ἐν
ταύτῃ δύο κόρακας εἶναι φασι μόνους, ὡς Καλλίμα-
χος ἐν τοῖς Θαυμασίοις καὶ Θεόπομπος.[1] ὅταν δὲ ἄλ-
λους ἐκνεοσσεύσωσιν, ἴσους αὐτοὺς καταλιπόντες ἀπ-
έρχονται.

[1] BNJ 115 F 267a

409 Steph. Byz. θ 40 Billerbeck s.v. Θήβη

Θήβη· πόλις Βοιωτίας . . . ἔστι καὶ ἄλλη Αἰγυπτία,
περὶ ἧς Καλλίμαχός φησιν ὅτι κατὰ τὰς Αἰγυπτίας
Θήβας ἐστὶ σπήλαιον, ὃ ταῖς ἡμέραις πληροῦται ἀνέ-
μου, κατὰ δὲ τὰς τριακάδας οὐ πνεῖ παντελῶς.

(XLIV) 173. [He says that] Theopompus says that the Venetians, who live around the Adriatic Sea, at the time of sowing send gifts to the jackdaws, and these are barley cakes and bread. And after offering them these things and providing for them, they depart. And that a great number of birds remain on the borders of this place, and that two or three after flying in and inspecting [the offerings] fly back again just like some ambassadors or scouts. And if the crowd . . .

408 Stephanus of Byzantium

Krannon: it is city of Thessaly . . . and another city of Athamania different from Pelasgian Crannon. In this one they say that there are only two crows, as Callimachus says in the *Wonders* and Theopompus. And whenever they hatch others, they depart leaving the same number behind.

409 Stephanus of Byzantium

Thebes: city of Boeotia. . . . There is another in Egypt about which Callimachus says in Egyptian Thebes there is a cave which is full of wind during the day, but on the thirtieth, it does not blow at all.

410 Ex. Vat. *De rebus mir.* c. 15[1]

Καλλίμαχός φησιν ἐν Θράκῃ δύο ποταμοὺς εἶναι Κέ-
ρωτα καὶ Μηλέα ὀνομαζομένους· τῶν δὲ προβάτων
περὶ τὸ συλλαμβάνειν ὄντων τὰ μὲν ἀπὸ τοῦ Κέρωτος
πίνοντα μέλανας ἄρνας τίκτειν, τὰ δὲ ἀπὸ τοῦ Μη-
λέως λευκούς, τὰ δὲ ἀπ' ἀμφοτέρων τῶν ὑδάτων ποι-
κίλα.

[1] E. L. De Stefani, ed., *SIFC* 11 (1903): 97

411 Plin. *HN* 31.9

in Aenaria insula calculosis mederi . . . idem contigit in
Velino lacu potantibus, item in Syriae fonte iuxta Taurum
montem auctor est M. Varro et in Phrygiae Gallo flumine
Callimachus. Sed ibi in potando necessarius modus, ne
lymphatos agat, quod in Aethiopia accidere his qui e fonte
Rubro bibere Ctesias[1] scribit.

[1] F11a Lenfant 2004

ΠΕΡΙ ΛΟΓΑΔΩΝ

412 Schol. Ambr. (K) ad Theoc. *Id.* 2.120a

μᾶλα μὲν ἐν κόλποισι Διωνύσοιο φυλάσσων· Καλ-
λίμαχος ἐν τῷ Περὶ λογάδων(?) τὸν Διονύσου στέφα-
νον ἐκ μήλων εἶναί φησιν, ἐξ ὧν καὶ τὸν Ἱππομένην

410 Vatican Excerpt, *On Miraculous Things*

Callimachus says in Thrace there are two rivers called the Ceron and the Meleus. When sheep gather around, those drinking from the Ceron gives birth to black lambs, those drinking from the Meleus, white ones, and those drinking water from both, lambs of variegated color.

411 Pliny the Elder, *Natural History*

Varro says that [the waters] on the island of Aenaria[1] cure stones . . . and likewise for those drinking [the waters] in lake Velinus[2] and the same in a fountain of Syria near mount Taurus, and Callimachus [says] in the river Gallus in Phrygia. But there moderation in drinking is necessary to avoid delirium, which happens to those in Ethiopia who drink from the Red fountain, as Ctesias writes.

[1] An island off the coast of Campania, now called Ischia (App. *BCiv.* 5.8.71).   [2] Lake Velinus was located in the Rieti valley in central Italy. It was drained in 271 BC by the consul Manius Curius Dentatus.

PERI LOGADŌN

412 Ambrosian Scholia to Theocritus, *Idylls*

Keeping safe in [my] lap the apples of Dionysus:[1] Callimachus in the *Peri logadōn* (?) says that the crown of Dionysus is [made] from apples, which Hippomenes[2] took

[1] On the apples of Dionysus, cf. Philit. fr. 17 Lightfoot (14 Kuchenmüller).   [2] Suitor of Atalanta who won her hand in a footrace when he distracted her by tossing Aphrodite's golden apples at her feet (Apollod. *Bibl.* 3.9.2).

λαβεῖν Ἀφροδίτης αἰτησαμένης, ὡς Διόδωρος ὁ ποιητὴς ἐν Κορινθι‹α›κοῖς.

ΜΟΥΣΕΙΟΝ

Suda κ 227 (v. test. 1 in indice operum).

ΜΗΝΩΝ ΠΡΟΣΗΓΟΡΙΑΙ
ΚΑΤΑ ΕΘΝΟΣ ΚΑΙ ΠΟΛΕΙΣ

Suda κ 227 (v. test. 1 in indice operum).

ΚΤΙΣΕΙΣ ΝΗΣΩΝ ΚΑΙ ΠΟΛΕΩΝ
ΚΑΙ ΜΕΤΟΝΟΜΑΣΙΑΙ

Suda κ 227 (v. test. 1 in indice operum).

412a (SH 291A) P.Turner 9 (fr. 1 + 2.3 in librorum indice)

Καλλιμάχου Κ[τίσεις?

ΠΕΡΙ ΝΥΜΦΩΝ

413 Stob. Flor. 1.49.50

. . . διαβόητον μὲν τοίνυν Στυγὸς ὕδωρ κατὰ τὴν Ἀρκαδίαν οἱ ἱστορικοὶ ἀναγεγράφασιν, ὧν ἐστι, καὶ Ἡρόδοτος . . . Καλλίμαχος δ' ἐν τῷ Περὶ νυμφῶν

after he had asked Aphrodite, as Diodorus the poet [says] in the *Corinthians*.

MUSEUM

Suda κ 227 (see T 1 on the list of Works).

NAMES OF THE MONTHS BY TRIBES AND CITIES

Suda κ 227 (see T 1 on the list of Works).

FOUNDATIONS OF ISLANDS AND CITIES AND THEIR CHANGES OF NAME

Suda κ 227 (see T 1 on the list of Works).

412a (*SH* 291A) Turner papyrus (list of books)
The *Foundations* (?) of Callimachus

ON NYMPHS

413 Stobaeus, *Anthology*

. . . Historians have written about the famous water of the Styx in Arcadia, among whom is even Herodotus[1] . . . Callimachus in his work *On Nymphs* even tells about the

[1] Hdt. 6.74.

συγγράμματι καὶ τὸ ἰδίωμα τοῦ ὕδατος ἀφηγεῖται
λέγων οὕτω· "Στύξ· ἐν Νωνακρίνη τῆς Ἀρκαδίας ὕδωρ
ἐστὶ τὸ διακόπτον πάντα τὰ ἀγγεῖα πλὴν τῶν κερα-
τίων."

ΠΕΡΙ ΟΡΝΕΩΝ

414 Ath. 9.388d

Καλλίμαχος δ᾽ ἐν τῷ Περὶ ὀρνίθων διεστάναι φησὶ
πορφυρίωνα πορφυρίδος, ἰδίᾳ ἑκάτερον καταριθμού-
μενος· τὴν τροφήν τε λαμβάνειν τὸν πορφυρίωνα ἐν
σκότῳ καταδυόμενον, ἵνα μή τις αὐτὸν θεάσηται·
ἐχθραίνει γὰρ τοὺς προσιόντας αὐτοῦ τῇ τροφῇ.

415 Ath. 9.389b

ὁ πέρδιξ . . . ἐστὶ δὲ τὸ ζῷον κακόηθες καὶ πανοῦρ-
γον, ἔτι δὲ ἀφροδισιαστικόν· διὸ καὶ τὰ ᾠὰ τῆς θη-
λείας συντρίβει, ἵνα ἀπολαύῃ τῶν ἀφροδισίων. ὅθεν
ἡ θήλεια γιγνώσκουσα ἀποδιδράσκουσα τίκτει.᾽ τὰ
αὐτὰ ἱστορεῖ καὶ Καλλίμαχος ἐν τῷ Περὶ ὀρνέων.

416 Ath. 9.394d

Καλλίμαχος δ᾽ ἐν τῷ Περὶ ὀρνέων ὡς διαφορὰς ἐκ-
τίθεται φάσσαν, πυραλλίδα, περιστεράν, τρυγόνα.

peculiarity of the water saying, "Styx: In Nonacrina[2] of Arcadia is water that breaks every container except [those made] of horn."

[2] A town in Arcadia in the central Peloponnese.

ON BIRDS

414 Athenaeus, *The Learned Banqueters*

Callimachus in his *On Birds* says that the *porphyris* is distinguished from the purple gallinule (*porphyriōn*), and catalogs the two separately. In addition, [he claims] that the purple gallinule goes down into the dark to feed, so that no one can see it; because it hates to have anyone come near when it is eating.

415 Athenaeus, *The Learned Banqueters*

The partridge . . . is a malicious, mischievous creature, and also libidinous. It therefore crushes the female's eggs, so that it can enjoy having sex with her. As a result, the female, knowing this, flees when she gives birth. Callimachus says the same things in *On Birds*.

416 Athenaeus, *The Learned Banqueters*

Callimachus in *On Birds* sets out the differences between the ringdove, *pyrallis*, pigeon, and turtledove.

417 Ath. 9.395ef

τῆς δὲ νήττης καὶ κολυμβάδος, ἀφ' ὧν καὶ τὸ νή-
χεσθαι καὶ κολυμβᾶν εἴρηται, μνημονεύει μετὰ καὶ
ἄλλων λιμναίων πολλῶν Ἀριστοφάνης ἐν Ἀχαρνεῦσι
διὰ τούτων·

    νάσσας κολοιὼς ἀτταγᾶς φαλαρίδας τροχίλως
      κολύμβως.

μνημονεύει αὐτῶν καὶ Καλλίμαχος ἐν τῷ Περὶ ὀρ-
νέων.

418 Ath. 9.391c

Καλλίμαχος δέ φησι δύο γένη εἶναι σκωπῶν καὶ τοὺς
μὲν φθέγγεσθαι, τοὺς δὲ οὔ. διὸ καὶ καλεῖσθαι τοὺς
μὲν σκῶπας αὐτῶν, τοὺς δ' ἀείσκωπας.

419 Hsch. s.v. σιαλενδρίς

σιαλενδρίς· ποιὸς ὄρνις παρὰ Καλλιμάχῳ.

420 Schol. ad Ap. Rhod. 1.1049–50

ἠΰτε κίρκους . . . ὑποτρέσσωσι πέλειαι· ἠΰτε κίρκους·
εἶδος ἱέρακος. ἔστι δὲ ἱεράκων γένη ἕξ, ὡς Καλλίμα-
χος ἐν τοῖς Περὶ ὀρνέων.

417 Athenaeus, *The Learned Banqueters*

Aristophanes[1] mentions the duck (*nēttē*) and the grebe (*kolumbas*), from which the verbs *nēchesthai* (to swim) and *kolumbān* (to dive) are derived, along with many other marsh birds, in the following passage:

> ducks (*nassas*), jackdaws, francolins, coots, plovers, grebes (*kolumbōs*).

Callimachus also mentions them in *On Birds*.

[1] *Ach.* 875–76.

418 Athenaeus, *The Learned Banqueters*

Callimachus says that there are two kinds of *scōps*,[1] and that one produces a call, while the other does not, therefore some of them are called *skōpes* and others *aeiskōpes*.

[1] A small owl.

419 Hesychius

sialendris: A type of bird according to Callimachus.

420 Scholia to Apollonius of Rhodes, *Argonautica*

like hawks . . . the doves give ground: like hawks, in the manner of a hawk. There are six kinds of hawks, as Callimachus [says] in *On Birds*.

421 Schol. (V Ald.) ad Ar. Av. 302–4

. . . ὁ δὲ ἐλεᾶς μήποτε ἐλείας ἐστὶν ἐν τοῖς Καλλιμά-
χου ἀναγραφόμενος φησὶ γάρ· "ἔλεια μικρόν, φωνῇ
ἀγαθόν."

422 Schol. (V Ald.) ad Ar. Av. 303

κεβλήπυρις· μήποτε οὐχ ἕν ἐστιν ἀλλὰ δύο φησὶν ὁ
Σύμμαχος· καὶ γὰρ ἐν τοῖς Καλλιμάχου ἀναγέγρα-
πται κέβλη.

423 Schol. (V Ald.) ad Ar. Av. 304

πορφυρίς· ἡ πορφυρὶς ἀναγέγραπται καὶ ἡ κολυμβὶς
δὲ φαίνεται καὶ ὁ δρύοψ καὶ ἡ ἀπελίς, κερχνῇς δὲ οὐκ
ἀναγέγραπται, ἀλλὰ κέρχνη.

424 Schol. (RV Ald.) ad Ar. Av. 765

φυσάτω πάππους· Εὐφρόνιος φησι πάππον ὄρνεόν τι
εἶναι· πρὸς τὸ ὄνομα οὖν παίζει . . . Καλλίμαχος οὐκ
ἀναγράφει τὸν πάππον.

425 Schol. (RV Ald.) ad Ar. Av. 882–84

καὶ φλέξιδι . . . καὶ αἰγιθάλῳ· ἐπισκεπτέον περὶ τού-
των ἐκ τῆς τῶν ζῴων ἱστορίας τίς ὁ τέτραξ καὶ φλέξις

421 Scholia to Aristophanes, *Birds*

. . . The *eleās* is perhaps spelled *eleias* in the works of Callimachus for he says, "the eleia is small, but has a good voice."

422 Scholia to Aristophanes, *Birds*

keblēpuris: Symmachus[1] says [the name] is never in one part, but in two. And in the work of Callimachus is it written *keblē*.

[1] Roman statesman, orator, and epistolographer (4th c. AD).

423 Scholia to Aristophanes, *Birds*

porphyris: [The name of the bird] is spelled *porphyris* and *kolymbis* appears and *dryops* and *apelis*,[1] but *kerchnē* is written, not *kerchneis*.

[1] All the bird's names are spelled with a final sigma except *cerchne*.

424 Scholia to Aristophanes, *Birds*

Let him be born a *pappus*: Euphorion[1] says that the *pappus* is some kind of bird; regarding the name, he is jesting . . . Callimachus does not write about the *pappus*.

[1] Poet and scholar (3rd c. BC).

425 Scholia to Aristophanes, *Birds*

and to the phlexis . . . and the titmouse: It is necessary to inquire about these from a history of animals what the

καὶ ἐλασᾶς. ἡ γὰρ βάσκα καὶ καταράκται εἰσὶ παρὰ
Καλλιμάχῳ ἀναγεγραμμέναι.

426 Schol. (RV Ald.) ad Ar. *Av.* 1181

γύψ, κύμινδις, αἰετός· τὴν κύμινδιν οὐκ ἀνέγραψεν ὁ
Καλλίμαχος· μήποτε οὖν κίσινδις γραπτέον·

427 Schol. B ad Hom. *Il.* 10.274

. . . Καλλίμαχος δὲ ἐν τῷ Περὶ ὀρνέων οὐ τὸν πύγαρ-
γόν φησιν εἶναι τὸν ἐν τῇ ὀχείᾳ τοὺς ὀφθαλμοὺς
αἱμάσσοντα, ἀλλὰ τὸν πελλόν, γράφων ὧδε, "ἀστε-
ρίας, ὁ δ᾽ αὐτὸς καλεῖται ὄκνος· οὗτος οὐδὲν ἐργάζε-
ται. πελλός· οὗτος ὅταν ὀχεύῃ, κραυγάζει καὶ ἐκ τῶν
ὀφθαλμῶν ἀφίησιν αἷμα, καὶ τίκουσιν ἐπιπόνως αἱ
θήλειαι. λευκός· οὗτος ἀνωδύνως ἐν ἀμφοτέροις ἀπαλ-
λάσσεται."

428 Schol. (s s³ s⁴ Tzetzes) ad Lyc. *Alex.* 513

τῇ δισαρπάγῳ κρεκί· κρέξ ὄρνεόν ἐστι θαλάσσιον
ποικίλον ἴβιδι ἐοικός ὡς Ἡρόδοτος . . . Καλλίμαχος
δὲ ἐν τοῖς Περὶ ὀρνέων φησὶ τοῖς γαμοῦσι δυσοιώνι-
στον εἶναι.

tetrax is and the *phlexis* and the *elasās*. The *basca* and *cataractae* are written about by Callimachus.

426 Scholia to Aristophanes, *Birds*

the vulture, *cymindis*, eagle: Callimachus did not write about the *cymindis*. It should never be spelled *cisindis*.

427 Scholia to Homer, *Iliad*

... Callimachus in *On Birds* says that the male eagle does not have red eyes in breeding, but dusky, writing as follows,[1] "the hawk, the one called 'Fear'; this one does nothing. 'Dusky'; this one whenever it mounts, it screams and blood discharges from its eyes and the females give birth with difficulty. [A third hawk is called] 'White'; this one delivers free of pain for both [male and female]."

[1] Callimachus distinguishes three kinds of hawks.

428 Tzetzes on Lycophron, *Alexandra*

the twice-ravaged *krex*: the *krex* is a seabird of varigated color like the ibis, according to Herodotus.[1] Callimachus in *On Birds* says that it is the worst omen for marriages.

[1] Hdt. 2.76.

ΠΙΝΑΚΕΣ ΤΩΝ ΕΝ ΠΑΣΗΙ ΠΑΙΔΕΙΑΙ
ΔΙΑΛΑΜΨΑΝΤΩΝ ΚΑΙ ΩΝ
ΣΥΝΕΓΡΑΨΑΝ ΕΝ ΒΙΒΛΙΟΙΣ Κ΄ ΚΑΙ Ρ΄

Titulus in *Suda* (v. test. 1).

429 Diog. Laert. 8.86

Εὔδοξος Αἰσχίνου Κνίδιος, ἀστρολόγος, γεωμέτρης,
ἰατρός, νομοθέτης. οὗτος τὰ μὲν γεωμετρικὰ Ἀρχύτα
διήκουσε, τὰ δ᾽ ἰατρικὰ Φιλιστίωνος τοῦ Σικελιώτου,
καθὰ Καλλίμαχος ἐν τοῖς Πίναξί φησι.

430 Ath. 15.669d–e

ἀλλ᾽ ἵνα κἀγώ, φησίν, μνημονεύσω τῶν τοῦ Χαλκοῦ
ποιητοῦ καὶ ῥήτορος Διονυσίου—Χαλκοῦς δὲ προση-
γορεύθη διὰ τὸ συμβουλεῦσαι Ἀθηναίοις χαλκῷ νο-
μίσματι χρήσασθαι, καὶ τὸν λόγον τοῦτον ἀνέγραψε
Καλλίμαχος ἐν τῇ τῶν Ῥητορικῶν ἀναγραφῇ—λέξω
τι καὶ αὐτὸς ἐκ τῶν Ἐλεγείων.

431 Schol. (RV) ad Ar. *Av.* 692

Προδίκῳ· ὅτι οὐκ ὀρθῶς Καλλίμαχος τὸν Πρόδικον ἐν
τοῖς ῥήτορσι καταλέγει, σαφῶς γὰρ ἐν τούτοις φιλό-
σοφος.

INDEX OF ALL THOSE PREEMINENT
IN LITERATURE AND OF THEIR
WRITINGS IN 120 BOOKS

429 Diogenes Laertius, *Lives of Eminent Philosophers*

Eudoxus[1] of Cnidos, son of Aeschines, an astrologer, geometer, physician, lawgiver. He studied geometry with Archytas and medicine with Philistion of Sicily, as Callimachus says in his *Pinakes*.

[1] 4th c. BC. Also a student of Plato.

430 Athenaeus, *The Learned Banqueters*

But, so that I too, he said, may quote from the works of the poet and orator Dionysius Chalcus[1]—he was called Chalcus (Brazen) because he advised the Athenians to use bronze coins, and Callimachus recorded this speech in his *Index of Speeches*—I myself will recite a passage from the *Elegies*.

[1] 5th c. BC.

431 Scholia on Aristophanes, *Birds*

to Prodicus: That Callimachus counts Prodicus[1] incorrectly among the orators, clearly as far as these [birds] are concerned he is a philosopher.

[1] Philosopher and orator (5th c. BC) who appears in several Platonic dialogues.

432 Dion. Hal. *Epist.* 4 ad Amm.

ἐπὶ δὲ Διοτίμου τοῦ μετὰ Καλλίστρατον ἐν Ἀθηναίοις
πρώτην εἶπε δημηγορίαν, ἣν ἐπιγράφουσιν οἱ τοὺς
ῥητορικοὺς πίνακας συντάξαντες Περὶ τῶν Συμμο-
ριῶν.

433 Ath. 13.585b

ἐμμελὴς δ᾽ ἦν πάνυ ἡ Γνάθαινα καὶ οὐκ ἀνάστειος
ἀποφθέγξασθαι, ἥτις καὶ νόμον συσσιτικὸν συνέγρα-
ψεν, καθ᾽ ὃν δεῖ τοὺς ἐραστὰς ὡς αὐτὴν καὶ τὴν θυ-
γατέρα εἰσιέναι, κατὰ ζῆλον τῶν τὰ τοιαῦτα συντα-
ξαμένων φιλοσόφων. ἀνέγραψε δ᾽ αὐτὸν Καλλίμαχος
ἐν τῷ τρίτῳ πίνακι τῶν Νόμων καὶ ἀρχὴν αὐτοῦ τήνδε
παρέθετο· "ὅδε ὁ νόμος ἴσος ἐγράφη καὶ ὅμοιος." στί-
χων τριακοσίων εἴκοσι τριῶν.

434 Ath. 6.244a

τοῦ Χαιρεφῶντος καὶ σύγγραμμα ἀναγράφει Καλ-
λίμαχος ἐν τῷ τῶν παντοδαπῶν Πίνακι γράφων οὕ-
τως· "δεῖπνα ὅσοι ἔγραψαν· Χαιρεφῶν Κυρηβίωνι."
εἶθ᾽ ἑξῆς τὴν ἀρχὴν ὑπέθηκεν· "ἐπειδή μοι πολλάκις
ἐπέστειλας." στίχων τριακοσίων ἑβδομήκοντα πέντε.

435 Ath. 14.643e

οἶδα δὲ καὶ Καλλίμαχον ἐν τῷ τῶν παντοδαπῶν
συγγραμμάτων Πίνακι ἀναγράψαντα πλακουντοποι-

432 Dionysius of Halicarnassus, *Letter to Ammaeus*

When Diotimus was presiding (the one after Callistratus), he [sc. Demosthenes] made the first speech to the Athenians, which those who assembled the index of orations called *On the Navy Boards*.

433 Athenaeus, *The Learned Banqueters*

Gnathaena was very proper and not boorish in conversation, and put together a set of dinner regulations, which her lovers had to follow when they visited her and her daughter in emulation of the philosophers who composed such things. Callimachus cataloged it in the third index of his *Laws* and quoted its beginning, which is as follows: "This law was written to be equitable and the same for all." 323 lines.

434 Athenaeus, *The Learned Banqueters*

Callimachus includes a prose piece by Chaerephon in his *Catalog of Miscellaneous Works*, writing as follows: "Those who wrote about dinner parties: Chaerephon to Cyrebion."[1] Then at once he appends the beginning: "Since you often wrote to me." 375 lines of text.

[1] A parasite (Ath. 6.242d).

435 Athenaeus, *The Learned Banqueters*

I know that Callimachus in his *Catalog of Miscellaneous Works* recorded discourses on the art of cake-making

ικὰ συγγράμματα Αἰγιμίου καὶ Ἡγησίππου καὶ Μη-
τροβίου, ἔτι δὲ καὶ Φαίστου.

436 Ath. 1.4e

ὅτι Ἀρχέστρατος ὁ Συρακούσιος ἢ Γελῷος ἐν τῇ ὡς
Χρύσιππος ἐπιγράφει Γαστρονομίᾳ, ὡς δὲ Λυγκεὺς
καὶ Καλλίμαχος Ἡδυπαθείᾳ, ὡς δὲ Κλέαρχος Δει-
πνολογίᾳ, ὡς δ' ἄλλοι Ὀψοποιίᾳ—ἐπικὸν δὲ τὸ ποί-
ημα, οὗ ἡ ἀρχή· "ἱστορίης ἐπίδειγμα ποιούμενος Ἑλ-
λάδι πάσῃ"—φησί·

437 Ath. 2.70b

Ἑκαταῖος δ' ὁ Μιλήσιος ἐν Ἀσίας Περιηγήσει, εἰ
γνήσιον τοῦ συγγραφέως τὸ βιβλίον· Καλλίμαχος
γὰρ Νησιώτου αὐτὸ ἀναγράφει.

438 Ath. 6.252c

Ἀττάλου δὲ τοῦ βασιλέως ἐγένετο κόλαξ καὶ διδά-
σκαλος Λυσίμαχος, ὃν Καλλίμαχος μὲν Θεοδώρειον
ἀναγράφει, Ἕρμιππος δ' ἐν τοῖς Θεοφράστου μαθη-
ταῖς καταλέγει. οὗτος δ' ὁ ἀνὴρ καὶ Περὶ τῆς Ἀττάλου
παιδείας συγγέγραφε βίβλους πᾶσαν κολακείαν ἐμ-
φαινούσας.

---

[1] Historian (3rd c. BC; *BNJ* 170 T 1).   [2] Attalus I of
Pergamum (r. 241–197 BC).   [3] Theodorus the Atheist (Diog.
Laert. 2.97).   [4] Peripatetic philosopher called "the Callima-
chean" (end of 3rd c. BC; fr. 56 Wehrli, suppl. vol. 1).

by Aegimus, Hegesippus, and Metrobius, as well as by Phaestus.[1]

[1] None of the authors can be identified.

436 Athenaeus, *The Learned Banqueters*

Archestratus of Syracuse or Gela[1] in the work entitled according to Chrysippus[2] the *Gastronomy*, but according to Lynceus[3] and Callimachus, the *Life of Pleasure*, and according to Clearchus[4] the *Science of Dining*, but according to other authorities the *Art of Cooking*—the poem is in epic verse and begins: "presenting my research to all Greece"[5]—he says . . .

[1] T 2 Olsen-Sens.   [2] *SVF* vol. 3, p. 199 fr. 6.
[3] fr. 21a Dalby 2000.   [4] fr. 79a Wehrli.
[5] Archestratus fr. 1 Olson-Sens (*SH* 191).

437 Athenaeus, *The Learned Banqueters*

Hecataeus[1] of Miletus in the *Guide to Asia*,[2] if the book is actually his; because Callimachus ascribes the same one to Nesiotes.[3]

[1] Hecataeus of Miletus (5th–6th c. BC), historian and mythographer.   [2] *BNJ* 1 T 15a.   [3] Otherwise unknown.

438 Athenaeus, *The Learned Banqueters*

Lysimachus[1] was a flatterer and teacher of King Attalus[2] whom Callimachus describes as a follower of Theodorus,[3] but Hermippus[4] lists him with the students of Theophrastus. This man (Lysimachus) wrote books on the education of Attalus that displayed every kind of flattery.

439 Ath. 8.336d

Ἄλεξις δ' ἐν Ἀσωτοδιδασκάλῳ, φησὶ Σωτίων ὁ Ἀλεξανδρεὺς ἐν τοῖς Περὶ τῶν Τίμωνος Σίλλων· ἐγὼ γὰρ οὐκ ἀπήντησα τῷ δράματι· . . . οὐδ' ἀναγραφῆς ἀξιωθέν τινι σύνοιδα· οὔτε γὰρ Καλλίμαχος οὔτε Ἀριστοφάνης αὐτὸ ἀνέγραψαν, ἀλλ' οὐδ' οἱ τὰς ἐν Περγάμῳ ἀναγραφὰς ποιησάμενοι.

440 Ath. 11.496e–f

Δίφιλος Αἱρησιτείχει (τὸ δὲ δρᾶμα τοῦτο Καλλίμαχος ἐπιγράφει Εὐνοῦχον) λέγει δὲ οὕτως·

440a (*SH* 292) Phil. Herenn. in Ammon. *Diff.* 202 (Parisinus 80, p. 53 Nickau)

καὶ Ἀριστοφάνης ὁ γραμματικὸς ἐν τῷ πρὸς τοὺς Πίνακας Καλλιμάχου περὶ Ἀντιφάνους διαστέλλει τὴν τάξιν.

439 Athenaeus, *The Learned Banqueters*

Alexis[1] in *The Instructor in Profligacy* says Sotion[2] of Alexandria in his works about the *Silloi* of Timon[3]—I never encountered the play myself . . . nor do I know anyone who thought it worthy to be cataloged; for neither Callimachus nor Aristophanes[4] cataloged it, and neither did those who made catalogs in Pergamum.

[1] Alexis of Thurii, poet of middle comedy (3rd–2nd c. BC). Antiphanes is another middle comic poet treated in the *Pinakes* (*SH* 292). [2] Biographer and doxographer (1st c. BC).

[3] Follower of the Skeptical philosopher Pyrrho of Elis (4th c. BC). His *Silloi* parody Greek philosophers (Clayman 2009).

[4] Aristophanes of Byzantium (3rd–2nd c. BC), fourth Librarian at Alexandria, grammarian and editor of Homer and other Greek poets.

440 Athenaeus, *The Learned Banqueters*

Diphilus[1] in *The Man Who Captured Walls* (fr. 5.1–2?)— Callimachus titles this play *The Eunuch*—says the following . . .

[1] Diphilus of Sinope (4th–3rd c. BC), important poet of New Comedy.

440a (*SH* 292) Philo of Byblos, *Lexicon* in Ammonius, *On the Differences of Synonymous Expressions*

And Aristophanes the grammarian in his *Against the Pinakes of Callimachus* differs from the [chronological] order as regards Antiphanes.

441 Choerob. in Theodos. (*Gramm. Gr.* vol. 4.1, p. 139.6 Hilgard)

ἔστι δὲ προσθεῖναι ἐν τῷ κανόνι τοῦ τεχνικοῦ "χωρὶς τοῦ υἱέσι παρ' Ἀθηναίοις" . . . "καὶ τοῦ δρομέσι" παρὰ Καλλιμάχῳ· ἐκεῖνος γὰρ οὕτως ἐπέγραψεν', ὀφείλων ἐπιγράψαι δρομεῦσι· δρομεύς γάρ ἐστιν ἡ εὐθεῖα τῶν ἑνικῶν· ἔτι δὲ σημειούμεθα καὶ τὸ δρομέσι παρὰ τῷ Καλλιμάχῳ·

442 Diog. Laert. 9.23–24

Παρμενίδης . . . καὶ αὐτὸς δὲ διὰ ποιημάτων φιλοσοφεῖ, καθάπερ Ἡσίοδός τε καὶ Ξενοφάνης καὶ Ἐμπεδοκλῆς . . . καὶ δοκεῖ πρῶτος πεφωρακέναι τὸν αὐτὸν εἶναι Ἕσπερον καὶ Φωσφόρον, ὥς φησι Φαβωρῖνος ἐν πέμπτῳ Ἀπομνημονευμάτων (οἱ δὲ Πυθαγόραν· Καλλίμαχος δέ φησι μὴ εἶναι αὐτοῦ τὸ ποίημα.)

441 Choeroboscus

In the artistic canon it is possible to attribute to Callimachus "apart from him in the presence of the sons (*huiesi*) of the Athenians" . . ."and the runners (*dromesi*)." That man wrote it this way, but one ought to write *dromeusi*. *Dromeus* is the correct form of the singular and yet we note *dromesi* in Callimachus.[1]

[1] Pfeiffer notes that these excerpts from Herodian's *On the Inflection of Nouns* show that Callimachus wrote the following in his *Catalog of Poets*: "Simonides; epinicia for runners."

442 Diogenes Laertius, *Lives of Eminent Philosophers*

Parmenides[1] . . . philosophized through his poems like Hesiod and Xenophanes[2] and Empedocles.[3] . . . and he seems to have been the first to observe Hesperus and Phosphorus[4] as Favorinus[5] says in Book 5 of his *Memorabilia*. (Others say it was Pythagoras.[6] Callimachus says that the poem is not his.)

[1] Parmenides of Elea (6th–5th c. BC; DK 28), presocratic philosopher.   [2] Xenophanes of Colophon (6th–5th c. BC; DK 21), presocratic philosopher and critic of religion and society.

[3] Empedocles of Acragas (5th c. BC; DK 3), presocratic philosopher and cosmogonist.   [4] The evening and morning stars, respectively. (Both in fact refer to the planet Venus.)

[5] Favorinus of Arelate (1st–2nd c. AD), academic philosopher and orator during the Second Sophistic.   [6] Pythagoras of Samos (6th–5th c. BC; DK 14), philosopher, religious leader, mathematician, and music theorist.

443 Dion. Hal. *Dem.* 13

ὁ δὲ πρὸς τὴν ἐπιστολὴν καὶ τοὺς πρέσβεις τοὺς
παρὰ Φιλίππου ῥηθεὶς λόγος, ὃν ἐπιγράφει Καλλίμα-
χος ὑπὲρ Ἀλοννήσου, ὁ τὴν ἀρχὴν τήνδε ἔχων . . .
ὅλος ἐστὶν ἀκριβὴς καὶ λεπτὸς καὶ τὸν Λυσιακὸν χα-
ρακτῆρα ἐκμέμακται εἰς ὄνυχα.

444 Dion. Hal. *Dinarch.* 10

Δημόσιοι λόγοι γνήσιοι . . . Κατὰ Θεοκρίνου ἔνδει-
ξις· "τοῦ πατρός, ὦ ἄνδρες." τοῦτον Καλλίμαχος ἐν
τοῖς Δημοσθένους φέρει.

445 Harpocrates s.v. ἐνεπίσκημμα

ἐνεπίσκημμα· . . . ἔστι δὲ καὶ λόγος τις ἐπιγραφόμε-
νος Δημοσθένους πρὸς Κριτίαν περὶ τοῦ ἐνεπισκήμ-
ματος, ὃν Καλλίμαχος μὲν ἀναγράφει ὡς γνήσιον,
Διονύσιος δὲ ὁ Ἁλικαρνασσεὺς ὡς ψευδεπίγραφον.

446 Phot. *Bibl.* (cod. 265 p. 491 b 31)

. . . καὶ τὸν ὑπὲρ Σατύρου δὲ λόγον τῆς ἐπιτροπῆς
πρὸς Χαρίδημον· οἱ μὲν πρὸς τὴν κρίσιν ἔχοντες τὸ

---

1 Charidemus (4th c. BC), Greek mercenary.

443 Dionysius of Halicarnassus, *On Demosthenes*

The speech in which he opposed Philip's[1] letter and
the ambassadors with him, which Callimachus calls *For
Halonnesus*, and which begins:[2] . . . is altogether precise
and spare and fits the stylistic model of Lysias[3] to a tee.

[1] Philip II of Macedon, father of Alexander the Great.
[2] Dem. *Or.* 7.1. [3] Lysias of Syracuse (5th–4th c. BC),
speechwriter at Athens whose plain style came to represent the
purest Attic.

444 Dionysius of Halicarnassus, *On Dinarchus*

Genuine public speeches (on Dinarchus)[1] . . . the indict-
ment against Theocrinus, "of the father, gentlemen." Cal-
limachus ascribes this speech to Demosthenes.[2]

[1] Dinarchus of Corinth (4th–3rd c. BC), Peripatetic and
speechwriter. [2] The speech (Dem. *Or.* 58) is extant.

445 Harpocrates

enepiskēmma (property claim against the state): . . . there
is a speech called *Demosthenes Against Critias:*[1] *Concern-
ing a Property Claim*, which Callimachus says is genuine,
but Dionysius of Halicarnassus says is wrongly ascribed.

[1] Athenian tragedian and public figure; friend of Socrates and
one of the Thirty Tyrants.

446 Photius, *Library*

. . . the speech against Charidemus[1] on the guardianship
of Satyrus. Those with unfailing judgment say that it is by

ἀσφαλὲς Δημοσθένους λέγουσιν εἶναι, ὁ δὲ Καλλίμα-
χος, οὐδ᾽ ἱκανὸς ὢν κρίνειν, Δεινάρχου νομίζει.

447 Dion. Hal. *Dinarch.* 1

ἅμα δ᾽ ὁρῶν οὐδὲν ἀκριβὲς οὔτε Καλλίμαχον οὔτε
τοὺς ἐκ Περγάμου γραμματικοὺς περὶ αὐτοῦ γράψαν-
τας, ἀλλὰ παρὰ τὸ μηδὲν ἐξετάσαι περὶ αὐτοῦ τῶν
ἀκριβεστέρων ἡμαρτηκότας, ὡς μὴ μόνον ἐψεῦσθαι
πολλὰ ἀλλὰ καὶ λόγους τοὺς οὐδὲν μὲν αὐτῷ προσ-
ήκοντας ὡς Δεινάρχου τούτῳ προστίθεσθαι, τοὺς δ᾽
ὑπ᾽ αὐτοῦ γραφέντας ἑτέρων εἶναι λέγειν·

448 Dion. Hal. *Isae.* 6

ἔστι δὴ καὶ παρὰ τῷ Λυσίᾳ τις ὑπὲρ ἀνδρὸς ξένου
δίκην φεύγοντος περὶ κλήρου ποιούμενος τὴν ἀπολο-
γίαν. τοῦτον ἐπιγράφει τὸν λόγον Καλλίμαχος Περὶ
Φερενίκου ὑπὲρ τοῦ Ἀνδροκλείδου Κλήρου καὶ ἔστι
πολλοῖς πρότερον ἠγωνισμένος ἔτεσι θατέρου.

449 Harpocrates s.v. Ἴων

Ἴων· Ἰσοκράτης ἐν τῷ Περὶ τῆς ἀντιδόσεως. Ἴωνος
τοῦ τῆς τραγῳδίας ποιητοῦ μνημονεύοι ἂν νῦν ὁ ῥή-
τωρ, ὃς ἦν Χῖος μὲν γένος, υἱὸς δ᾽ Ὀρθομένους, ἐπί-
κλησιν δὲ Ξούθου· ἔγραψε δὲ καὶ μέλη πολλὰ καὶ

Demosthenes, but Callimachus, who is not able to judge, believes that it is by Dinarchus.

447 Dionysius of Halicarnassus, *On Dinarchus*

At the same time, however, after I saw that neither Callimachus nor the grammarians from Pergamum had written anything accurate about Dinarchus, and that on account of not studying him more precisely they had made mistakes, so that not only did they say many things that were not true, but also ascribed speeches to Dinarchus that were not his and said that his speeches were written by others.

448 Dionysius of Halicarnassus, *On Isaeus*

There is a speech by Lysias on behalf of an alien defending him against a charge concerning an inheritance. Callimachus entitles the speech *Concerning Pherenicus: On the Inheritance of Androclides* and it was argued many years before that one.[1]

[1] The case of the metic Eumathes defended by Isaeus (Dion. Hal. *Isae.* 5).

449 Harpocrates

Ion: Isocrates in the speech on the antidosis.[1] The speaker might now recall Ion the tragic poet who was born in Chios, the son of Orthomenes of Zuthos. He wrote many

[1] Isoc. 15. A defense of rhetoric and of his life as a teacher of rhetoric in the form of a fictionalized lawsuit written as if Isocrates had been accused of corrupting his students.

τραγῳδίας καὶ φιλόσοφόν τι σύγγραμμα τὸν Τριαγ-
μὸν ἐπιγραφόμενον, ὅπερ Καλλίμαχος ἀντιλέγεσθαί
φησιν †ὡς Ἐπιγένους.†

450 Schol. (DEFGQ) ad Pind. *Pyth.* 2 inscr.

Γέγραπται μὲν Ἱέρωνι ἅρματι νικήσαντι, ἄδηλον δὲ
εἰς ποῖον ἀγῶνα. διεστασίασται γὰρ οὐ μετρίως τοῖς
πρὸ ἡμῶν. οἱ μὲν γὰρ οὐδὲ ὅλως ἐπίνικον αὐτὸν εἶναί
φασι, Τίμαιος δὲ θυσιαστικήν, Καλλίμαχος, Νεμεα-
κήν; Ἀμμώνιος καὶ Καλλίστρατος, Ὀλυμπιακήν; ἔνιοι
Πυθικήν, ὡς Ἀπολλώνιος ὁ εἰδογράφος, ἔνιοι δὲ Παν-
αθηναϊκήν.

450a (*SH* 293) *P.Oxy.* 2368, P^2 183

ταύτην τ]ὴν ᾠδὴν Ἀρίσταρχ(ος) [....διθ]υραμβικὴν
εἶ[ναι φησι]ν διὰ τὸ παρειλή[φθαι ἐν α]ὐτῇ τὰ περὶ
Κασ[σάνδρας,] ἐπιγράφει δ' αὐτὴν [... Κάσσ]ανδραν
πλανη[θέντα δ' α]ὐτὴν κατατάξαι [ἐν τοῖς Π]αιᾶσι
Καλλίμαχον [.......]οὐ συνέντα ὅτι [..ἐπίφθ]ε{γ}γμα
κοινόν ἐ[στι καὶ δ]ιθυράμβου . . .

poems and tragedies and a philosophical work called the *Triagmos*,[2] which Callimachus says Epigenes[3] disputed.

[2] The *Triagmos* or *Triagmoi* was apparently a philosophical treatise on the theory of triads.   [3] Possibly the comic poet Epigenes of Athens (4th c. BC).

450 Scholia to Pindar, *Pythian Odes*

It is written for Hieron[1] who was victorious in a chariot race, but it is unclear in which contest. There is disagreement, not moderate, among our predecessors. Some say that this is not altogeher an epinician, Timaeus [says] it is a ritual ode; Callimachus, a *Nemean*; Ammonius[2] and Callistratus,[3] an *Olympian*; some, a *Pythian*, like Apollonius the Eidographer;[4] and some a *Panathenaic*.

[1] Hieron I, tyrant of Syracuse (r. 478–467 BC).
[2] Perhaps Ammonius of Alexandria, pupil of Aristarchus.
[3] Grammarian at Alexandria (2nd c. BC)
[4] Head of the Library at Alexandria (3rd–2nd c. BC).

450a (*SH* 293) Oxyrhynchus papyrus

Aristarchus says that the ode is a dithyramb because it treats the matter of Cassandra. He entitled it *Cassandra*, that Callimachus was wrong when he classified it among the *Paeans*, that he did not understand that the refrain is also common to the dithramb.

451 Schol. (MNO) ad Eur. *Andr.* 445

εἰλικρινῶς δὲ τοὺς τοῦ δράματος χρόνους οὐκ ἔστι
λαβεῖν· οὐ δεδίδακται γὰρ Ἀθήνησιν. ὁ δὲ Καλλίμα-
χος ἐπιγραφῆναί φησι τῇ τραγῳδίᾳ Δημοκράτην.

452 Tatianus, *Ad Gr.* c. 31 (p. 31.24 Schwartz); Euseb.
Praep. evang. 10.11.3

. . . περὶ γὰρ τῆς Ὁμήρου ποιήσεως γένους τε αὐτοῦ
καὶ χρόνου καθ᾽ ὃν ἤκμασε· προηρεύνησαν πρεσβύ-
τατοι μὲν Θεαγένης τε ὁ Ῥηγῖνος κατὰ Καμβύσην
γεγονὼς καὶ Στησίμβροτος ὁ θάσιος . . . ἔπειτα
γραμματικοί Ζηνόδοτος, Ἀριστοφάνης, Καλλίμοχος
. . .

453 *Suda* o 251

ἐπιγέγρπται δὲ ἐν τῷ τάφῳ αὐτοῦ τόδε τὸ ἐπίγραμμα,
ὃ ὑπὸ τῶν Ἰητῶν ἐποιήθη, ὥς φησι Καλλίμαχος.

451 Scholia to Euripides, *Andromache*

It is not possible to determine the date of this drama[1] accurately. It is not recorded in the *didascaliae* at Athens. Callimachus says that Democrates was given credit for the tragedy.

[1] Euripides' *Andromache*.

452 Tatianus, *Oration to the Greeks*; Eusebius, *Preparation for the Gospel*

. . . about the poetry of Homer, his birth and the age at which he reached his acme. The oldest who first investigated it were Theagenes of Rhegium,[1] born during the reign of Cambyses and Stesimbrotus of Thasus[2] . . . then the grammarians Zenodotus,[3] Aristophanes,[4] and Callimachus . . .

[1] Theagenes of Rhegium (6th c. BC; DK 8), philosopher.
[2] Stesimbrotus of Thasus (5th c. BC; *BNJ* 107 F 21), sophist and historian.   [3] Zenodotus of Ephesus (3rd c. BC), first Librarian of Alexandria.   [4] Aristophanes of Byzantium (2nd–3rd c. BC), fourth Librarian of Alexandria.

453 *Suda*

This epitaph is written on his[1] tomb which was made by the people of Ios,[2] as Callimachus says.

[1] Homer's.   [2] Greek island in the Aegean Sea between Naxos and Thera; claimed to be the burial place of Homer (Paus. 10.24.2).

CALLIMACHUS

ΠΙΝΑΞ ΚΑΙ ΑΝΑΓΡΑΦΗ
ΤΩΝ ΚΑΤΑ ΧΡΟΝΟΥΣ ΚΑΙ ΑΠ
ΑΡΧΗΣ ΓΕΝΟΜΕΝΩΝ ΔΙΔΑΣΔΑΛΩΝ

Titulus in *Suda* (v. test. 1).

454 Schol. (Ald.) ad Ar. *Nub.* 553

Εὔπολις μὲν τὸν Μαρικᾶν πρώτιστος παρείλκυσεν·
δῆλον ὅτι πρότερος ὁ Μαρικᾶς ἐδιδάχθη τῶν δευτέ-
ρων Νεφελῶν. Ἐρατοσθένης δέ φησι Καλλίμαχον
ἐγκαλεῖν ταῖς διδασκαλίαις, ὅτι φέρουσιν ὕστερον
τρίτῳ ἔτει τὸν Μαρικᾶν τῶν Νεφελῶν, σαφῶς ἐνταῦθα
εἰρημένου, ὅτι πρῶτος καθεῖται.

455 Schol. (V Ald.) ad Ar. *Av.* 1242

Λικυμνίαις βολαῖς· ἐν Λικυμνίῳ δράματι Εὐριπίδου
εἰσήχθη τις κεραυνοβολούμενος. ὁ μὲν Καλλίμαχος
"γράφων οὕτως 'Λικυμνίαις βολαῖς,'" φησί, "ταύτης
τῆς διδασκαλίας οὐδὲ μέμνηται." ἐν δὲ ἐνίοις τῶν
σχολικῶν ὑπομνήμασι ταυτὶ γέγραπται, "ἴσως ὁ Λι-
κύμνιος ἐνεπύρισέ τινων οἰκίας." ἐν δὲ τοῖς ἐπιγεγραμ-
μένοις Ἀπολλωνίου ταῦτα γέγραπται ὅτι ἡμίφλεκτόν
τινα εἰσάγει . . .

INDEX AND REGISTER
OF THE DRAMATIC POETS
IN ORDER FROM THE BEGINNING

454 Scholia to Aristophanes, *Clouds*

Eupolis first presented Maricas:[1] It is clear that Maricas was presented earlier than the second version of the *Clouds*.[2] Eratosthenes says that Callimachus claims in the *Didascaliae* that they brought *Maricas* out in the third year after the *Clouds*, clearly saying here that it was produced earlier.

[1] A fictional comic character representing Hyperbolus.

[2] Eupolis, an important comic poet and rival of Aristophanes, produced his *Maricas* in 421 BC. Aristophanes' *Clouds* was presented in 423 BC, but the surviving text is a revision of the original that was never produced.

455 Scholia to Aristophanes, *Birds*

with Licymnian blows: In the Licymnian drama of Euripides someone who was struck by a thunderbolt is brought in. Callimachus says "writing 'by Lycymnian blows' is not recorded in the *Didascaliae*." In some scholarly commentaries it is explained in this way: "Perhaps Licymnius[1] burned down someone's house." In the epigrams of Apollonius it says that he brought in someone half-burned . . .

[1] Son of Electryon and Mideia, slain by Tlepolemus (Pind. *Ol.* 7.29).

456 *IG* XIV, 1098a, 1097, 1098 = *IGUR* 216, 215, 218

haec tria fragmenta Romae reperta reliquiae sunt ingentis
πίνακος τῶν διδασκάλων, quem apographon esse libri
Callimachei nullo epitomatore intercedente iudicavit A.
Koerte.[1]

[1] Pf. vol. 1, 350.

ΠΙΝΑΞ ΤΩΝ ΔΗΜΟΚΡΙΤΟΥ ΓΛΩΣΣΩΝ
ΚΑΙ ΣΥΝΤΑΓΜΑΤΩΝ

Suda κ 227 (v. test. 1 in indice operum).

ΠΕΡΙ ΤΩΝ ΕΝ ΤΗΙ
ΟΙΚΟΥΜΕΝΗΙ ΠΟΤΑΜΩΝ

Titulus in *Suda* (v. test. 1).

457 Schol. ad Euphor. (?); *P.Oxy.* 2085

Ὀρνεὰς ὅτι ποταμ[ος ἐστιν Ἀργ]είας ἐν ταῖς Χιλι-
ά[σιν εἴρηκ]ε̣ν καὶ 'ὁ Μάρμαρος δὲ τ̣[ῆς Εὐβοί]ας̣ (?)
ἐν τῷ Περὶ ποταμῶ[ν Καλ]λίμαχος εἴρη(κεν)· Νῆριν
δ[ὲ ποτα]μὸν μὲν οὐκ οἶδα.

456 Three Greek Inscriptions

These three fragments, discovered at Rome, are of the large *Index of Dramatic Poets* that Koerte[1] judged to be a copy of the book of Callimachus, not an abridgment.

[1] Alfred Koerte, "Inschriftliches zur Geschichte der attischen Komödie," *RhM.* 60 (1905): 425–47; Benjamin W. Millis and S. Douglas Olson, eds., *Inscriptional Records for the Dramatic Festivals at Athens* (Brill: Leiden/Boston, 2012), 225–29.

INDEX OF THE GLOSSES AND WRITINGS OF DEMOCRITUS

Suda κ 227 (see T 1 on the list of Works).

ON RIVERS OF THE INHABITED WORLD

457 Scholia to Euphorion (?); Oxyrhynchus papyrus

The Orneas is a river of Argos he[1] said in the *Chiliads* and the Marmarus[2] [is a river] of Euboea Callimachus said in *On Rivers*. I do not know the river Neris.

[1] Euphorion of Chalcis (3rd c. BC), Librarian at Antioch, poet, and scholar. Author of the *Chiliads*.   [2] Not otherwise known.

458 Strabo 9.1.19

οἷον ἐν τῇ συναγωγῇ τῶν ποταμῶν ὁ Καλλίμαχος
γελᾶν φησίν, εἴ τις θαρρεῖ γράφειν τὰς τῶν Ἀθη-
ναίων παρθένους "ἀφύσσεσθαι καθαρὸν γάνος Ἠρι-
δάνοιο," οὗ καὶ τὰ βοσκήματα ἀπόσχοιτ᾽ ἄν.

459 Schol. ad Ap. Rhod. 1.1165a

Καλλίμαχος δὲ ἱστορεῖ περὶ τοῦ ποταμοῦ ἐν τῷ Περὶ
τῶν κατὰ τὴν Ἀσίαν ποταμῶν καὶ Δημήτριος ὁ Σκή-
ψιος ἐν Τρωικῷ διακόσμῳ.

ΠΡΟΣ ΠΡΑΞΙΦΑΝΗΝ

460 Vit. Arat. I 9.6 (Vat. Gr. 191) Martin

Ἀντίγονος γάρ, ᾧ συνεγένετο Ἄρατος, κατὰ τὸν πρῶ-
τον καὶ δεύτερον γέγονε Πτολεμαῖον . . . μέμνηται
γοῦν αὐτοῦ καὶ Καλλίμαχος ὡς πρεσβυτέρου οὐ μό-
νον ἐν τοῖς Ἐπιγράμμασιν, ἀλλὰ καὶ ἐν τοῖς Πρὸς
Πραξιφάνην, πάνυ ἐπαινῶν αὐτὸν ὡς πολυμαθῆ καὶ
ἄριστον ποιητήν.

458 Strabo, *Geography*

For example, in his *Collection of Rivers*, Callimachus says that he laughs if anyone is bold enough to write that the virgins of Athens "draw pure water from the Eridanus,"[1] which even cattle avoid.

[1] A quote from an unknown poem in hexameters.

459 Scholia to Apollonius of Rhodes, *Argonautica*

Callimachus writes about the river[1] in his *On Rivers in Asia* and Demetrius the Skeptic[2] in the *Trojan Catalogue*.

[1] The Rhyndacus in northwestern Anatolia forming the border between Mysia and Bithynia (Strabo 12.8.11).
[2] Demetrius the Skeptic, also known as Demetrius the Cynic (1st c. AD), philosopher and friend of Seneca.

AGAINST PRAXIPHANES

460 *Life of Aratus*

Aratus, who was a contemporary of Antigonus, lived at the time of the first and second Ptolemy . . . and Callimachus remembered him as an older man not only in his *Epigrams*,[1] but also in the *Against Praxiphanes*,[2] praising him much as a polymath and the best poet.

[1] *Epigr.* 27.   [2] Praxiphanes of Mytilene, Peripatetic philosopher, pupil of Theophrastus, grammarian.

ΥΠΟΜΝΗΜΑΤΑ

461 Eust. ad *Od*. 12.85 (p. 1714.43 van der Valk)

ἰστέον δὲ ὅτι ἐπιρρεπὴς ὁ μῦθος εἰς τὰ κυνώδη φάσ-
ματα, ὃς καὶ τὴν Ἑκάβην ἀπεκύνωσε· καὶ τὴν Ἑκά-
την δὲ κυνὸς κεφαλὴν ἔχουσαν πλάττει. καὶ Καλλί-
μαχος οὖν ἐν ὑπομνήμασι τὴν Ἄρτεμιν ἐπιξενωθῆναί
φησιν Ἐφέσῳ υἱῷ Καΰστρου, ἐκβαλλομένην δὲ ὑπὸ
τῆς γυναικὸς, τὸ μὲν πρῶτον μεταβαλεῖν αὐτὴν εἰς
κύνα, εἶτ' αὖθις ἐλεήσασαν ἀποκαταστῆσαι εἰς ἄν-
θρωπον, καὶ αὐτὴν μὲν αἰσχυνθεῖσαν ἐπὶ τῷ συμβε-
βηκότι ἀπάγξασθαι, τὴν δὲ θεὸν περιθεῖσαν αὐτῇ τὸν
οἰκεῖον κόσμον Ἑκάτην ὀνομάσαι.

462 *P.Oxy*. 1802 col. ii, 43

μελῳδία ἡ τραγῳδία τὸ παλαιὸν ἐλέγετο, ὡς Καλ-
λίμαχος ἐν Ὑπομνήμασιν.

463 Harpocration s.v. Ἄκη

Ἄκη· πόλις αὕτη ἐν Φοινίκῃ . . . ἣν Νικάνωρ ὁ Περὶ
μετονομασιῶν γεγραφὼς καὶ Καλλίμαχος ἐν τοῖς
Ὑπομνήμασι τὴν νῦν Πτολεμαΐδα καλουμένην φασὶν
εἶναι. Δημήτριος δὲ ἰδίως τὴν ἀκρόπολιν τῆς Πτολε-
μαΐδος πρότερον Ἄκην ὀνομάσθαι φησίν.

COMMENTARIES

461 Eustathius on Homer, *Odyssey*

One must see that the myth that turned Hecabe into a dog inclines to dog-like phantoms. For he makes Hecate with the head of a dog. And Callimachus in his *Commentaries* says that Artemis was entertained by Ephesus the son of Caystrus and when she was cast out by his wife she first changed her into a dog, and then taking pity on her restored her as a human; she, being dishonored, hanged herself as a consequence of what happened and the god named the local area Hecate for her.

462 *Oxyrhynchus Glossary*

In antiquity tragedy was called *melōidia*, as Callimachus [says] in the *Commentaries*.

463 Harpocration

Ake: this is a city in Phoenicia . . . which Nicanor, writing in his *On Changes of Name*,[1] and Callimachus in the *Commentaries* say is now called Ptolemais. Demetrius, who saw the acropolis of Ptolemais, says that it was formerly called Ake.

[1] *FHG* vol. 3, p. 633, fr. 5.

464 Schol. ad Ap. Rhod. 1.1116

καὶ πεδίον Νηπήιον· Ἀπολλόδωρος[1] δέ φησι Νηπείας πεδίον ἐν Φρυγίᾳ. ὁ δὲ Καλλίμαχός φησιν ἐν Ὑπομνήμασι Νέμεσιν εἶναι τὴν τὸ πεδίον κατέχουσαν.

[1] *BNJ* 244 F 175

INCERTI LIBRI

465 Ath. 3.72a

Ὅτι Καλλίμαχος ὁ γραμματικὸς τὸ μέγα βιβλίον ἴσον ἔλεγεν εἶναι τῷ μεγάλῳ κακῷ.

466 Schol. Ambr. ad Theoc. *Id.* 2.12

τᾷ χθονίᾳ Ἑκάτᾳ· Καλλίμαχος κατὰ λέξιν ὧδέ φησιν· "τῇ Δήμητρι μιχθεὶς ὁ Ζεὺς τεκνοῖ Ἑκάτην διαφέρουσαν ἰσχύϊ καὶ μεγέθει τῶν θεῶν." ἣν ὑπὸ γῆν πεμφθῆναι ὑπὸ τοῦ πατρὸς πρὸς Περσεφόνης ζήτησιν. καὶ νῦν Ἄρτεμις καλεῖται καὶ Φύλαξ καὶ Δαδοῦχος καὶ Φωσφόρος καὶ χθονία.

464 Scholia to Apollonius of Rhodes, *Argonautica*

and the plain of Nepeia: Apollodorus[1] says that the plain of Nepeia is in Phrygia. Callimachus says in his *Commentaries* that it is Nemesis who possesses the plain.[2]

[1] Apollodorus of Athens (2nd c. BC), student of Aristarchus, Librarian at Alexandria, and Homeric scholar.   [2] *Hec.* 116.

UNCERTAIN BOOKS

465 Athenaeus, *The Learned Banqueters*

The grammarian Callimachus used to say that a big book is the same as a big evil.

466 Scholia to Theocritus, *Idylls*

to Hecate of the Underworld: Callimachus, as the saying goes, says this: "After Zeus had sex with Demeter, she gave birth to Hecate, who differed in strength and size from the gods." She was sent under the earth by her father to seek Persephone. And now she is called Artemis and Guardian and Torchbearer and Light-bringer and Goddess of the Underworld.

FRAGMENTS OF
UNCERTAIN LOCATION

FRAGMENTA INCERTAE SEDIS

467 Ammon. *In Arist. de int. comm.* 2 (*Commentaria in Aristotelem Graeca* 4.5, p. 38 Busse)

τὸ ἄνθρωπος ὄνομα καὶ τὸ μέροψ καὶ τὸ βροτὸς σημαίνει ταὐτόν . . . διὸ καὶ τὸ "ἐδείμαμεν—μορτοῖς" φησὶν ὁ Κυρηναῖος,

<blockquote>ἐδείμαμεν ἄστεα μορτοί[1]</blockquote>

[1] μορτοί *Etym. Orion.*: μορτοῖς Ammonius

468 [Ammon.] *Diff.* 122 (p. 31 Nickau)

καὶ τὰ συγγράμματα ἐκάλουν οἱ παλαιοὶ γράμματα. Καλλίμαχος πού φησι,

<blockquote>γράμματα δ᾽ οὐχ εἴλισσεν ἀπόκρυφα</blockquote>

469 Antig. Car. *Hist. mir.* 45.2 (p. 37 Musso)

ἔστι δὲ χωλὸν τὸ ὄρνεον, ὅθεν καὶ Καλλίμαχος ὁ ἐκ τῆς Αἰγύπτου περίτρανος εἶναι βουλόμενος ἔφησεν προείπας ὑπὲρ ἄλλου τινὸς ὀρνέου,

<blockquote>αἴγιθος ἀμφιγυήεις</blockquote>

FRAGMENTS OF
UNCERTAIN LOCATION

467 Ammonius, *Commentary on Aristotle*

The words *anthrōpos* and *merops* and *brotos* mean the same thing . . . therefore the Cyrenean[1] says,

> We mortals built cities

[1] That is, Callimachus of Cyrene.

468 Pseudo-Ammonius, *On the Differences of Synonymous Expressions*

The ancients called written works *grammata*. Callimachus says somewhere,

> he did not unroll writings that were secret

469 Antigonus Carystius, *Collection of Wonderful Tales*

The bird is lame, and from this, Callimachus, the one from Egypt, wishing to be very clear, said this concerning some other bird,

> the [bird called] *aegithus*, [is] lame in both feet

470

a Apollod. (*BNJ* 244 F 157a5); Strab. 7.3.6

ἐπιτιμᾷ δὲ καὶ τοῖς Σικελίαν τὴν πλάνην λέγουσι . . .
καὶ τοῖς μὲν ἄλλοις συγγνώμην εἶναι, Καλλιμάχῳ δὲ
μὴ πάνυ . . . ὃς τὴν μὲν Γαῦδον Καλυψοῦς νῆσόν
φησι.

Γαῦδος

b [Ammon.] *Diff.* p. 103 Valckenaer (p. 352 Nickau)

ὀλίγον καὶ μικρὸν διαφέρει· τὸ μὲν γὰρ ὀλίγον ἐπ᾽
ἀριθμοῦ, τὸ δὲ μικρὸν ἐπὶ μεγέθους τάσσεται. Ἀρι-
στόνικος ἐν ὑπομνήματι . . . Καλλίμαχος ἐν β᾽ Αἰτίων
στοιχείῳ· "ὀλίγην—Καλυψοῦς." φασὶ δὲ οὕτω ὀλίγην
μικρὰν ὑπαλλακτικῶς . . . καὶ Ὅμηρος, "δίφρον . . .
ὀλίγην τε τράπεζαν" (*Od.* 20.259).

ὀλίγην νησῖδα Καλυψοῦς

471 Ap. Dysc. *Pron.* (*Gramm. Gr.* vol. 1.1, p. 113
Schneider)

Ἡσίοδος . . . ἐπίμεμπτός ἐστιν εἰπὼν . . . ἐν ᾧ ἑνικῷ
ἀντὶ πληθυντικοῦ ἐχρήσατο· καὶ Καλλίμαχος·

Μοῦσαί νιν ἑοῖς ἐπὶ τυννὸν ἔθεντο
⟨γούνασι⟩[1]

[1] Sugg. Toup.

470

a Apollodorus; Strabo, *Geography*

He censures those who say that [Odysseus'] wandering took place around Sicily . . . and he pardons others, but not at all Callimachus, who says that Gaudus is the island of Calypso.

> Gaudus

b Pseudo-Ammonius, *On the Differences of Synonymous Expressions*

Few (*oligon*) differs from small (*mikron*): Few relates to number, and small to size. Aristonicus in his *Commentary* [says] . . . Callimachus in a verse in Book 2 of the *Aetia*: "the small (*oligēn*) island of Calypso." He says in this way he varies *mikron* with *oligon* . . . like Homer, "a stool . . . and a small (*oligān*) table" (*Od.* 20.259).

> the small island of Calypso

471 Apollonius Dyscolus, *On Pronouns*

Hesiod[1] . . . is criticized, saying that . . . he used a singular form instead of a plural, like Callimachus,

> the Muses placed him, a child,
> on their knees

[1] *Op.* 58.

472 Ap. Dysc. *Pron.* (*Gramm. Gr.* vol. 1.1, p. 109.25 Schneider)

τὸ μέντοι "ἀλλ᾽ αἰεὶ φρεσὶν ᾗσιν ἔχων" ἀντὶ τοῦ ἐμαῖς· εὐλόγως ὑπ᾽ Ἀριστάρχου ὑπωπτεύετο ὡς νόθον, καθὸ ἀδιάπτωτος ἐν ἀντωνυμίαις. πλεῖστα γοῦν ἔστ παρ᾽ ἑτέροις εὑρεῖν, "σφέτερον πατέρα" ἀντὶ τοῦ ὑμέτερον, ἀντὶ τοῦ τεά "τοι—εά" παρὰ Καλλιμάχῳ.

†τοι κήδεα λέξον ἑά

473

a Ap. Dysc. *Adv.* (*Gramm. Gr.* vol. 1.1, p. 157.13 Schneider)

ὅτι γὰρ καὶ δύο συλλαβῶν ἀπόκοπα γίνονται, ἐν τῷ Περὶ παθῶν ἐδείχθη. τό τε γὰρ πρόπαρ οὕτως ἔχει, καὶ τὸ μάκαρ, πηδά, καὶ τὸ ὑμέν παρὰ Καλλιμάχῳ.

b Hellad. *Chrest.* ap. Phot. *Bibl.* (p. 531a8)

τὸ δὲ μάκαρ ἐκ τοῦ μακάριος ἀποκέκοπται, ὥσπερ καὶ τὸ ὑμέναιε γέγονεν ἀποκοπὲν ὑμέν.

474 Ap. Dysc. *Coni.* (*Gramm. Gr.* vol. 1.1, p. 238.17 Schneider)

. . . τοῦ Καλλιμάχου,

†περσιητ᾽ ἕνεκεν πένθος ἀπωμόσατ[ο[1]

---

[1] Pf. ad loc: locus lacunis nimis deformatus de argumento, de sententiarum conexu, de supplementis.

472 Apollonius Dyscolus, *On Pronouns*

"Always having in my (*hēisin*) chest"[1] instead of in my (*emais*) chest: Aristarchus suspected with reason that it is spurious, since Homer is faultless in his use of pronouns. But a great number of examples can be found in others, [for instance] "your (*spheteron*) father"[2] instead of your (*humeteron*) father, and instead of your (*tea*) cares, "your (*hea*) cares" in Callimachus.

> tell about your cares

[1] Hom. *Od.* 13.320.   [2] Hes. *Op.* 2.

473

a Apollonius Dyscolus, *On Adverbs*

That two of the syllables are created by *apocopē* (cutting off) is shown in *On Modifications*. In Callimachus the parts that come first are *makar*, *pēda*, and (*h*)*ymen*.

b Helladius, *Chrestomathy* in Photius, *Library*

makar is cut from *makarios*, just as (*h*)*ymen* is cut from *hymenaie*.

474 Apollonius Dyscolus, *On Conjunctions*

. . . [an example from] Callimachus,

> she[1] swore off grief on account of Hecate[2]

[1] Perhaps Demeter.   [2] Perseia, daughter of Perses, but also "the Destroyer."

475 Artem. 4.84 Pack

τοῖς δ' ἀπόροις μικρὰ παντελῶς, καὶ μάλιστά γε οἱ
ἀγαθοί . . . ὀρθῶς γοῦν καὶ τὸ Καλλιμάχειον ἔχει·

αἰεὶ τοῖς μικκοῖς μικκὰ διδοῦσι θεοί

476 Ath. 1.24b

οἱ δὲ νεώτεροι καὶ ἐπὶ τοῦ πληρωθῆναι τιθέασι τὸ
πάσασθαι. Καλλίμαχος,

μύθου δὲ πασαίμην

ἥδιον

477 Ath. 13.571a

Ἔτι πολλὰ τοῦ Κυνούλκου θέλοντος λέγειν καὶ τοῦ
Μάγνου ἐπιρραπίσαι βουληθέντος αὐτὸν εἰς τιμὴν
τοῦ Μυρτίλου, φθάσας ὁ Μυρτίλος ἔφη· "οὐχ—καλέ-
σαι" φησὶν ὁ Καλλίμαχος,

οὐχ ὧδ' ἐμόγησαν
ἐλπίδες ὥστ' ἐχθρῶν συμμαχίην καλέσαι

478 Ath. 2.69c

καὶ Καλλίμαχος δέ φησιν ὅτι ἡ Ἀφροδίτη τὸν Ἄδω-
νιν ἐν θριδακίνῃ κρύψειεν, ἀλληγορούντων τῶν ποιη-
τῶν ὅτι ἀσθενεῖς εἰσι πρὸς ἀφροδίσια οἱ συνεχῶς
χρώμενοι θρίδαξι.

118

475 Artemidorus, *Interpretation of Dreams*

Always small things to the poor, especially the good . . .
rightly therefore Callimachus says:

> Always the gods give small things to small people.

476 Athenaeus, *The Learned Banqueters*

But more recent authors also use *pateomai* to mean to be
full. Callimachus,

> for me to have my fill of a story would be sweeter

477 Athenaeus, *The Learned Banqueters*

Although Cynulcus[1] still had much that he wanted to say,
and Ulpian[2] was eager to attack him in defense of Myrtilus,
Myrtilus[3] began speaking first: As Callimachus says,

> My situation is not so
> hopeless that I have to call on enemies for assistance.

[1] A Cynic philosopher who takes an anti-Attic position in
Athenaeus' *The Learned Banqueters*.　　[2] Ulpian of Tyre, and
therefore the "Syrian." An important jurist and politician who
plays the role of symposiarch in the *Deipnosophistae*.

[3] Myrtilus of Thessaly, a grammarian and cynic, like Cynulcus.

478 Athenaeus, *The Learned Banqueters*

And Callimachus claims that Aphrodite hid Adonis in a
bed of lettuce, which is the poets' way of saying allegori-
cally that men who eat lettuce continually become weak
in respect to their sexual power.

CALLIMACHUS

479 Caes. Bass. *De met.* (*Gramm. Lat.* vol. 6, p. 258.25 Keil)

de hendecasyll. Phalaecio . . . altera divisio est cuius feceram mentionem, cum de epodo Callimachi dicerem hoc exemplo: "siccas ducite machinae carinas." nam priores duo pedes . . . heroum, reliqua pars ithyphallicum facit.

480 Choerob. in Theodos. *Alex. can.* (*Gramm. Gr.* vol. 4.1, p. 115 Hilgard)

ἐπειδὴ δὲ κατὰ τὸν Θουκυδίδην "ἀρχόμενοι πάντες ὀξύτερον ἀντιλαμβάνονται," καὶ Καλλίμαχος δὲ τὸ αὐτὸ τοῦτο λέγει·

ἀρχόμενοι μανίην ὀξυτάτην ἔχομεν

481 Choerob. in Theodos. *Alex. can.* (*Gramm. Gr.* vol. 4.1, p. 268 Hilgard)

ὅτι δὲ καὶ τοῦ τάλας τάλαντος ἦν ἡ γενική, δηλοῖ ὁ Ἱππῶναξ εἰπών "τι τῷ τάλαντα Βουπάλῳ συνῴκησας;" καὶ ὁ Καλλίμαχος γινώσκει τὴν διὰ τοῦ ν̄τ κλίσιν ἐν οἷς φησιν,

οἱ δὲ τὸν αἰνοτάλαντα κατέστεψαν

479 Caesius Bassus, *On Meter*

About the hendecasyllabic Phalaecean[1] . . . there is another division, of which I made mention when I spoke about an epode of Callimachus using this example: "take down the dry ships with an engine." For the first two feet . . . are dactyls and the second part makes an ithyphallic.

[1] The Phalacean is an Aeolic meter usually analyzed as a glyconic followed by a bacchiac (or catalectic iamb); Bassus is suggesting that it could also be understood as two dactyls followed by an ithyphallic.

480 Choeroboscus

Since according to Thucydides[1] "at the beginning everyone is seized with the greatest enthusiasm," and Callimachus says the same thing:

> At the beginning we have the most acute madness.

[1] Thuc. 2.8.2.

481 Choeroboscus

And that the genitive of *talas* was *talantos* is clear from Hipponax who says, "Why did you live with the wretched (*talanti*) Bupalus?"[1] And Callimachus knows the inflection with *nt* where he says,

> They garlanded the one who is most miserable.

[1] Hippon. 15 West (12 D[3]).

482 Choerob. in Theodos. *Alex. can.* (*Gramm. Gr.* vol. 4.2, p. 119 Hilgard)

τὸ ᾔδειν οἱ Ἴωνες λέγουσιν ᾔδεα κατὰ διάλυσιν, ὡς παρὰ Καλλιμάχῳ,

ᾔδεα μᾶλλον ἔγωγε

483 Choerob. in Theodos. *Alex. can.* (*Gramm. Gr.* vol. 4.1, p. 130 Hilgard)

ἔστι γὰρ τῇ ὑσμίνῃ καὶ τῇ Δωδώνῃ διὰ τοῦ η καὶ ῑ, καὶ γίνονται κατὰ μεταπλασμὸν τῇ ὑσμῖνι καὶ τῇ Δωδῶνι διὰ τοῦ ῑ μόνον, οἷον ὡς παρὰ τῷ ποιητῇ· "μέμασαν δὲ καὶ ὣς ὑσμῖνι μάχεσθαι" καὶ παρὰ Καλλιμάχῳ·

μή με τὸν ἐν Δωδῶνι λέγοι μόνον οὕνεκα χαλκόν ἤγειρον

484 Choerob. in Theodos. *Alex. can.* (*Gramm. Gr.* vol. 4.1, p. 113 Hilgard)

τινὲς δὲ ἠθέλησαν τὸ λ τελικόν λέγειν τῶν ἀρσενικῶν ὀνομάτων, ἐπειδὴ τὸ βάκαλ κλινόμενον εὑρέθη οἷον ὁ βάκαλ του βάκαλος καὶ οἱ βάκαλες ὡς παρὰ Καλλ.,

†τέκνα σοὶ μὲν βάκαλες†

482 Choeroboscus

In reference to *ēidein* (I had known) the Ionians say *ēidea*
by resolving the diphthong, as in Callimachus,

> I had certainly known

483 Choeroboscus

The forms are *husminēi* and *dōdōnēi* with the eta and iota,
and *hysmīni* and *dōdōni* are made by metaplasty with the
iota alone, such as [this example] from the Poet: "they
were eager to fight in battle (*hysmini*),"[1] and from Callim-
achus,

> may no one say that I only banged the brass in
> Dodona (*Dōdōni*)[2]

[1] Hom. *Il.* 8.56.   [2] At the oracle of Zeus at Dodona in
Epirus there were bronze cauldrons that resounded simultane-
ously when one was touched (Serv. ad Verg. *Aen.* 3.466). The
expression refers to someone who makes a lot of noise signifying
nothing.

484 Choeroboscus

Some wished to say that lambda is a termination for mas-
culine nouns since Bacal is found declined this way: *Bakal*
(nominative), *Bakalos* (genitive), and *Bakales*[1] (nomina-
tive plural), as in Callimachus,

> your children Bacales[2]

[1] An indigenous people in Libya (Hdt. 4.171).
[2] The text is corrupt.

123

485 Choerob. in Theodos. *Alex. can.* (*Gramm. Gr.* vol. 4.1, p. 152 Hilgard)

οἱ Δωριεῖς τῶν εἰς ειϛ διὰ τῆς ει διφθόγγου ἀποβάλλουσι τὸ ῑ, οἷον χαρίεις χαρίες, τιμήεις τιμῆες, Μαλόεις Μαλόες· τοιοῦτον γάρ ἐστι καὶ παρὰ Καλλιμάχῳ "ὁ—χορός" ἀντὶ τοῦ Μαλόεις.

ὁ δ᾽ ἀείδων Μαλόες ἦλθε χορός

486 Choerob. in Theodos. *Alex. can.* (*Gramm. Gr.* vol. 4.1, p. 155 Hilgard)

τὸ δὲ κύριον ὄνομα τὸ Κόμης διχῶς εὑρέθη κλινόμενον παρὰ τοῖς ἀρχαίοις· εὑρίσκεται γὰρ Κόμου ἡ γενική, Ἰωνικῶς δὲ καὶ Κόμεω, ὥσπερ Ἀτρείδης Ἀτρείδεω καὶ Κομάδης τὸ πατρωνυμικόν, ὥσπερ Βορεάδης, Αἰνειάδης, Κλευάδης, εὑρίσκεται δὲ καὶ διὰ τοῦ τοϛ κλινόνενον τῷ λόγῳ τῶν ἰαμβικῶν, οἷον Κόμητος, ὡς παρὰ τῷ Καλλιμάχῳ·

δημεχθέα Χέλλωνα κακόκνημόν τε Κόμητα

487 Choerob. in Theodos. *Alex. can.* (*Gramm. Gr.* vol. 4.1, p. 265 Hilgard)

τοῦτο γὰρ ὁ Καλλίμαχος διὰ τοῦ ε ἔκλινεν, εἰπών·

ἀλλ᾽ ἀντὶ βρεφέων πολιὸν νέον εἴρενα μέσσον

485 Choeroboscus

The Dorians drop the iota from the diphthong *ei* of words ending in *-eis*, for example *charieis* becomes *charies*, *timēeis* becomes *timēes*, and *Maloeis*, *Maloes*. Such is the case even in Callimachus. Instead of *Maloeis* he says,

> the chorus of Maloes[1] came singing

[1] Apollo Maloes had a shrine and festival in Malea outside of Mytilene on Lesbos (Thuc. 3.3.3).

486 Choeroboscus

The proper name Comes is found declined in two ways by the ancients; the genitive *Komou* and in Ionic *Komeō* like *Atreidēs*, *Atreideō* and the patronymic *Komadēs*, like *Boreadēs*, *Aineiadēs*, *Kleuadēs*; and it is found declined with *-tos* in the writing of the iambic poets like *Komētos*, as in Callimachus,

> Chellon hated by the people and Comes with weak
>   legs

487 Choeroboscus

Callimachus declined this word (*eirēn*) with epsilon, saying:

> After infancy, old age, youthful adolescence and
>   middle age (*eirena*)[1]

[1] The four ages of man.

488 Choerob. in Theodos. *Alex. can.* (*Gramm. Gr.* vol. 4.1, p. 287 Hilgard)

. . . ἔτι σεσημείωται τὸ Ἄτραξ Ἄτραγος διὰ τοῦ γ̄ κλιθέν (ἔστι δὲ ἔθνος), περὶ οὗ ἔστιν εἰπεῖν ὅτι τοῦτο ἀναλογώτερόν ἐστι διὰ τοῦ κ̄ κλινόμενον, οἷον Ἄτρα-κος, ὡς παρὰ Καλλιμάχῳ,

Ἀτράκιον δήπειτα λυκοσπάδα πῶλον ἐλαύνει

489 Pf. = *Hec.* 163

490 Pf. = *Hec.* 173

491 [Plut.] *Cons. ad Apoll.* 113e–f

Δῆλον οὖν ὅτι καὶ ὁ λεγόμενος ἄωρος θάνατος εὐ-παραμύθητός ἐστι διά τε ταῦτα καὶ τὰ προειρημένα ἐν τοῖς ἔμπροσθεν,

μεῖον ἐδάκρυσεν Τρωίλος ἢ Πρίαμος[1]

[1] Cf. Cic. *Tusc.* 1.93, non male ait Callimachus "multo saepius lacrimasse Priamum quam Troilum."

492 Clem. Alex. *Protr.* 2.29.4

Σκύθαι δὲ τοὺς ὄνους ἱερεύοντες μὴ παυέσθων, ὡς Ἀπολλόδωρός φησι καὶ Καλλίμαχος·

Φοῖβος Ὑπερβορέοισιν ὄνων ἐπιτέλλεται ἱροῖς

488 Choeroboscus

... Yet [the form] *Atrax, Atragos* appears declined with a gamma (it is an ethnic name); about this one can say that it is analogous to *Atrax, Atrakos* declined with a kappa, as in Callimachus,

> then he drives the Atracian[1] colt with a wolf bit[2]

[1] Atrax or Atracia is a city in Thessaly (Ov. *Her.* 17.248).
[2] A hook-shaped, jagged bit used for fractious horses (Plut. *Quaest. conv.* 641f).

489 Pf. = *Hecale* 163

490 Pf. = *Hecale* 173

491 Pseudo-Plutarch, *Consolation to Apollonius*

It is clear that even the death that is called untimely is easily consoled by the same words that were said above.

> Troilus cried less than Priam[1]

[1] Priam, king of Troy, weeps in the presence of Achilles, who killed his sons, including Hector and Troilus, defenders of the city (Hom. *Il.* 24.507–12, 255–59).

492 Clement of Alexandria, *Protrepicus*

May the Scythians not cease to sacrifice asses, as Apollodorus[1] says and Callimachus:

> Phoebus orders the Hyperboreans[2] to sacrifice asses

[1] Apollodorus of Athens (2nd c. BC; *BNJ* 244 F 126a), historian and grammarian.   [2] A mythical northern people associated with Apollo (Hdt. 4.32–35). On their annual gifts to Delos, see *Aet.* 186.

493 Clem. Alex. *Strom.* 5.14.100 (2)

γήινον μὲν οἱ φιλόσοφοι παρ' ἕκαστα τὸ σῶμα ἀνα-
γορεύσιν . . . Καλλ. δὲ διαρρήδην γράφει· . . . πάλιν
τε αὖ ὁ αὐτός τε,

εἴ σε Προμηθεύς
ἔπλασε, καὶ πηλοῦ μὴ 'ξ ἑτέρου γέγονας

494 Ath. 1.8e

ταῦτα οἴκοθεν ἔχων εἰς τὸ συμπόσιον ἦλθον καὶ προ-
μελετήσας, ἵνα κἀγὼ τὸ στεγανόμιον κομίζων παρα-
γένωμαι,

ἄκαπνα γὰρ αἰὲν ἀοιδοί
θύομεν

495 Didym. *Dem.* (*P.Berol.* 9780 col. XIV, 34)

κ[αὶ] ἔστιν ὁ λόγος τὰ νῦν τῷ Δη[μ]οσθένε[ι π]ερ[ὶ]
τῆς Μεγαρικῆς Ὀργάδ[ος], ἧς καὶ Καλλίμαχός που
μνημονεύων φησ[ί]·

Νισαίης ἀγλῖθες ἀπ' Ὀργάδος

493 Clement of Alexandria, *Stromata*

The philosophers say that the body is made of earth in each case . . . Callimachus writes clearly,[1] . . . and again [he writes],

> if Prometheus[2] made you,
> and you were not created from another clay

[1] *Ia.* 192.1–3.　　[2] The Titan god who defied Zeus and became the archetypical craftsman. In an Aesopic fable (240 Perry) he molds men and animals from clay.

494 Athenaeus, *The Learned Banqueters*

I came to the symposium bringing these things from home and I took care to be here with the rent money,

> we bards always make smokeless sacrifices

495 Didymus, *On Demosthenes* (Berlin papyrus)

There is a saying as regards the present discusssion in Demosthenes about Megarian Orgas, which Callimachus recalls somewhere and says,

> heads of garlic from Nisaean Orgas[1]

[1] Nisaea was the old port of Megara (Thuc. 4.66.4), and Orgas, a nearby town.

CALLIMACHUS

496 (*SH* 295; 496 + 533 Pf.) *Epimer. Hom.* λ 38 s.v. λαός
(vol. 2, p. 472.56 Dyck);[1] *Et. Gud.* s.v. μάταιος (p. 380.20
Sturz)

λαοὶ Δευκαλίωνος ὅσοι γενόμεσθα γενέθλης
πουλὺ θαλασσαίων μυνδότεροι νεπόδων

[1] γίνεται δὲ λαὸς . . . παρὰ τὸ λαλῶ . . . ἄλλοι δὲ παρὰ
τοὺς λᾶας ὠνομάσθαι,

497 *Epimer. Hom.* π 169 s.v. παρείατο (vol. 2, p. 641
Dyck)

παρείατο· Καλλ.,

κούρη δὲ παρείατο δακρυχέουσα

498 *Et. Gen.* B s.v. ἄκμον

ἄκμον· σημαίνει τόν τε σίδηρον, ἐφ' οὗ οἱ χαλκεῖς
τύπτουσι, καὶ τοῦ Οὐρανοῦ τὸν πατέρα· οὕτως γὰρ
αὐτὸν γενεαλογοῦσι. Καλλίμαχος,

τῷ περὶ δινήεντ' Ἀκμονίδην ἔβαλεν

499 *Et. Gen.* B s.v. ἀκουός

ἀκουός· Καλλ.,

ἀλλ' ἐπακουούς
οὐκ ἔσχεν

130

496 (*SH* 295; 496 + 533 Pf.)[1] *Epimerismi Homerici*; *Etymologicum Gudianum*

As many as we were became the people of Deucalion,[2] much dumber than the children of the sea.

[1] J. Irigoin (*REG* 73 [1960]: 439–47) joined these fragments to form an elegiac couplet (*SH* 295).   [2] Deucalion survived the mythical flood and with his wife, Pyrrha, repopulated the world (Pind. *Ol.* 9.41–53).

497 *Epimerismi Homerici*

pareiato (she took a seat): Callimachus,

the girl sat down weeping

498 *Etymologicum Genuinum*

akmon (anvil): it means an iron object which bronze workers strike, and also Acmon is the father of Uranus. They give him this genealogy. Callimachus,

around it he cast the whirling son of Acmon

499 *Etymologicum Genuinum*

akouos (a listener): Callimachus,

but he did not have
listeners

500 *Et. Gen.* AB s.v. ἀλίαστος

ἀλίαστος· . . . παρὰ τὸ λιάζω . . . ἢ παρὰ τὸ ἀλῶ
ῥῆμα . . . γίνεται ἀλίζω, ὡς φοιτῶ φοιτίζω. Καλλ.,

φοιτίζειν ἀγαθοὶ πολλάκις ἤιθεοι
εἰς ὀάρους ἐθέλουσιν

501 *Et. Gen.* AB s.v. Ἅλυς

Ἅλυς· οἷον "ἀκτῇ ἐπὶ προβλῆτι ῥοαὶ Ἅλυος ποταμοῖο
δεινὸν ἐρεύγονται· μετὰ τὸν δ᾽ ἀγχίρροος Ἴρις." Ἅλυς
ποταμὸς Παφλαγονίας κατὰ Σινώπην, χωρίζων Χά-
λυβας καὶ Λευκοσύρους τοὺς ἐν Πόντῳ. . . . Ἴριν δὲ
αὐτὸν λέγει Καλλ.

502 *Et. Gen.* AB s.v. ἀμαλή

ἀμαλή· ἡ μάλη—ἡ λέξις Μακεδόνων—ὅθεν καὶ πρό-
μαλος εἴρηται . . . ἐστὶ δὲ ⟨καὶ⟩ ἀπαλή, καὶ τροπῇ
ἀμαλή, Καλλ.

ἣν μο⟨ύ⟩νη ῥύετο παῖς ἀμαλή

503 *Et. Gen.* B s.v. Μιμαλλόνες

Μιμαλλόνες· ἐκλήθησαν κυρίως αἱ ⟨. . .⟩ γυναῖκες—
πολεμικαὶ γὰρ—παρὰ τὸ μιμεῖσθαι τοὺς ἄνδρας· ἤτοι
διὰ Μακεδονικὴν ἱστορίαν, ἥτις κεῖται ἐν τοῖς Καλλι-
μάχου.

500 *Etymologicum Genuinum*

aliastos (undaunted): . . . parallel to *liazdō* (draw back) . . . or the word *alō* . . . is parallel to *alizō* (assemble) like *phoitō* to *phoitizō* (frequent). Callimachus,

Noble young men often wish to spend time in conversation.

501 *Etymologicum Genuinum*

Halys: for example, "on the jutting headland the streams of the river Halys roar terribly; and into it the Iris flows nearby." The Halys[1] is a river of Paphlagonia opposite Sinope dividing the Chalybes[2] and the Leucosyri[3] in Pontus[4] . . . Callimachus says that it is the same as the Iris.

[1] The Halys flows between Syria and Paphlagonia, emptying into the Black Sea (Hdt. 1.6). [2] A people in Pontus famous for ironworking (Hdt. 1.28). [3] Cappadocians (Strabo 12.3.9).
[4] On the south shore of the Black Sea.

502 *Etymologicum Genuinum*

amalē: the Macedonian form *malē* is derived from this one, from which *promalos* also comes . . . there is also (*h*)*apalē* and by a change in form *amalē*. Callimachus,

which (city) the tender girl alone defended

503 *Etymologicum Genuinum*

Mimallones: women are rightly called Mimallones who are warlike by imitating (*mimeisthai*) men; indeed, according to a Macedonian history which is in Callimachus' (*Aetia*?).[1]

[1] Or according to Schneider (fr. 401), his *Commentaries*.

504 *Et. Gud.* s.v. Ἄρειος πάγος

Ἄρειος πάγος· δικαστήριον Ἀθήνησιν οὕτω καλούμε-
νον. Καλλίμαχος,

αἱ δὲ πάγον φορέουσιν ἔπ᾽ Ἄρεος

505 *Et. Gen.* AB s.v. Ἀσσύριοι

Ἀσσύριοι· τὸ ἔθνος· Καλλ.,

ἡ μὲν ἀπ᾽ Ἀσσυρίων ἡμεδαπὴ στρατιή

506 *Et. Gen.* AB s.v. Ἀσσύριοι

καί,

ἥμισυ μὲν Πέρσαι†, ἥμισυ δ᾽ Ἀσσύριοι

507 *Et. Gen.* B. s.v. ἀτμήν, ἀτμένος

ἀτμήν, ἀτμένος· ὁ δοῦλος. Καλλ.,

Φιλαδελφείων† ἄτμενος ἦα δόμων[1]

[1] corr. Dilthey et Diels (D'Alessio 2007, vol. 2, 710–11n28)

508 *Et. Gen.* B. s.v. βλωμός

βλωμός· ὁ ψωμός. Καλλ.,

ὅσον βλωμοῦ πίονος ἠράσατο

504 *Etymologicum Gudianum*

Areopagos (Hill of Ares):[1] what the Athenians call the court of justice. Callimachus,

the [roads] lead to the Hill of Ares

[1] A large rock below the Acropolis in Athens where capital crimes were tried under the democracy.

505 *Etymologicum Genuinum*

Assyrioi (Assyrians): a people. Callimachus,

the native army of Assyrians

506 *Etymologicum Genuinum*

and,

half Persians, half Assyrians[1]

[1] See *Fr. Inc. Sed.* 505 above.

507 *Etymologicum Genuinum*

atmēn, atmenos: a slave. Callimachus,

I was a slave[1] in the court of the Philadelphi.[2]

[1] Or "of a slave." The text is corrupt.
[2] Ptolemy II Philadelphus and his sister/wife, Arsinoe II.

508 *Etymologicum Genuinum*

blōmos: a morsel. Callimachus,

as much as he desired a rich morsel

509 *Et. Gen.* AB s.v. Βούχετα ἢ Βουχέτιον

Βούχετα ἢ Βουχέτιον· ἔστι δὲ πόλις τῆς Ἠπείρου . . .
μέμνηται δὲ τοῦ ἐθνικοῦ Καλλ. οἷον,

> ἐξ ἁλὸς οὐ †δίκην ἀνέρα Βουχέτιον
> ἕλκειν

510 *Et. Gen.* s.v. AB γέγειος

γέγειος· ὁ ἀρχαῖος. καὶ γέγειαι. εἴρηται παρ' Ἑκα-
ταίῳ καὶ Καλλιμάχῳ,

> ἢ ῥ' ὅτι τὼς ὁ γέγειος ἔχει λόγος

511 *Et. Gen.* B s.v. γενὴ καὶ γενέθλη

γενὴ καὶ γενέθλη· . . . Καλλ.,

> τὴν δὲ γενὴν οὐκ οἶδα

512 *Et. Gen.* B s.v. γλαρίς

γλαρίς· λιθοξοϊκὸν ἐργαλεῖον. Καλλ.,

> καὶ γλαρίδες σταφύλη τε καθιεμένη τε μολυβδίς

513 *Et. Gen.* B s.v. γραίδιον

γραίδιον· . . . ἔστι γραῦις, γραϋδι παρὰ Καλλιμάχῳ
. . . οὕτως οὖν καὶ γραῦις γραύιδος, γραυίδιον· καὶ
. . . γραΐδιον.

509 *Etymologicum Genuinum*

Bucheta or Buchetion is a city of Epirus . . . Callimachus mentions a local custom such as,

> it is not right for a man from Bucheta to take something[1] from the sea

[1] Perhaps a kind of sacred fish, as Bentley conjectured.

510 *Etymologicum Genuinum*

gegeios: ancient. Also *gegeiai* (feminine plural). It is used by Hecataeus[1] and Callimachus,

> truly, [I say] that the ancient story has it this way

[1] *BNJ* 1 F 362.

511 *Etymologicum Genuinum*

genē kai genethlē (family): . . . Callimachus,

> I do not know the family

512 *Etymologicum Genuinum*

glaris: an instrument for cutting stone. Callimachus,

> and the chisels, the plummet of a level, and the sinking lead weight[1]

[1] The equipment for house-building (Pollux 10.147).

513 *Etymologicum Genuinum*

graidion: . . . it is an old woman (*gravis*, *gravidi*) in Callimachus, and so the forms of the noun are *gravis*, *gravidos*, *gravidion*; and . . . *graïdion*.

514 *Et. Gen.* AB s.v. Γραικός

Γραικός· Καλλ.,

   Γραικοὶ καὶ γαίης ἡμετέρης ἀδαεῖς

515 *Et. Gen.* B s.v. δάκετον

δάκετον· θηρίον ἑρπετόν. παρὰ τὸ δάκνω δάκνετον καὶ δάκετον, καὶ δάκετος. Καλλ.,

   ξεῖνος Ἐχιδναῖον νέρθεν ἄγων δάκετον

516 *Et. Gen.* B s.v. δεκάφυια

δεκάφυια· τὰ δεκαπλάσια. Καλλ.,

   τῶν ἔτι σοὶ δεκάφυια φάτο ζωάγρια τίσειν

517 *Et. Gen.* AB s.v. Δελφοί

Δελφοί· καὶ Δελφός. Καλλ.,

   καὶ Δελφὸς ἀνὴρ ἐμοὶ ἱεροεργός

514 *Etymologicum Genuinum*

Graikos (Greek): Callimachus,

> the Greeks are ignorant of our land[1]

[1] Since ancient Greeks called themselves Hellenes, a non-Greek must be speaking.

515 *Etymologicum Genuinum*

daketon: a creeping animal. The forms of *daknō*: *dakneton*, *daketon*, and *daketos*. Callimachus,

> the stranger driving up from below the Echidnean beast[1]

[1] Cerberus, the three-headed dog who guards the underworld, is the son of Echidna, so the stranger must be Heracles (Bacchyl. *Ep.* 5.56–62).

516 *Etymologicum Genuinum*

dekaphuia: ten times. Callimachus,

> he said he would still pay you tenfold ransom for them[1]

[1] Perhaps addressed to a deity for the lives or well-being of some other persons, as is commonly found in epigrams (e.g., *Epig.* 53–54; see D'Alessio 2007, vol. 2, 713).

517 *Etymologicum Genuinum*

Delphoi (Delphians): and *Delphos* (masculine singular). Callimachus,

> and a man from Delphi was the sacrificing priest for me

518 *Et. Gen.* B s.v. δῆρις

δῆρις· ἡ μάχη . . . ἢ παρὰ τὸ δαίω, τὸ σφάζω καὶ
κόπτω, γίνεται ὄνομα δάϊς βαρύτονον· Καλλ.,

ἐς δάϊν ἐρχομενάων

519 Pf. = *Hec.* 167

520 *Et. Gen.* B s.v. δίασμα

δίασμα· ἡ πρώτη τοῦ ἱματίου ἐργασία· Καλλ.,

εἰ δέ ποτε προφέροιντο διάσματα, φάρεος ἀρχήν

521 *Et. Gen.* B s.v. Διόσκορος

Διόσκορος· . . . δεῖ σημειώσασθαι τὸ "Διόσθυος"
παρὰ Καλλιμάχῳ· ἐν συνθέσει γὰρ ὂν ἐφύλαξε τὸ σ.
ἐστὶ δὲ ὄνομα μηνός.

522 *Et. Gen.* B s.v. δύπτης

δύπτης· δύπται λέγονται αἱ αἴθυιαι. καὶ ὁ δύπτης (?).
Καλλίμαχος,

δύπται δ' ἐξ ἁλὸς ἐρχόμενοι
ἔνδιοι καύηκες

518 *Etymologicum Genuinum*

dēris: battle . . . or in reference to a feast, slaughter and dismembering; the word *daïs* has an unaccented final syllable. Callimachus,

> of the women coming into battle

519 Pf. = *Hecale* 167

520 *Etymologicum Genuinum*

diasma (warp): the preliminary steps in making a cloak. Callimachus,

> if ever they brought forward the warp, the beginning of a mantle

521 *Etymologicum Genuinum*

Dioskoros: . . . In Callimachus the form *Diosthyos* must be noted. In composition it retained the sigma. It is the name of a month.[1]

[1] Diostheos is a month name in Rhodes (*IG* XII.1, 762.4).

522 *Etymologicum Genuinum*

dyptēs (diver): shearwaters are called divers. And (in the singular?), diver. Callimachus,

> divers coming from the sea, at midday, the terns

523 *Et. Mag.* s.v. εἶαρ (p. 294.48 Lasserre)

εἶαρ· τὸ αἷμα. καὶ εἰαροπώτης, ὁ αἱματοπότης· ὡς φησι Καλλ.,

$$\text{τὸ δ' ἐκ μέλαν εἶαρ ἔδαπτεν}$$

524 *Et. Gen.* B s.v. Εἰνατία

Εἰνατία· ἐπίθετον τῆς Εἰλειθυίας. Καλλ.,

$$\text{Εἰνατίην ὁμόδελφυν ἐπ' ὠδίνεσσιν ἰδοῦσα}$$

525 Pf. = *Hec.* 26

526 *Et. Gen.* B s.v. ἐλινύω

ἐλινύω· ἐνδίδωμι, ἀναπαύομαι. Θεόκριτος καὶ Καλλ.

$$\text{οὐδὲ βοὴ κήρυκος ἐλίνυσεν}$$

527 *Et. Gen.* B s.v. ἐμπελάτειρα

ἐμπελάτειρα· ἡ ἑταίρα· ἀπὸ τοῦ ἐμπελάζειν πᾶσι. Καλλ.

$$\text{τοὺς αὐτῷ σκοτίους ἐμπελάτειρα †καὶ ἔτεκε γυνή†}$$

523 *Etymologicum Magnum*

eiar: blood. And blood drinker, the blood drinker; as Callimachus says,

> he ate up the black blood

524 *Etymologicum Genuinum*

Einatia: epithet of Eileithuia. Callimachus,

> (she) looking at her own sister Einatia[1] in the pains of childbirth

[1] Eileithuia, goddess of childbirth, was honored as Einatia at a cult site in Crete (Steph. Byz. ε 21 Billerbeck). The sister of Eileithuia is Hebe (Pind. *Nem.* 7.1–4), who may be the subject here. Eileithuia was the mother of Eros (Paus. 9.27.2).

525 Pf. = *Hecale* 26

526 *Etymologicum Genuinum*

elinuō: to concede, to cease. Theocritus[1] and Callimachus,

> nor did the cry of the herald abate

[1] Theoc. *Id.* 10.51.

527 *Etymologicum Genuinum*

empelateira (companion): the hetaera, from drawing near to all. Callimachus,

> drawing near to him in darkness; †and the woman gave birth† to them[1]

[1] The text is corrupt.

527a Pf. = *Hec.* 177

528 *Et. Gen.* B. s.v. ἠλεός

ἠλεός· μάταιος, μαινόμενος, μωρός. Καλλ.,

ὁ δ' ἠλεὸς οὔτ' ἐπὶ σίττην

βλέψας

528a *Et. Gen.* B s.v. ἠλεός (supra fr. 528)

ἠλεὰ μὲν ῥέξας, ἐχθρὰ δὲ πεισόμενε

529 *Et. Gen.* B s.v. ἠλιτόμηνος καὶ ἀλιτήμερος

ἠλιτόμηνος καὶ ἀλιτήμερος· σημαίνει δὲ τὸν ἑπταμη-
νιαῖον γεννηθέντα παῖδα, ὥς φησι Καλλ.,

τὸν οὐκ ἔπλησε φέρουσα
μήτηρ †οὓς ὥδινε μῆνας†

530 *Et. Gen.* AB s.v. ἴσανδρος

ἴσανδρος· παρὰ τὸ ἴσος γέγονε καὶ τοῦ ἀνδρὸς ἴσαν-
δρος· γράφεται δὲ τοῦ ῑ . . . καὶ παρὰ τοῖς ἐποποιοῖς
εὑρίσκεται συνεσταλμένον, ὡς παρὰ Καλλιμάχῳ,

χολῇ δ' ἴσα γέντα πάσαιο

527a Pf. = *Hecale* 177

528 *Etymologicum Genuinum*

ēleos: foolish, mad, moronic. Callimachus,

> the madman . . . not after seeing the nuthatch[1]

[1] A bird of good omen (*Ia.* 191.56).

528a *Etymologicum Genuinum* (above fr. 528)

> You, who after doing foolish things, will suffer hateful ones.[1]

[1] A reference to the "law of Rhadamanthys" that whatever one has done in life, one will suffer in the afterlife (Hes. fr. 286 M.-W.).

529 *Etymologicum Genuinum*

untimely born and unlucky: it means a child born in the seventh month, as Callimachus says,

> The mother, carrying the child, had not filled out the months when she gave birth

530 *Etymologicum Genuinum*

isandros (like a man): it is made from *isos* (equal) and *andros* (man). It is written with a long iota . . . and in epic poetry the short form is found as in Callimachus,

> may you taste guts like bile

531 *Et. Gen.* B s.v. κιβισις

κιβισις· σημαίνει κιβωτὸν ἢ πήραν. Καλλ.,

  εἰ γὰρ †ἐπιθήσει πάντα† ἐμὴ κίβισις

532 *Et. Gen.* AB s.v. Κῶος

Κῶος· σὺν τῷ ῑ γράφεται, ἐπειδὴ εὕρηται κατὰ διά-
στασιν. Καλλ.,

  τῷ ἴκελον τὸ γράμμα τὸ Κώϊον

533 v. 496

534 *Et. Gen.* AB s.v. ὄλπις

ὄλπις· Καλλίμαχος,

  καί ῥα παρὰ σκαιοῖο βραχίονος ἔμπλεον ὄλπιν

535 *Et. Gen.* A s.v. πλειότερος

πλειότερος· κατασκευάζεται οὕτως . . . οὐ πάντα τὰ
εἰς ων ὀνόματα ποιοῦσι συγκριτικά . . . τὸ οὖν παρὰ
Καλλιμάχῳ,

  ὄφρα σε πλειοτέρῃ δεῦρο δέχωμ'

531 *Etymologicum Genuinum*

kibisis: it means pouch or wallet. Callimachus,

> if my wallet will contain everything

532 *Etymologicum Genuinum*

Kōios (Coan): is written with iota, when it is found in diaeresis. Callimachus,

> Coan writing[1] is like it

[1] This may refer to the work of the fourth-century poet Philitas of Cos, whom Callimachus admired (*Aet.* 1.9–12; Harder vol. 2, 32–44).

533 see 496

534 *Etymologicum Genuinum*

olpis (oil flask): Callimachus,

> and from the left arm a full oil flask[1]

[1] These were used for anointing in the gymnasia (Theoc. *Id.* 2.156).

535 *Etymologicum Genuinum*

pleioteros (more complete): it is constructed in this way . . . not all words make comparatives with omega + nu . . . an example in Callimachus,

> so that I may receive you here with more complete

536 *Et. Gen.* B s.v. τέρπνιστος

τέρπνιστος· Καλλίμαχος,

   τέρπνιστοι δὲ τοκεῦσι τόθ᾽ υἱέες

537 *Et. Gen.* B s.v. Τρῳάς

Τρῳάς· ἔχει τὸ ῑ, ἐπειδὴ εὕρηται κατὰ διάστασιν
"Τρωϊάδας γυναῖκας"· καὶ παρὰ Καλλιμάχῳ

[lacuna]

538 *Et. Gen.* AB s.v. φείδομαι

φείδομαι· . . . φιδός ὄνομα, τὸ σημαῖνον τὸ φειδωλός,
ἐπεκράτησε διὰ τοῦ ῑ, ὡς παρὰ Καλλιμάχῳ οἷον,

         Μουσέων δ᾽ οὐ μάλα φιδὸς ἐγώ

539 *Et. Gen.* B s.v. φιαρός

φιαρός· ὁ λαμπρός. Καλλίμαχος,

         φιαρὴ τῆμος ἄνεσχεν ἕως

540 *Et. Gen.* B v. χύτλα

χύτλα· κυρίως τὰ μεθ᾽ ὕδατος ἔλαια, καταχρηστικῶς
δὲ καὶ τὰ ἐναγίσματα. Καλλίμαχος,

   χύτλων ἀντιάσαντες

536 *Etymologicum Genuinum*

terpnistos (most delightful): Callimachus,

Most delightful to parents, then, are sons

537 *Etymologicum Genuinum*

Trōias (Trojan woman) has the iota when it is found in diaeresis, as in "Trojan women"[1] and in Callimachus:

[citation missing]

[1] E.g., Hom. *Il.* 9.139.

538 *Etymologicum Genuinum*

pheidomai (I am sparing): . . . the word is *phīdos*, the meaning is parsimonious; it has a long iota, as in Callimachus, for example,

I am by no means sparing of the Muses

539 *Etymologicum Genuinum*

phiaros: shining. Callimachus,

then the bright dawn rose

540 *Etymologicum Genuinum*

chytla (libations): properly olives with water, incorrectly used of offerings for the dead. Callimachus,

after receiving libations

541 Euseb. *Chron.* 193

ἱστοροῦσι δὲ οἱ περὶ Ἀριστόδημον τὸν Ἠλεῖον, ὡς
ἀπ᾽ εἰκοστῆς καὶ ἑβδόμης ὀλυμπιάδος ἤρξαντο οἱ
ἀθληταὶ ἀναγράφεσθαι . . . πρὸ τοῦ γὰρ οὐδεὶς ἀνε-
γράφη, ἀμελησάντων τῶν πρότερον· τῇ δὲ εἰκοστῇ
ὀγδόῃ τὸ στάδιον νικῶν Κόροιβος Ἠλεῖος ἀνεγράφη
πρῶτος. καὶ ἡ ὀλυμπιὰς αὕτη πρώτη ἐτάχθη, ἀφ᾽ ἧς
Ἕλληνες ἀριθμοῦσι τοὺς χρόνους. τὰ δ᾽ αὐτὰ τῷ
Ἀριστοδήμωι καὶ Πολύβιος ἱστορεῖ. Καλλίμαχος δὲ
δεκατρεῖς Ὀλυμπιάδας ἀπὸ Ἰφίτου παρεῖσθαί φησι
μὴ ἀναγραφείσας, τῇ δὲ τεσσαρεσκαιδεκάτῃ Κόροι-
βον νικῆσαι.

542 Eust. ad *Od.* 8.20 (p. 1584.17 van der Valk)

ὁ μάσσων γίνεται ἐκ τοῦ μακρός καὶ ὁ βράσσων ἐκ
τοῦ βραχύς καὶ ὁ ἐλάσσων ἐκ τοῦ ἐλαχός, ὁ παρὰ
Καλλ. κεῖται.

543 Eust. ad *Il.* 8.518 (p. 727.21 van der Valk)

ἀπόμουσος ὁ ἄμουσος, καὶ ἀπότριχες παρὰ Καλλι-
μάχῳ οἱ ἄνηβοι, ἀλλὰ δηλαδὴ ἀπόδρομοι ἐν Κρήτῃ
οἱ μήπω τῶν κοινῶν δρόμων μετέχοντες ἔφηβοι.

541 Eusebius, *Chronicon*

The followers of Aristodemus[1] the Elean write that champions were first entered into the public record after the 27th Olympiad (780 BC) . . . before that no one was entered because in previous times they did not care. But in the 28th Olympiad (776 BC) Coroebus the Elean was victorious in the stadion and he was the first to be inscribed. And this same Olympiad was the first from which the Greeks calculate their chronology. Polybius[2] writes the same as Aristodemus. Callimachus says that there were thirteen Olympiads from the time of Iphitus[3] that were not recorded and that Coroebus was victorious in the fourteenth.[4]

[1] Historian (1st or 2nd c. BC; *BNJ* 414 F 1). [2] *BNJ* 254 F 2a. [3] King of Elis who restored the Olympic games after the Dorian invasion at the request of the Oracle at Delphi (Paus. 5.4.5–6). [4] Perhaps a reference to Callimachus' *On Contests* (*Fr. Doct.* 403), as suggested by Pfeiffer vol. 1, 388.

542 Eustathius on Homer, *Odyssey*

Massōn (larger) comes from *makros* (large) and *brassōn* (shorter) from *brachys* (short) and *elassōn* (smaller) from *elachos* (small) which is in Callimachus.

543 Eustathius on Homer, *Iliad*

Apomousos means uncultured (lit., Museless) and youths in Callimachus are *apotriches* (hairless) but clearly the *apodromoi* (raceless) in Crete are the ephebes who do not yet participate in the public races.

544 Eust. ad *Il.* 6.135 (p. 629.56 van der Valk)

βουπλὴξ δὲ βούκεντρον . . . εὕρηται καὶ ὀρθοπλὴξ
ἵππος . . . καὶ μεθυπλήξ, ὡς Καλλίμαχος,

   τοῦ < ˘ > μεθυπλῆγος φροίμιον Ἀρχιλόχου

545 Eust. ad *Il.* 20.207 (p. 1204.3 van der Valk)

. . . Καλλίμαχος δὲ ἄλλως ὀνόμασαι θελήσας οἶος
ἐκεῖνος Ὑδατοσύδνην λέγει μεταποιήσας τὴν Ἁλο-
σύδνην.

546 Eust. ad *Od.* 1.155 (p. 1404.38 van der Valk)

ἀναβάλλεται δὲ καὶ ὕδωρ, διὰ σωλήνων ἢ κίονος ἢ
οὕτω πως ἀναβαῖνον, ἢ καὶ ἄλλως ἀναπηδῶν, ὡς δη-
λοῖ παρὰ Καλλιμάχῳ τὸ,

               κρήνη
λευκὸν ὕδωρ ἀνέβαλλεν

547 Eust. ad *Od.* 7.107 (p. 1571.57 van der Valk)

καιροσέων δ' ὀθονέων· . . . καίρωμα, ὅ ἐστι μίτωμα·
καῖρος δέ φασι καὶ καίρωμα, τὸ διάπλεγμα ὃ οὐκ ἐᾷ
τοὺς στήμονας συγχέεσθαι, ἐξ οὗ καὶ καιρωστρίδες

544 Eustathius on Homer, *Iliad*

Bouplēx, an ox goad . . . is found and an *orthoplēx* (rearing) horse, . . . and *methyplēx* (struck by wine) as in Callimachus,

> the prelude of wine-struck Archilochus[1]

[1] Archilochus of Paros (7th c. BC; cf. Archil. fr. 120 West). On the meter, see D'Alessio 2007, vol. 2, 721n54.

545 Eustathius on Homer, *Iliad*

. . . Callimachus wished to use a different name and he alone calls the Nereid Hydatosydne (Water-child), modeled on [Homeric] Halosydne (Sea-child).[1]

[1] An epithet of Thetis (Hom. *Il.* 20.207; cf. *Od.* 4.404).

546 Eustathius on Homer, *Odyssey*

And the water leaps up through channels or a column or somehow rising up or otherwise gushing, as is clear from Callimachus,

> the spring
>
> casts up clear water

547 Eustathius on Homer, *Odyssey*

and from the closely woven fabrics: . . . *kairōma*, which is the thread of the warp; they say both *kairos* and *kairōma*,[1] the woof that does not allow the threads to commingle, from which come *kairōstrides* (weavers) and *kairōstrides*

[1] Cf. *Fr. Inc. Sed.* 640.

ἢ καιρωστρίδες γυναῖκες παρὰ Καλλ., ἀντὶ τοῦ ὑφάν-
τριαι. οὗ δὴ Καλλιμάχου καὶ τὸ,

ὑδάτινον καίρωμα ⟨∪–⟩ ὑμένεσσιν ὁμοῖον

548 Eust. ad *Od.* 8.324 (p. 1599.25 van der Valk)

θηλύτεραι δὲ θεαί· ἄλλως δὲ θηλύτεραι γυναῖκες κατὰ
τοὺς παλαιοὺς αἱ εὔκαρποι καὶ πολυφόροι. ὅθεν καὶ
"θῆλυς ἐέρση" (*Od.* 5.467), ἡ τοῦ εὐκαρπεῖν καὶ πολυ-
φορεῖν αἰτία· ὅθεν καὶ Καλλίμαχος,

θηλύτατον πεδίον

549 Eust. ad *Od.* 14.350 (p. 1761.45 van der Valk)

ἐφόλκαιον· τὸ δὲ ῥῆμα, ἐξ οὗ καὶ τὸ ἐφόλκαιον καὶ τὸ
ἐφόλκιον, ποιεῖ καὶ τὸ ἐφόλκον, ὃ δηλοῖ τὸ ἐπαγωγόν,
ὡς Καλλ.,

ἔχοιμί τι παιδὸς ἐφολκόν

550 Gal. in Hippoc. Περὶ ἀγμῶν 3.51 (vol. 18.2, p. 611
Kühn)

ὥσπερ καὶ Καλλίμαχος,

ὃ πρὸ μιῆς ὥρης θηρίον οὐ λέγεται

gynaikes (weaving women) in Callimachus, instead of *hyphantriae*,[2] of which Callimachus writes,

> a diaphanous web . . . like a membrane

[2] Female weavers.

548 Eustathius on Homer, *Odyssey*

very tender goddesses: otherwise, according to the ancients, very fertile women who bore many children. From this also "tender dew" (*Od.* 5.467), the cause of fruitfulness and productivity. From this also Callimachus,

> the most fertile plain

549 Eustathius on Homer, *Odyssey*

epholkaion (lading plank): the word (from which come *epholkaion* and *epholkion*) also has the form *epholkon*, which means lure, as Callimachus,

> Would that I had some lure to attract a boy

550 Galen on Hippocrates, *On Fractures*

As also Callimachus says,

> The beast is not spoken of before the first hour[1]

[1] The ape, which is a bad omen if mentioned early in the morning.

551 Gal. *Gloss. Hippoc.* s.v. πολυγράῳ (vol. 19, p. 132 Kühn)

πολυγράῳ· πολυφάγῳ "καὶ—κηδεμόνα." Καλλίμαχος, ἀντὶ τοῦ κατέφαγε.

> καὶ γόνος αἰζηῶν ἔγραε κηδεμόνα

552 Pf. = *Hec.* 169

553 Gell. *NA* 4.11.2

opinio vetus falsa occupavit et convaluit Pythagoram philosophum non esitavisse ex animalibus, item abstinuisse fabulo, quem Graeci κύαμον appellant; ex hac opinione Callimachus poeta scripsit,

> καὶ κυάμων ἄπο χεῖρας ἔχειν, ἀνιῶντος ἐδεστοῦ,
> κἠγώ, Πυθαγόρης ὡς ἐκέλευε, λέγω

554 Hephaest. *Ench. de Met.* 15.8 (p. 50.9 Consbruch)

ἄλλο δὲ (sc. τῶν παρ᾽ Ἀρχιλόχῳ ἀσυναρτήτων) τὸ ἐκ δακτυλικῆς τετραποδίας καὶ τοῦ αὐτοῦ ἰθυφαλλικοῦ . . . τοῦτο παρὰ τοῖς νεωτέροις πολὺ τὸ μέτρον ἐστίν, ὥσπερ καὶ παρὰ Καλλιμάχῳ,

> Τόν με παλαιστρίταν ὀμόσας θεὸν ἑπτάκις
> φιλήσειν

---

[1] E.g., Archil. fr. 188 West.　　[2] *Epig.* 39.　　[3] Hermes, patron deity of the wrestling school (Pl. *Lys.* 203a, 206d).
[4] Apparently, the first verse of an epigram.

551 Galen, *Glossary of Words in Hippocrates*

polygraōi (excessive eating): gluttony . . . instead of *kate-phage* (he ate excessively) Callimachus [uses the synonym *egrae*:

> and the seed devoured the protector of men[1]

[1] The text and its meaning are disputed. Pfeiffer (vol. 1, 393) suggests that the passage is about the death of Heracles.

552 Pf. = *Hecale* 169

553 Gellius, *Attic Nights*

Pythagoras the philosopher vigorously held the old and false conviction not to eat animals and likewise to abstain from beans, which the Greeks call *kyamon*; of this tenet the poet Callimachus wrote,

> To hold back the hands from beans, a vexacious food,
> I, too, command as Pythagoras[1] ordered.

[1] Pythagoras of Samos (6th–5th c. BC; DK 14), philosopher, religious leader, mathematician, and music theorist. Cf. *Ia.* 191.56–63.

554 Hephaestion, *Handbook on Meter*

Another of the asynarteta in Archilochus consists of a dactylic tetrameter and the same ithyphallic meter.[1] . . . This meter is often used by the more recent poets, as also in Callimachus,[2]

> after swearing by me, the god of the *palaestra*,[3] that
> he would kiss (someone) seven times[4]

555 Heraclit. gram. *Quaest. Hom.* 66.9 Buffière

πιθανῶς δὲ καὶ τὴν νῆσον ἐν ᾗ ταῦτα διέπλασε, Φά-
ρον ὠνόμασεν, ἐπειδήπερ ἐστὶ τὸ φέρσαι γεννῆσαι,
καὶ τὴν γῆν ἀφάρωτον ὁ Καλλίμαχος εἶπε τὴν ἄγο-
νον,

†ἀφάρωτος οἷον γυνή†

556 Hdn. Περὶ μονήρος λέξεως (vol. 2, p. 915.17 Lentz)

τὰ περισπώμενα, εἰ λέγοιτο ἐν πλείοσι συλλαβαῖς,
διὰ τοῦ ō λέγεται. Δημοφόων· Καλλίμαχος,

νυμφίε Δημοφόων, ἄδικε ξένε

557 Pf. = *Aet.* 54e

558 Hdn. Περὶ ὀρθογραφίας 1 (cod. Lipsiensis Tischen-
dorf 2, fol. 22ʳ, A 15–20; p. 305 Reitzenstein)

Πτῷον ὄρος σὺν/[τῷ ῑ. Πίνδαρος· "κα]ί ποτε τὸν τρι-
κάρα[νον Πτῴου κευθ]μῶνα κατέσχεθε κού[ρα]."[1]
τοῦτο ὅτε κτητ]ικόν τύπον ἔχει, σὺν/[τῷ ῑ, ὅτε δὲ κύ-
ριον,] τὸ ω συνέσταλται· [Πτοῖον γὰρ Καλλί/]μαχος.

[1] Pind. fr. 51b S.-M.

555 Heraclitus grammaticus, *Homeric Questions*

Plausibly he [Homer] named the island on which he created these things Pharos,[1] since *phersai* means to beget, and Callimachus said land that was unplowed was unproductive.

†unplowed, like a woman†

[1] Hom. *Od.* 4.354–424.

556 Herodian, *On Rare Words*

As regards circumflexes, if a word has multisyllables, it is written with omicron, [for instance,] *Dēmophoōn*. Callimachus,

O bridegroom Demophoön,[1] unjust stranger

[1] Demophon, son of Theseus, on his way home from Troy was shipwrecked at Rhodope, where he met the queen, Phyllis. He promised to marry her when he returned, but when it was clear that he would not, she hanged herself in grief (Ov. *Her.* 2).

557 Pf. = *Aetia* 54e

558 Herodian, *On Spelling*

Mt. Ptoion, with iota. Pindar, "And once the youth inhabited the three-peaked cavern of Ptoïon." It has this form when it is possessive, with the iota; when it is nominative, it is contracted with omega. For example, Callimachus [writes] *Ptoion*.

559 Hdn. Περὶ ὀρθογραφίας 1 (cod. Lipsiensis Tischendorf 2, fol. 22ᵛ, 10–13; p. 305 Reitzenstein)

Πρῳζόν· Καλλίμα[χος . . .

560 Ioannes Charax, Περὶ ἐγκλινομένων (*Anecd. Gr.* vol. 3, p. 1154 Bekker)

"ὅτις σφεας εἰσαφίκηται" "ἦρχε δ᾽ ἄρά σφιν." αὗται παραλόγως ἐνεκλέθησαν . . . καὶ παρὰ Καλλιμάχῳ,

τόξού σφεων τις ἄριστα Κυδωνίου

561 Hdn. excerpt. *De encl.* (cod. Laur. 57, 26 fol.˙ 68; p. 326.1 Reitzenstein)

ad ἐσμέν et ἐμέν· γρῆές—αἴτιος†, Καλλιμάχου,

γρῆές ἐμεν †κορεης δ᾽ οὐκ αἴτιος†

562 (562 Pf. + *SH* 296) *P.Oxy.* 2375, col. II

νηματαχρη[
καυστιρου[
   αλλοτεδη[
τευχηστ.[
5   εἰς δάιν ὀπ[λισμὸν† ἵππιον Ἄργος ἔχει
αἰεὶ γαρ κ.. [
...[.]....[.].. [

559 Herodian, *On Spelling*

Prōizon (lately): Callimachus . . .

560 Ioannes Charax, *On Enclitics*

"whoever approaches them (*spheas*)" (Hom. *Od.* 12.40)
"and he led them (*sphin*)" (Hom. *Il.* 14.134). And these
[pronouns in sigma-phi] unexpectedly are enclitics . . . also
in Callimachus,

> Some one of them (*spheōn*) best with the Cydonian[1]
>   bow

[1] Cretan (*Hymn* 1.45, 3.197). On Cretan bowmen, cf. *Epig.* 37.

561 Herodian, *On Enclitics* (excerpts)

on *esmen* and *emen*: . . . of Callimachus,

> we are old women †not responsible for the girl†[1]

[1] Text and meaning are uncertain.

562 (562 Pf. + *SH* 296) Oxyrhynchus papyrus

> the threads [of fate] . . . of burning . . . at one time
> . . . a warrior . . . for the battle Argos has a cavalry
> shield, for always . . . [

563 Hsch. s.v. ἄοζοι

ἄοζοι· μάγειροι. ὑπηρέται, θεράποντες, ἀκόλουθοι.
Καλλίμαχος

[lacuna]

564 Hsch. s.v. θύα

θύα· ἀρτύματα. Κύπριοι. ἔνιοι τὰ ἀρώματα· Καλλίμα-
χος

[lacuna]

565 Hsch. s.v. κάππα

κάππα· τινὲς δὲ τὸ ἐλάχιστον· οὐκ εὖ. καὶ γὰρ παρὰ
Καλλιμάχῳ γράφεται κόππα.

566 Hsch. s.v. καταριστήν (?)

καταριστήν (?)· ὀρθὴν †δουριστήν†. παρὰ Καλλι-
μάχῳ τὴν χάλαζαν.

567 Hsch. s.v. νεκάδεσσι

νεκάδεσσι· νεκυάδεσι· ταῖς τῶν νεκρῶν τάξεσι· νε-
κροῖς. ἐλέγχεται δὲ ὁ Καλλίμαχος νεκάδας ψιλῶς τὰς
τάξεις νενοηκώς·

ἡδομένη νεκάδεσσιν †ἐπι σκυρῶν† πολέμοιο

563 Hesychius

aozoi: cooks. Attendants, henchmen, followers. Callimachus

[citation missing]

564 Hesychius

thya: spices. Cyprians. Some [say] aromatics: Callimachus

[citation missing]

565 Hesychius

kappa: some say it means the least, incorrectly. In Callimachus it is written *koppa*.

566 Hesychius

kataristēn (hail?): correct . . . In Callimachus, *chalazan* (hail).[1]

1 Perhaps the storm in the *Hecale* (fr. 257 Schn.).

567 Hesychius

nekadessi: corpses; the array of corpses; the dead. Callimachus examines [the scene] reflecting on an array of stripped corpses:

taking pleasure[1] in the corpses . . . of the battle

1 Bentley suggests the subject is Athena (*Hymn* 5.43–44).

568 Hsch. s.v. †χρεμέδα· ἠγῇ†

†χρεμέδα· ἠγῇ†·[1] ὡς Καλλίμαχος

[1] χρεμετᾷ· ἠχεῖ coni. Salmasius et Voss.

569 Hyg. *Poet. astr.* 2.18 (Eur in *Melanipp.* fr. 488 N.[2], pp. 576–77 Collard-Cropp)

Euripides autem in Melanippa Hippen Chironis Centauri filiam . . . dicit; quae cum aleretur in monte Pelio et studium in venando maximum haberet. Quodam tempore ab Aeolo . . . persuasam concepisse, cumque iam partus appropinquaret, profugisse in silvam . . . cum parens eam persequeretur, dicitur illa petisse a deorum potestate ne pariens a parente conspiceretur. Quae deorum voluntate, postquam peperit, in equam conversa inter astra est constituta . . . Callimachus autem ait, quod desierat venari et colere Dianam, in quam supra diximus speciem eam Dianam convertisse.

570 Hyg. *Poet. astr.* 2.34

alii dicunt cum Callimacho, cum Dianae vim voluerit afferre (sc. Orion), ab ea sagittis esse confixum et ad sidera propter venandi consimile studium deformatum.

571 [Lucian] *Amores* 49

δεῖ δὲ τῶν νέων ἐρᾶν, ὡς Ἀλκιβιάδου Σωκράτης, ὃς ὑπὸ μιᾷ χλαμύδι πατρὸς ὕπνους ἐκοιμήθη. καὶ ἔγωγε

568 Hesychius

[corrupt text]: as in Callimachus

569 Hyginus, *Astronomy*

Euripides in his *Melanippe* says that Hippe was the daughter of Chiron the Centaur . . . when she was raised on Mt. Pelion, had the greatest enthusiam for hunting. At some time she became pregnant after being seduced by Aeolus, and when the birth was imminent, she fled into the forest . . . when her parent followed, it is said that she asked by the power of the gods that she not be seen by her parent while giving birth. By the wish of the gods, after she gave birth she was turned into a horse and set among the stars . . . Callimachus says that she abandoned hunting and that in anger Artemis turned her into the shape we mentioned above.

570 Hyginus, *Astronomy*

Some say with Callimachus, when [Orion] wished to assault Diana, he was pierced by her with arrows and transformed into a constellation on account of the same enthusiasm for hunting.

571 Pseudo-Lucian, *Amores*

It is necessary to love young men as Socrates loved Alcibiades, who under one cloak was lulled to sleep by a

τὸ Καλλιμάχειον ἐπὶ τέλει τῶν λόγων ἥδιστα προσ-
θείην ἂν ἅπασι κήρυγμα,

αἴθε γὰρ ὦ κούροισιν ἐπ' ὄθματα λίχνα φέροντες,
Ἐρχίος ὡς ὑμῖν ὥρισε παιδοφιλεῖν,
ὧδε νέων ἐρόῳτε· πόλιν κ' εὔανδρον ἔχοιτε

572 Or. *Etym.* s.v. ἀλιτήριος (p. 32.12 Sturz)

ἀλιτήριος· . . . ἀλίτης . . . καὶ παρώνυμον ἀλιτήρ, ὡς
ἀρότης ἀροτήρ· Καλλίμαχος,

ἀρότας κύματος Ἀονίου

573 Or. *Etym.* s.v. ὀλοφυρόμενος (p. 113.20 Sturz)

ὀλοφυρόμενος· κυρίως τὸ μετὰ τιλμοῦ τῶν τριχῶν
κλαίειν. Καλλίμαχός φησι,

ὠλόψατο χαίτας

574 Or. *Etym.* s.v. φάτνη (p. 162.21 Sturz)

φάτνη· . . . δύναται δὲ καὶ παρὰ τὸ πατῶ τὸ ἐσθίω·
ὅτι δὲ πατῶ ἐπὶ τοῦ ἐσθίω κεῖται, τίθησι τοῦτο καὶ
Καλλ. λέγων,

ὁ δὴ μήκωνα πατεῖται

father. And I would most happily add to the end of my discourse the pronouncement of Callimachus to all,

> O you who cast your lewd eyes at young men, would that you love the young in this way, as Erchius[1] ordered you to love. Then, you would have a city of just men

[1] Otherwise unknown.

572 Orion of Thebes, *Etymologicon*

alitērios (guilty): . . . *alitēs* (sinner) . . . and its derivative *alitēr*, like *arotēs* (plowman) and *arotēr*. Callimachus,

> plowmen of the Aonian[1] Sea

[1] The Boeotian Sea. Aonia as an ancient name for Boeotia (*Hymn* 4.75).

573 Orion of Thebes, *Etymologicon*

olophyromenos (lamenting): in the proper sense, to weep along with tearing one's hair. Callimachus says,

> she tore out her hair

574 Orion of Thebes, *Etymologicon*

phatnē (taste): . . . it is possible to say to taste instead of to eat because tasting relates to eating; Callimachus does this, saying,

> he tastes the poppy seed

575 Or. *Etym.* s.v. χεά καὶ χειά (p. 165.2 Sturz)

χεά καὶ χειά· ὁ φωλεός· . . . καὶ μετὰ περισσοῦ τοῦ
ō Καλλίμαχος,

> †οἱ δ᾽† ὥστ᾽ ἐξ ὀχεῆς ὄφις αἰόλος αὐχέν᾽
> ἀνασχών[1]

[1] ἀνασχών Ruhnken (v. Hollis, 334): ἀναύχην Or.

576 Phlegon, *Mir.* 4 (*BNJ* 257 F 36.4–10)

Ἱστορεῖ δὲ καὶ Ἡσίοδος καὶ Δικαίαρχος καὶ Κλέαρ-
χος καὶ Καλλίμαχος καὶ ἄλλοι τινὲς περὶ Τειρεσίου
τάδε.

Τειρεσίαν τὸν Εὐήρους ἐν Ἀρκαδίᾳ ἐν τῷ ὄρει
τῷ ἐν Κυλλήνῃ ὄφεις ἰδόντα ὀχεύοντας τρῶσαι
τὸν ἕτερον καὶ παράχρημα μεταβαλεῖν τὴν
ἰδέαν· γενέσθαι γὰρ ἐξ ἀνδρὸς γυναῖκα καὶ μι-
χθῆναι ἀνδρί. τοῦ δὲ Ἀπόλλωνος αὐτῷ χρήσα-
ντος, ὡς ἐὰν τηρήσας ὀχεύοντας ὁμοίως τρώσῃ
τὸν ἕνα ἔσται οἷος ἦν, παραφυλάξαντα τὸν Τει-
ρεσίαν ποιῆσαι τὰ ὑπὸ τοῦ θεοῦ ῥηθέντα καὶ
οὕτως κομίσασθαι τὴν ἀρχαίαν φύσιν. Διὸς δὲ
ἐρίσαντος Ἥρᾳ καὶ φαμένου ἐν ταῖς συνουσί-
αις πλεονεκτεῖν τὴν γυναῖκα τοῦ ἀνδρὸς τῇ τῶν
ἀφροδισίων ἡδονῇ, καὶ τῆς Ἥρας φασκούσης
τὰ ἐναντία, δόξαι αὐτοῖς μεταπεμψαμένοις ἐρέ-
σθαι τὸν Τειρεσίαν διὰ τὸ τῶν τρόπων ἀμφοτέ-

575 Orion of Thebes, *Etymologicon*

chea and *cheia*: a lair (*phōleos*) . . . and with the unusual omicron Callimachus,

> So the slippery snake, raising his neck from his hole

576 Phlegon, *On Wonders*

Hesiod, Dicaearchus, Clearchus, Callimachus, and some others say this about Teiresias,

> Tiresias, son of Eueres saw some snakes copulating on Mt. Cyllene in Arcadia. He wounded one and immediately changed his form. He went from being a man to a woman, and had intercourse with a man. Apollo than prophesied to him that if he saw snakes copulating again and wounded one, he would change back to his original form, which he did. When Zeus quarreled with Hera about whether a man or a woman had more pleasure from sex (Zeus said the woman, Hera the opposite), they asked Tiresias because he had experienced it both ways.

ρων πεπειρᾶσθαι. τὸν δὲ ἐρωτώμενον ἀποφήνα-
σθαι, διότι μοιρῶν οὐσῶν δέκα τὸν ἄνδρα
τέρπεσθαι τὴν μίαν, τὴν δὲ γυναῖκα τὰς ἐννέα.
τὴν δὲ Ἥραν ὀργισθεῖσαν κατανύξαι αὐτοῦ
τοὺς ὀφθαλμοὺς καὶ ποιῆσαι τυφλόν, τὸν δὲ
Δία δωρήσασθαι αὐτῷ τὴν μαντικὴν καὶ βιοῦν
ἐπὶ γενεὰς ἑπτά.

577 Phlegon, *Mir.* 5 (*BNJ* 257 F 36.4–10)

Οἱ αὐτοὶ ἱστοροῦσιν κατὰ τὴν Λαπιθῶν χώραν γενέ-
σθαι Ἐλάτῳ τῷ βασιλεῖ θυγατέρα ὀνομαζομένην
Καινίδα. ταύτῃ δὲ Ποσειδῶνα μιγέντα ἐπαγγείλασθαι
ποιήσειν αὐτῇ ὃ ἂν ἐθέλῃ, τὴν δὲ ἀξιῶσαι μεταλλά-
ξαι αὐτὴν εἰς ἄνδρα ποιῆσαί τε ἄτρωτον. τοῦ δὲ Πο-
σειδῶνος κατὰ τὸ ἀξιωθὲν ποιήσαντος μετονομασθῆ-
ναι Καινέα.

578 Phot. *Lex.* s.v. τριττύαν θυσίαν (vol. 2, p. 227
Naber)

τριττύαν θυσίαν· Καλλίμαχος μὲν τὴν ἐκ κριοῦ, ταύ-
ρον καὶ κάπρου.

579 Plin. *HN* 3.152

Illyrici ora mille amplius insulis frequentatur . . . ab Issa
Corcyra Melaena cognominata cum Cnidiorum oppido
distat xxv, inter quam et Illyricum Melite, unde catulos
Melitaeos appellari Callimachus auctor est.

And he replied that a man has one-tenth the pleasure as a woman. Hera in anger gouged out his eyes and made him blind, but Zeus gave him the art of prophecy and a lifetime of seven generations.

577 Phlegon, *On Wonders*

The same authors write that in the land of the Lapiths a daughter named Cainis was born to King Elatus. Poseidon had intercourse with her and promised to do for her whatever she wished. She asked him to turn her into a man and make her invulverable. After Poseidon did what she asked, her name was changed to Caineus.

578 Photius, *Lexicon*

the threefold sacrifice: Callimachus [says] it consists of a ram, a bull, and a boar.

579 Pliny the Elder, *Natural History*

More than a thousand islands crowd the shore of Illyricum[1] . . . Twenty-five miles from Issa is Corcyra (the one called Melaena), with a town founded by the Cnidians, and between this one and Illyricum is Melite, from which Melitean terriers are named according to Callimachus.

[1] A Roman province in Pliny's time along the east coast of the Adriatic Sea.

580 Plin. *HN* 4.65

Cyclades: prima earum Andrus cum oppido abest a Ge-
raesto x̄, a Ceo, x̄x̄x̄v̄īīī. Ipsam Myrsilus Cauron, deinde
Antandron cognominatam tradit, Callimachus Lasiam, alii
Nonagriam, Hydrusam, Epagrim.

581 Plin. *HN* 4.69

Sporades: Telos unguento nobilis, a Callimacho Agathusa
appellata.

582 Plin. *HN* 4.70

Melos cum oppido quam Aristides Mimblida appellat;
Aristoteles, Zephyriam; Callimachus, Mimallida . . .

583 Plin. *HN* 4.73

Insula Samothace . . . Callimachus eam antiquo nomine
Dardaniam vocat.

580 Pliny the Elder, *Natural History*

Cyclades: the first of these is Andros with a city ten miles distant from Geraestus, and thirty-eight from Ceos. This one Myrsilus[1] says was named Caurus and then Antandrus; Callimachus, Lasia, and others say Nonagria, Hydrusa, and Epagris.[2]

[1] Myrsilus of Methymna (3rd c. BC; *BNJ* 477 F 12); he wrote a history of Lesbos and *Historical Paradoxes*.   [2] The source may be Callimachus' treatise *Foundations of Islands and Cities and Their Changes of Name* (Fr. Doct. 412).

581 Pliny the Elder, *Natural History*

Sporades: Telos known for its balm was called Agathusa by Callimachus.

582 Pliny the Elder, *Natural History*

Melos with a town [of the same name] which Aristides[1] calls Mimblis; Aristotle, [calls it] Zephyria, and Callimachus, Mimallis . . .

[1] Aristides (2nd c. BC; *BNJ* 444 F 6), author of *On the Foundation of Cnidus.*

583 Pliny the Elder, *Natural History*

The island of Samothrace[1] . . . Callimachus calls it by its ancient name, Dardania.

[1] Island in the northern Aegean off Thrace, where there was an important sanctuary of the Great Gods (Hdt. 2.51) that was significant to Ptolemy II and his sister/wife, Arsinoe II, who built a large propylon gate and tholos there.

584 Pliny *HN* 5.28

(Syrtis minor—litus inter duas Syrtis—Syrtis maior) . . . in
intimo sinu fuit ora Lotophagon . . . ad Philaenorum Aras;
ex harena sunt hae. ab his non procul a continente palus
vasta amnem Tritonem nomenque ab eo accipit, Pallantias
appellata Callimacho et citra Minorem Syrtim esse dicta,
multis vero inter duas Syrtis.

585 Pf. = *Hec.* 157

586 [Plut.] *Placit. phil.* 1.7.3 (881a)

ἀναιρείσθω γάρ φησίν, ὁ ποιητικὸς λῆρος σὺν Καλ-
λιμάχῳ τῷ λέγοντι,

εἰ θεὸν οἶσθα,
ἴσθ᾽ ὅτι καὶ ῥέξαι δαίμονι πᾶν δυνατόν

587 *Suda* κ 2113

Κόροιβος· ὄνομα κύριον. καὶ μωρός τις μετρῶν τὰ
κύματα, Καλλίμαχος,

ἑπτὰ σοφοὶ χαίροιτε—τὸν ὄγδοον, ὥς τε
Κόροιβον,
οὐ συναριθμέομεν—

584 Pliny the Elder, *Natural History*

(The lesser Syrtis—the shore between the two—the greater Syrtis) . . . in the innermost gulf was the Coast of the Lotus-eaters . . . near the Altars of the Philaeni; these are made from sand. And from these, not far from the continent, is a large swamp into which flows the River Triton[1] and receives its name from it. It is called Pallantia[2] by Callimachus and he says it is on this side of the Syrtis Minor, but others that it is between the two Syrtes.

[1] Considered a local deity in Libya (Ap. Rhod. 4.1537–85).

[2] "Of Pallas," on account of the legend that she was born there (Aesch. *Eum.* 292–93).

585 Pf. = *Hecale* 157

586 Pseudo-Plutarch, *Placita philosophorum*

Let the argument be confuted, the poetic trash with Callimachus the speaker,

> if you know a god,
> know that it is possible for a deity to do everything

587 *Suda*

Coroebus: a proper name. And some moron counting the waves, Callimachus,

> Greetings to you, Seven Wise Men. The eighth, as
> it is Coroebus,[1] we do not include.

[1] The Phrygian fiancé of Cassandra, who came to Troy too late and became a paragon of stupidity (Ael. *VH* 13.15).

CALLIMACHUS

588 Procl. *In Resp.* 391b

τὰς . . . Ἕκτορος ἕλξεις περὶ τὸ σῆμα τὸ Πατρόκλου·
εἴρηται μὲν οὖν καὶ ὑπὸ τῶν **παλαιῶν**, ὡς Θετταλικόν
τι τοιοῦτον ἔθος ἦν καὶ ὁ Κυρηναῖος μαρτυρεῖ ποιη-
τής,

πάλαι δ᾿ ἔτι **Θεσσαλὸς** ἀνήρ
ῥυστάζει φθιμένων ἀμφὶ τάφον φονέας

589 Procl. *In Ti.* 21c

εἴπερ γάρ τις ἄλλος καὶ ποιητῶν ἄριστος κριτὴς ὁ
Πλάτων, ὡς καὶ Λογγῖνος συνίστησιν· Ἡρακλείδης
γοῦν ὁ Ποντικός φησιν, ὅτι τῶν Χοιρίλου τότε εὐ-
δοκιμούντων Πλάτων τὰ Ἀντιμάχου προύτίμησε καὶ
αὐτὸν ἔπεισε τὸν Ἡρακλείδην εἰς Κολοφῶνα ἐλθόντα
τὰ ποιήματα συλλέξαι τοῦ ἀνδρός· μάτην οὖν φληνα-
φῶσι Καλλ. καὶ Δοῦρις ὡς Πλάτωνος οὐκ ὄντος ἱκα-
νοῦ κρίνειν ποιητάς.

590 Pf. = *Aet.* 54b.23 (*SH* 257.23)

591 Pf. = *Hec.* 161

176

588 Proclus on Plato, *Republic*

the . . . dragging of Hector around the tomb of Patroclus:
It is said even by the ancients that it was some Thessalian
custom, and Callimachus the poet is a witness,

> long ago and even now a Thessalian man
> drags murderers about the tomb of the deceased

589 Proclus on Plato, *Timaeus*

Beyond any other, Plato was the best critic of poets, as
even Longinus[1] confirmed. Heraclides Ponticus[2] says that
he honored the works of Antimachus[3] above those of
Choerilus[4] (who was the most esteemed at the time), and
that he persuaded Heraclides to go to Colophon to collect
that man's poems. In vain Callimachus and Duris[5] blabber
about how Plato is not adequate to judge poets.

[1] Alleged author of *On the Sublime*, an influential work of
literary criticism dated to the first century AD.   [2] Fr. 6
Wehrli (2nd ed., 1969). Heraclides Ponticus (4th c. BC), student
of Plato, philosopher and astronomer.   [3] Antimachus of
Colophon (4th c. BC), editor of Homer who anticipated the Hel-
lenistic poets by incorporating scholarship into his epic (*Thebaid*)
and lyric (*Lyde*) poetry.   [4] Choerilus of Samos (*SH* 314–32),
author of the *Persica*, who announced at the end of the fifth
century that it was not possible to write epic poetry after Homer
(*SH* 317).   [5] Duris of Samos (4th–3rd c. BC; *BNJ* 76 F 83),
historian and tyrant.

590 Pf. = *Aetia* 54b.23 (*SH* 257.23)

591 Pf. = *Hec.* 161

592 Schol. M ad Aesch. *Eum.* 21

Παλλὰς Προναία· "χἠ—Προναίην" Καλλίμαχος,

χἠ Παλλάς, Δελφοί νιν ὄθ' ἱδρύοντο Προναίην

593 Schol. M Tr ad Aesch. *Eum.* 27

καὶ Ποσειδῶνος κράτος καλοῦσα· τὴν Πυθὼ τὴν
πρώην Ποσειδῶνος, ὑπὲρ ἧς Καλαύρειαν ἐδέξατο.
Καλλίμαχος,

μέσφα Καλαυρείης ἦλθεν ἐς ἀντίδοσιν

594 Schol. ad Ap. Rhod. 1.117

Φλίας . . . Ἀραιθυρέηθεν ἵκανεν . . . πηγῆσιν ἐφέ-
στιος Ἀσωποῖο· Ἀσωπός ποταμὸς Θηβῶν ἔχων τὰς
πηγὰς ἐν Ἀραιθυρέᾳ. ἐκεραυνώθη δὲ ὑπὸ Διὸς διώκων
αὐτὸν διὰ τὸ ἡρπακέναι τὴν θυγατέρα αὐτοῦ Αἴγιναν,
ὡς καὶ Καλλίμαχός φησιν.

592 Scholia to Aeschylus, *Eumenides*

Pallas Pronaia (Pallas Before the Temple): . . . Callimachus,

> And Pallas, when the Delphians dedicated her
> [statue] as "Before the Temple"

593 Scholia to Aeschylus, *Eumenides*

and calling on the strength of Poseidon: Pytho once belonged to Poseidon; he exchanged it for Calaureia.[1] Callimachus,

> until he[2] came to the exchange for Calaureia

[1] An island in the Saronic Gulf where there was a sanctuary of Poseidon. For the tradition that Poseidon exchanged Delos rather than Pytho for Calaureia, see Ephorus (*BNJ* 70 F 150).

[2] Perhaps Poseidon.

594 Scholia to Apollonius of Rhodes, *Argonautica*

Phlias[1] . . . came from Araethyrea . . . at home by the springs of Asopus: the Theban river Asopus with its springs in Araethyrea.[2] He was blasted by Zeus, who pursued him because he had raped his daughter Aegina, as Callimachus says.[3]

[1] Or Phleias, one of the Argonauts (Ap. Rhod. 1.115).

[2] The Peloponnesian Asopus in Sicyon, not to be confused with the more famous Asopus in Boeotia (Paus. 2.5.1).

[3] No quotation follows.

595 Schol. ad Ap. Rhod. 1.760–62c

Τιτυὸν μέγαν, ὅν ῥ' ἔτεκέν γε δῖ' Ἐλάρη, θρέψεν δὲ
καὶ ἂψ ἐλοχεύσατο Γαῖα· . . . δοκεῖ δὲ ἡ ἱστορία ἀπί-
θανος εἶναι καὶ ἄπιστος, ὅτι ἐκ δευτέρου ἡ Γῆ ἐγέν-
νησε τὸν Τιτυόν. ἀλλ' ἐροῦμεν, ὅτι οἱ ποιηταὶ τοὺς
τερατώδεις κατὰ τὸ σῶμα Γῆς εἶναί φασιν. οὕτω γὰρ
καὶ Καλλίμαχος τὰ δεινὰ τῶν θηρίων Γῆς εἶναι ἔφη.

596 Schol. ad Ap. Rhod. 1.1207b

Ὕλας χαλκέῃ σὺν κάλπιδι· . . . ἀπρεπὲς δὲ νεανίαν
ὑδρίαν βαστάζειν. Ὅμηρος δὲ πρεπόντως παρθένον.
πιθανώτερον δὲ ἦν ἀμφορέα εἰπεῖν, ὡς Καλλίμαχος.

597 Pf. = Aet. 60b (SH 286c)

598 Schol. ad Ap. Rhod. 2.4

Βιθυνὶς Μελίη· . . . Μελίαν δέ φησιν αὐτὴν διὰ τό
τινας τῶν νυμφῶν Μελίας καλεῖσθαι ἀπὸ Μελίας τῆς
Ὠκεανοῦ, ὥς φησι Καλλίμαχος (ἢ διὰ τὸ περὶ μελίας
δένδρα διατρίβειν καθάπερ Ἀμαδρυάδας).

FRAGMENTS OF UNCERTAIN LOCATION

595 Scholia to Apollonius of Rhodes, *Argonautica*

Great Tityus[1] whom glorious Elare bore, and Earth gave birth to him again and brought him up: . . . the story seems unbelievable and untrustworthy that Earth produced Tityus a second time. But we claim that the poets say the monsters are deep in the Earth. Even Callimachus said that the dreadful beasts were [sons] of Earth.

[1] One of the giants (Hom. *Od.* 11.576–77).

596 Scholia to Apollonius of Rhodes, *Argonautica*

Hylas with a bronze pitcher: . . . it is inappropriate for a young man to carry water. Homer[1] suitably [uses] a young woman [for this task]. And it would have been more plausible to call [the vessel] an amphora, as Callimachus.[2]

[1] *Od.* 7.20.   [2] No quotation follows.

597 Pf. = *Aetia* 60b (*SH* 286c)

598 Scholia to Apollonius of Rhodes, *Argonautica*

Melia from Bithynia: . . . he says that she is Melia because some of the nymphs are called Melia from Melia, the daughter of Ocean, as Callimachus says (or because they spend time in ash trees like Hamadryads).

599 Schol. ad Ap. Rhod. 2.866

Ἰμβρασίοισι παρ' ὕδασιν· Ἴμβρασος ποταμὸς Σά-
μου πρότερον Παρθένιος λεγόμενος, ὡς καὶ Καλλίμα-
χος,

ἀντὶ γὰρ ἐκλήθης Ἴμβρασε Παρθενίου

600 Schol. ad Ap. Rhod. 2.904–10

Καλλιχόροιο· ποταμὸς Παφλαγονίας ἱερὸς Διονύσου
περὶ Ἡράκλειαν, οὗ μέμνηται καὶ Καλλίμαχος. ἔξεισι
δὲ διὰ στομάτων δισσῶν.

601 Pf. = *Aet*. 113d.4 (*SH* 274.4)

602 Schol. ad Ap. Rhod. 4.1322

οἰοπόλοι δ' εἰμὲν χθόνιαι θεαὶ αὐδήεσσαι . . . περὶ
δὲ τῶν Νυμφῶν μέμνηται Καλλ. οὕτω λέγων,

δέσποιναι Λιβύης ἡρωΐδες, αἳ Νασαμώνων
αὖλιν καὶ δολιχὰς θῖνας ἐπιβλέπετε,
μητέρα μοι ζώουσαν ὀφέλλετε

---

[1] One of a number of references in Callimachus to the history
and myth of his native Cyrene. Others are in *Fr. Inc. Sed* 484, 584,

599 Scholia to Apollonius of Rhodes, *Argonautica*

by the waters of the Imbrasus: the Imbrasus river of Samos, earlier called the Parthenius,[1] as also Callimachus,

O Imbrasus, before you were called Pathenius

[1] The river Imbrasus of Samos changed its name to Parthenius because Hera was led there while still a young girl (Schol. ad Ap. Rhod. 1.187). For the cult of Hera at Samos, cf. *Aet.* 100–101a.

600 Scholia to Apollonius of Rhodes, *Argonautica*

of the Callichorus: the Paphlagonian River sacred to Dionysus[1] near Heraclea, which Callimachus mentions. It discharges through double mouths.

[1] When Dionysus left India he came to Thebes and held dances and rites in front of a cave by the river, which the neighbors called Callichorus (Ap. Rhod. 2.904–10).

601 Pf. = *Aetia* 113d.4 (*SH* 274.4)

602 Scholia to Apollonius of Rhodes, *Argonautica*

we are shepherds, goddesses of this land speaking with a human voice: . . . Callimachus says this about the Nymphs,

O mistress-heroines of Libya,[1] who keep watch over the homestead and the long shores of the Nasamonians,[2] make great my living mother

671, 673, 706, 716 (see D'Alessio 2007, vol. 2, 743n93). It is possible Callimachus included this material in a work dedicated to Cyrene: see L. Lehnus, *Eikasmos* 5 (1994): 189–207.

[2] An indigenous people whom the Greeks encountered in Libya (Hdt. 2.32, 4.172).

603 Schol. (VΘ Ald.) ad Ar. *Eq.* 821

μὴ σκέρβολλε πονηρά· μὴ λοιδόρει· δηλοῖ δὲ καὶ τὸ
κερτομεῖν. κεῖται δὲ νῦν ἡ λέξις ἀντὶ τοῦ μὴ ποίκιλλε.
καὶ Καλλίμαχος,

> σκέρβολα μυθήσαντο

604 Schol. (V Ald.) ad Ar. *Nub.* 333

κυκλίων τε χορῶν ᾀσματοκάμπτας· οἱ παλαιοὶ δια-
φθορὰν μουσικῆς ἡγοῦντο εἶναι τοὺς διθυράμβους,
καὶ προελθὼν αὐτῶν μᾶλλον καθάψεται λέγων . . .
καὶ Καλλίμαχος δὲ πρὸς αὐτοὺς ἀποτεινόμενος οὕτω
πως αὐτῶν καθάπεται,

> νόθαι δ᾽ ἤνθησαν ἀοιδαί

605 Schol. (V Ald.) ad Ar. *Vesp.* 62

μυττωτεύσομεν· . . . ἀντὶ τοῦ συντρίψομεν, δριμύξο-
μεν, ἐπικρανοῦμεν. μετενήνεκται δὲ ἀπὸ τῶν σκορό-
δων. μυττωτὸν γάρ ἐστι κυρίως τὸ ἐκ σκορόδων καὶ
τυροῦ καὶ ὄξους τρίμμα . . . εἴ γε καὶ ὁ Καλλίμαχός
φησιν,

> ἵν᾽ ἐτρίψαντο μυσωτόν

606 Schol. (V) ad Ar. *Pax* 28

τρίψας δι᾽ ἡμέρας ὅλης ὥσπερ γυναικὶ γογγύλην
μεμαγμένην· ὡς τῶν γυναικῶν ἑαυταῖς ἐπιμελέστερον

603 Scholia to Aristophanes, *Knights*

do not speak abusively: do not revile; it means to abuse.
Here the word is used instead of do not vilify. And Callimachus,

> they spoke abusively

604 Scholia to Aristophanes, *Clouds*

the song-twisters of the circular dances: the ancients
thought that dithyrambs were the ruination of music and
going forward he[1] assailed them saying (Ar. *Nub*. 969–72)
. . . and Callimachus, alluding to these, attacks them in this
way,

> bastard songs flourished

[1] Aristophanes.

605 Scholia to Aristophanes, *Wasps*

we will mash: . . . instead of we will grind together, we will
hash up, we will blend. He speaks metaphorically of garlic.
Muttōton is properly a compound of garlic and cheese and
vinegar . . . indeed Callimachus says,

> where they mashed the garlic paste[1]

[1] A mortar like the one on the head of Artemis of Leucadia
(*Aet*. 31g).

606 Scholia to Aristophanes, *Peace*

after rubbing it for the whole day like a round cake
kneaded by a woman: like women very carefully kneading,

185

τριβουσῶν, ὥστε μὴ διακεχύσθαι τὴν μᾶζαν διὰ τὸ ἄτριπτον εἶναι, ἀλλὰ συνεστράφθαι. παρατετήρηκε ταῦτα καὶ Σώφρων καὶ Καλλίμαχος,

γογγύλος ἐστὶ λίθος

607

a Schol. (RV) ad Ar. *Pax* 363

οὐδὲν πονηρόν, ἀλλ᾽ ὅπερ καὶ Κιλλικῶν· ὁ γάρ τοι Κιλλικῶν ἐπὶ πονηρίᾳ διαβόητός ἐστιν. φασὶ γὰρ αὐτὸν οἱ μὲν Σάμον ἢ Μίλητον προδοῦναι Πριηνεῦσι . . .

b *Suda* π 2040

ὕστερον μὲν οὖν παρὰ Θεαγένους τινὸς εἰσῆλθεν ὠνησόμενος κρέα. κἀκεῖνος ὑποδεῖξαι ἐκέλευσεν, πόθεν κόψαι θέλει. προτείνας δὲ τῇ χειρί, ἀπέκοψε τὴν αὑτοῦ χεῖρα καὶ εἶπε· "ταύτῃ τῇ χειρὶ οὐ προδώσεις πόλιν ἑτέραν." μέμνηται δὲ καὶ Καλλίμαχος·

μὴ σύ γε, Θειόγενες, κόψας χέρα Καλλικόωντος;

608 Pf. = *Hec.* 168

609 Schol. (RΘ Ald.) ad Ar. *Plut.* 386–88

τοὺς χρηστοὺς μόνους ἀπαρτὶ πλουτῆσαι ποήσω·

so that the bread does not become relaxed on account of inadequate pounding, but forms a compact body. Both Sophron[1] and Callimachus observe these things,

> the stone is round

[1] Fr. 39 Holdern.

607

a Scholia to Aristophanes, *Peace*

nothing grievous, but what Cillicon [did]: Cillicon was famous for his wickedness. They say that he betrayed either Samos or Miletus to the Prienians . . .

b *Suda*

Later [Cillicon] entered the house of a certain Theogenes to buy some meat, and he asked Cillicon to show him where he wanted him to cut. He put out his hand and Theogenes cut it off, saying "With this hand you will not betray another city." Callimachus mentions it too:

> Are you not Theogenes who cut off the hand of
>   Callicon?[1]

[1] Perhaps the opening verse of a dialogue with a statue; see L. Lehnus (1990) in *Scritti in onore di A. Grilli*, 286–89.

608 Pf. = *Hecale* 168

609 Scholia to Aristophanes, *Wealth*

From now on (*aparti*) I will make only the good wealthy:

ἀπαρτί ἐπίρρημά ἐστιν ὡς ἀμογητί . . . ἔσθ᾽ ὅτε γὰρ
καὶ χρονικὸν ἐπίρρημα δηλοῖ, ὡς Καλλίμαχος καὶ
Πλάτων.

610 Schol. (VG) ad Ar. *Plut.* 676–78

ὁρῶ τὸν ἱερέα τοὺς φθοῖς ἀφαρπάζοντα καὶ τὰς
ἰσχάδας ἀπὸ τῆς τραπέζης τῆς ἱερᾶς· οὕτως μονο-
συλλάβως σύνηθες αὐτοῖς (Ἀττικοῖς) λέγειν· Καλ-
λίμαχος,

†ὅδ᾽ αὖθις† παρὰ φθόϊας

611 Pf. = *Hec.* 172

612 Schol. ad Dionys. Per. 1

Ἀρχόμενος γαῖάν τε καὶ εὐρέα πόντον ἀείδειν· τὸ προ-
οίμιον οἰκεῖον ἔταξε τῇ ὑποθέσει καὶ οὐκ ἀσύμφωνον
τῷ σκοπῷ . . . προϊὼν δὲ μετ᾽ οὐ πολὺ συμπαραλαμ-
βάνει τὰς Μούσας, εὔνοιάν τινα παραφυλάττων ἅμα
τῇ τέχνῃ. παραιτεῖται δὲ τὸ ἀμάρτυρον, ἴσως ἐκ τοῦ
Καλλιμάχου τοῦτο μαθών, ἐπεὶ κἀκεῖνος "ἀμάρτον
οὐδὲν ἀείδω" φησί. διατετηρημένην δὲ ἐν τοῖς ἑξῆς
ἀποδιδοὺς ἑαυτῷ τὴν πίστιν ἐπάγει τὸ ἔπος, εἰπών
"ὑμεῖς δ᾽, ὦ Μοῦσαι, σοκλιὰς ἐνέποιτε κελεύθους."

ἀμάρτυρον οὐδὲν ἀείδω

aparti is an adverb like *amogēti*. . . . sometimes it is an adverb of time, as in Callimachus and Plato.[1]

[1] Pl. *Lys.* 215c. There is no illustrative quotation from Callimachus.

610 Scholia to Aristophanes, *Wealth*

I saw the priest snatching the cakes (*phthois*) and figs from the holy table: he writes *phthois* with one syllable in the customary Attic manner. Callimachus, [in contrast writes],

> beside the cakes[1]

[1] *phthoïas*, with three syllables.

611 Pf. = *Hecale* 172

612 Scholia to Dionysius Periegetes

Beginning to sing of the earth and wide sea: he has organized a suitable prologue with a hypothesis and not discordant with his goal . . . early on he does not much involve the Muses, securing their goodwill by means of his art. He rejects whatever is unattested, perhaps having learned this from Callimachus, since that [poet] says, "I sing nothing unattested," and arguing for his own trustworthiness in the following words: [Dionysius] introduces the poem, saying "May you tell, O Muses, of obscure paths."

> I sing nothing unattested[1]

[1] A much-quoted tag. In Callimachus, as here, it seems to be an argument for trusting the veracity of what is said. It need not have come from one of Callimachus' own prooemia (Pf. vol. 1, 418) nor must it be a literary manifesto (D'Alessio 2007, vol. 2, 746n99).

CALLIMACHUS

613 Schol. ad Dionys. Per. 100

ὁ Ἀδρίας παράκειται ἄχρι τῆς τῶν Ἰαπύγων οἵ εἰσιν
ἐν Ἰταλίᾳ· μέμνηται δὲ αὐτῶν καὶ Καλλίμαχος οὕτως,

Ἰηπύγων ἔγχος ἀπωσάμενοι

614 = 384.31 Pf.

615 Schol. ad Dionys. Per. 364

Ζεφύρου παραφαίνεται ἄκρη· τῇ δ' ὑπὸ Λοκροὶ ἔασιν·
οὗτος μὲν ἀπὸ Ζεφύρου ὄρους, ὁ δὲ Καλλίμαχος καὶ
ἄλλοι πολλοὶ Ἐπιζεφυρίους φασὶ τοὺς Λοκροὺς κα-
λεῖσθαι διὰ τὸ πρὸς ζέφυρον ἄνεμον κεῖσθαι.

616 Schol. ad Dionys. Per. 369

πτολίεθρον ἐϋστεφάνοιο Κρότωνος· ἐϋστεφάνοιο δὲ
Κρότωνος εἶπε διὰ τὰς νίκας τὰς ἐκ τῶν οἰκούντων,
ὥς φησι Καλλίμαχος.

617 Schol. ad Dionys. Per. 376

Τάρας δ' ἁλὸς ἐγγύθι ναίει, ἥν ποτ' Ἀμυκλαίων ἐπο-
λίσσατο καρτερὸς Ἄρης· ἥντινα Τάραντα θηλυκῶς δὲ
εἶπε. μέμνηται δὲ τῆς ἱστορίας καὶ Καλλίμαχος, λέ-
γων οὕτως,

613 Scholia to Dionysius Periegetes

The Adriatic extends as far as the land of the Iapygi, who are in Italy. Callimachus mentions them in this way,

> after they repelled the spear of the Iapygi[1]

[1] On their origins, see Hdt. 7.170.

614 = 384.31 Pf.

615 Scholia to Dionysius Periegetes

the peak of Zephyrus appears, under which are the Locrians: this is from Mt. Zephyrus, but Callimachus and many others say that the Epizephyrians are called Locrians on account of the wind lying to the west.[1]

[1] The Epizephyrians are one of three tribes of Locri. For an explanation of the name, see Harder vol. 2, 828–29.

616 Scholia to Dionysius Periegetes

the city of Croton, rich in crowns: He called Croton[1] well-crowned on account of the victories of the inhabitants, as Callimachus says.

[1] Greek city on the coast of Southern Italy. On its foundation, see Strabo 6.1.

617 Scholia to Dionysius Periegetes

Tarentum[1] is situated near the sea, which once from Amyclae mighty Ares founded: he called the same place Taras in the feminine form. Callimachus mentions the story, speaking like this,

[1] A Greek city in southern Italy (Strabo 6.1.2).

πάντες ἀφ᾽ Ἡρακλῆος ἐτήτυμον †ἔσσα κώμου†,
    ἔξοχα δ᾽ ἐν πεδίοις οἳ πόλιν ᾠκίσατε
< . . . . > Ἰταλῶν

618 Schol. ad Dionys. Per. 461

Αἰόλου· . . . εἷς δὲ τῶν υἱῶν αὐτοῦ Ἰόκαστος ὁ Ῥήγιον
ἔκτισε, πόλιν πρώην Ἐρυθρὰν καλουμένην, ὡς ὁ
Καλλίμαχος,

    Ῥήγιον ἄστυ λιπὼν Ἰοκάστεω Αἰολίδαο

619 Pf. = *Hec.* 159

620 Schol. Vat. ad Eur. *Hipp.* 402

ἐμοὶ γὰρ εἴη μήτε λανθάνειν καλά· Καλλίμαχος,

    ἄγνωτον μηδὲν ἔχοιμι καλόν

620a Schol. MB ad Eur. *Hec.* 934

λέχη δὲ φίλια μονόπεπλος λιποῦσα, Δωρὶς ὡς κόρα·
αἱ Λακεδαιμόνιαι κόραι διημερεύουσιν ἄζωστοι καὶ
ἀχίτωνες ἱματίδιον ἔχουσαι πεπορπημένον ἐφ᾽ ἑτέρου
τῶν ὤμων. καὶ Καλλίμαχος,

    ἔσκεν ὅτ᾽ ἄζωστος χἀτερόπορπος ἔτι

[come] you who are truly descendants of Heracles,
especially [you] who founded the city on the plains
. . . of the Italians

618 Scholia to Dionysius Periegetes

of Aeolus: . . . one of the sons of the same Jocastus who
founded Rhegium, the city long ago called Erythra, as
Callimachus,

> after leaving Rhegium, the city of Jocastus,[1] son of
> Aeolus

[1] On the mythical king Jocastus, see Timaeus (*BNJ* 566 F 164
sec. 8; cf. Diod. Sic. 5.8.1).

619 Pf. = *Hecale* 159

620 Vatican Scholia to Euripides, *Hippolytus*

may good things not escape my notice: Callimachus,

> may nothing good be hidden from me

620a Scholia to Euripides, *Hecuba* 934

leaving my own marriage bed wearing only a peplos, like
a Dorian girl: the Lacedaemonian girls pass the day with-
out belts and chitons, with a cloth pinned down on one
shoulder. Also Callimachus,

> it was the time when [a girl] still wore no belt and
> [her dress] was pinned on one side

621 Schol. MTAB ad Eur. *Phoen.* 134

Τυδεύς, Ἄρη δ᾽ Αἰτωλὸν ἐν στέρνοις ἔχει· ὡς ἔχοντος
αὐτοῦ ἐπὶ τῆς ἀσπίδος τὸν περὶ τοῦ συὸς πόλεμον.
Καλλίμαχος,

εἰμὶ τέρας Καλυδῶνος, ἄγω δ᾽ Αἰτωλὸν Ἄρηα

622 Schol. Vat. ad Eur. *Rhes.* 29

ἢ τὸν Εὐρώπας· . . . τὸν Σαρπηδόνα . . . διττὰς δὲ τὰς
Εὐρώπας ἀναγράφουσιν ἔνοι· μίαν μὲν Ὠκεανίδα ἀφ᾽
ἧς καὶ τὸ ἐν μέρος τῆς οἰκουμένης κληθῆναι, καθάπερ
Ἀπίων ἐν τοῖς Περὶ ἐπωνύμων καὶ Ἀριστοκλῆς ἐν τῷ
ᾱ τῆς Θεογονίας, ἑτέραν δὲ Φοίνικος ἢ Ἀγήνορος, ὡς
καὶ Εὐριπίδης καὶ ἄλλοι ἱστοροῦσιν, ἧς τοὺς περὶ τὸν
Μίνω γενέσθαι φασίν, ἔνιοι δέ εἰσιν οἳ καὶ παρὰ τὴν
αὐτὴν ὠνομάσθαι τὴν ἤπειρον, καθάπερ καὶ Καλλί-
μαχος, Ζηνόδοτος δὲ ἐξ αὐτοῦ.

623 Procl. *In Op.* 512

πνεύσαντος Βορέαο . . . θῆρες δὲ φρίσσουσ᾽, οὐρὰς
δ᾽ ὑπὸ μέζε᾽ ἔθεντο, τῶν καὶ λάχνη δέρμα κατάσκιον·
. . . εἴωθε γὰρ τὰ ζῷα διὰ τὸ ψῦχος τὰς οὐρὰς μεταξὺ

621 Scholia to Euripides, *Phoenician Women*

Tydeus, he has the Aetolian Ares in his breast: because he has on his shield the battle with the boar. Callimachus,

> I am the Calydonian[1] portent, and I bring the
> Aetolian[2] god of war

[1] On the hunt for the Calydonian boar, see Apollod. *Bibl.* 1.8.1–3; Ov. *Met.* 8.260–444.　　[2] Calydon was a city in the region of Aetolia near the west coast of Greece.

622 Vatican Scholia to Euripides, *Rhesus*

or the son of Europa: . . . Sarpedon . . . Some write that there were two Europas. One the daughter of Ocean,[1] from whom one part of the inhabited world is named, like Apion[2] in the *On Names* and Aristocles[3] in the first book of his *Birth of the Gods*, and another [Europa] who was the daughter of Phoenix or Agenor, as Euripides and others write, from whom they say the family of Minos was born, and there are some who say that the land was named from her, like Callimachus, and Zenodotus[4] after him.

[1] Hes. *Theog.* 357.　　[2] Apion (1st c. AD), grammarian and commentator on Homer (*Suda* α 3215).　　[3] Perhaps Aristocles of Messene (1st c. AD), Peripatetic philosopher (*Suda* α 3916).　　[4] Zenodotus (3rd c. BC), first Librarian at Alexandria and Homeric scholar (*Suda* ζ 75).

623 Proclus on Hesiod, *Works and Days*

when the North Wind blows . . . beasts shiver and put their tails between their legs, even those whose skin is covered with fur: . . . animals are accustomed on account of the

τῶν μηρῶν ἀποθλίβοντα ἐγγὺς τῶν αἰοίων ποιεῖν· ὡς καὶ παρὰ Καλλιμάχῳ,

†ἔζεσθαι θερμότατον ῥιζοῦχε Ποσειδῶν†

624 Schol. et paraphr. ad Hom. *Il.* 1.1 (*AO* vol. 4, p. 403.29 Cramer)

οἱ δὲ συνηγοροῦντες τῷ ἑνὶ λ φασὶν οὕτως· πρῶτον μὲν ἀπὸ τῆς ἀναλογίας ἵνα ᾖ ὅμοιον τῷ Ἰλεύς, βασιλεύς· εἶτα καὶ ἐκ τῆς ἐτυμολογίας, Ἀχιλεὺς γὰρ ἀπὸ τοῦ εἶναι ἄχος τοῖς Ἰλεῦσιν ἤγουν τοῖς Τρωσί, κατὰ φερωνυμίαν· ὑπὸ γὰρ θείας προνοίας, ὡς ἔφη Καλλίμαχος, ἐκλήθη οὕτως.

625 Pf. = *Aet.* 137a.14

626 Schol. AT ad Hom. *Il.* 6.305

πότνι' Ἀθηναίη ἐρυσίπτολι· πλεονασμὸς τοῦ ε̄ . . . παρὰ Καλλιμάχῳ,

τῶν οὐκ ἀγαθῶν ἐρυσίπτολιν

627 Schol. B ad Hom. *Il.* 7.231

τοῖοι· οἱ γλωσσογράφοι τὸ τοῖοι ἀντὶ τοῦ ἀγαθοί· ὅθεν καὶ Καλλίμαχος τῷ 'τοίων ἀεί' κέχρηται.

τοίων ἀεί†

cold to put their tails between their thighs near their genitalia. As also in Callimachus,

> that Poseidon sits at the hottest [place] at the root [of the earth][1]

[1] The text is damaged.

624 Scholia to Homer, *Iliad*

Those arguing [about the spelling of Achilles' name][1] in Book 11 of the *Odyssey* say this, first from analogy, that it is similar to *Ileus* and *basileus*. Then from etymology, that *Achileus* is from the pain (*achos*) [he caused] the people of Ilion, that is to say, to the Trojans, a name referring to the event. By divine foresight, as Callimachus said, he was named in this way.

[1] Whether it should be spelled with one lambda (*Achileus*) or two (*Achilleus*). Homer spells it both ways.

625 Pf. = *Aetia* 137a.14

626 Scholia to Homer, *Iliad*

Lady Athena, guardian of the city (*erysiptoli*): the redundancy of the [initial] epsilon . . . in Callimachus,

> the city-guardian of the wicked

627 Scholia to Homer, *Iliad*

such: The glossographers write such men instead of good men and from this Callimachus uses,

> always† of such

628 Schol. AD ad Hom. *Il.* 10.67

ἄνωχθι· ἐνεστῶτός ἐστι καὶ παρατατικοῦ μᾶλλον
ἤπερ παρακειμένου· ἀναλογώτερον δὲ παρὰ Καλλι-
μάχῳ,

ἄνωγε δὲ πορθμέα νεκρῶν

629 Pf. = *Hec.* 47.15

630 Schol. T ad Hom. *Il.* 16.234

Δωδώνης μεδέων δυσχειμέρου· οἱ περὶ Ζηνόδοτον πο-
λυπίδακος, διὰ τὸ Καλλιμάχου,

κρηνέων τ᾽ Εὐρώπῃ μισγομένων ἑκατόν

631 (631 Pf. + *SH* 297) Schol. T(B) ad Hom. *Il.* 16.235
ed. F. Montanari, *Athenaeum* 54 (1976): 139

ἀνιπτόποδες· οἱ φυλασσόμενοί τι μιαρὸν πατῆσαι, ἢ
μὴ προϊόντες τοῦ ἱεροῦ ὡς μὴ δεῖσθαι νίπτρων, καὶ
Καλλίμαχος,

```
      ] .παρα.. ο..[
      ]γυναικας .[
      ] .ς κατέχεας [
σάμβ]αλον αὐλείου[
5     ] .ου ἐλλειπε
      ]ντο μὴ εξιναι[
      ] ἔνεκ᾽ οὐδοῦ αυ[
```

628 Scholia to Homer, *Iliad*

Give an order: it is the present imperative and from the imperfect rather than the perfect. There is an analogous form in Callimachus,

> Give an order to the ferryman of the dead

629 Pf. = *Hecale* 47.15

630 Scholia to Homer, *Iliad*

ruling over stormy Dodona: the followers of Zenodotus[1] explain that it has many streams on account of Callimachus,

> a hundred springs mingling with the Europa

[1] Zenodotus (3rd c. BC), first Librarian at Alexandria and Homeric scholar (*Suda* ζ 75).

631 Scholia to Homer, *Iliad*

with unwashed feet:[1] those taking care not to tread on anything polluted or not leaving the shrine because they do not need water for washing, also Callimachus,

> Besides . . . women . . . you let fall . . . the sandal [at the entrance] of the court . . . he leaves . . . it is not

[1] Of the priests of Dodona called Selli, who do not wash their feet and sleep on the ground (*Il.* 16.234–35).

```
      ] σ[ά]μβαλον κα[
      ]υ                [
10    ]λιον             [
      ]χεισθαι    [
      ] ..             [
      ]ωι[ ]          [
      πο  λαν ...  [
```

632 Schol. A ad Hom. *Il.* 18.487

Ζεὺς Καλλιστοῦς τῆς Λυκάονος ἐρασθεὶς ἐμίσγετο
αὐτῇ λανθάνων Ἥραν. ἐπιγνοῦσα δὲ ἡ θεὸς μετέβα-
λεν αὐτὴν εἰς ἄρκτον, καὶ ὡς θηρίον Ἀρτέμιδι προσ-
έταξε τοξεῦσαι. Ζεὺς δὲ εἰς οὐρανὸν αὐτὴν ἀναγαγὼν
πρώτην κατηστέρισεν. ἡ ἱστορία παρὰ Καλλιμάχῳ.

633 Schol. ABT ad Hom. *Il.* 20.332

Αἰνεία, τίς σ' ὧδε θεῶν ἀτέοντα κελεύει ἀντί' Ἀχιλ-
λῆος πολεμίζειν; ἀτέοντα· ἀφροντιστοῦντα, φρενοβλα-
βοῦντα . . . Καλλίμαχος,

    Μουσέων †κενὸς† ἀνὴρ ἀτέει

634 Schol. BT ad Hom. *Il.* 21.536

μὴ οὖλος ἀνήρ· καὶ Καλλίμαχός φησιν,

    οὔλου μῆτερ Ἄρηος

allowed . . . as regards the threshold . . . the sandal and . . .

632 Scholia to Homer, *Iliad*

Zeus had sex with Callisto, the daughter of Lycaon, in secret from Hera, but the goddess discovered it and changed her into a bear. And she ordered Artemis to shoot her as if she were a wild beast. But Zeus transformed her first into a constellation and brought her into heaven. The story is in Callimachus.

633 Scholia to Homer, *Iliad*

Aeneas, who among the gods orders you who are distraught (*ateonta*) to fight against Achilles? *ateonta*: heedless, distraught . . . Callimachus,

> that man . . . of the Muses is distraught

634 Scholia to Homer, *Iliad*

that the destructive man may not: and Callimachus says,

> the mother[1] of deadly Ares

[1] Hera (*Il*. 5.892–93).

635 Schol. ad Hom. *Il.* 22.56

εἰσέρχεο τεῖχος . . . ὄφρα σαώσῃς Τρῶας· τεῖχος τὴν πόλιν. Καλλίμαχος,

ὁ δ᾽ ἐκ Λοκρῶν τείχεος Ἰταλικοῦ
παρῆν ἀμύντωρ

636 Schol. T ad Hom. *Il.* 24.254

Ἕκτορος ὠφέλετ᾽ ἀντὶ . . . πεφάσθαι· καὶ Καλλίμαχος,

μὴ ὀφέλετ᾽ ἀλλήλοισιν ἐπὶ πλέον ὄμματα δῦναι

637 Schol. MV ad Hom. *Od.* 2.134

ἐκ γὰρ τοῦ πατρὸς κακὰ πείσομαι, ἄλλα δὲ δαίμων δώσει· τὸ δὲ τοῦ πατρός . . . περὶ Ὀδυσσέως. οὐ γὰρ ἀπεγνώκει αὐτόν, ἐπειδή φησιν "ὀσσόμενος πατέρ᾽ ἐσθλὸν ἐνὶ φρεσίν." ἄλλως τε κατὰ Καλλίμαχον,

χαλεπὴ μῆνις ἐπιχθονίων

638 Schol. HMQR ad Hom. *Od.* 3.380

ἵληθι· ἀπὸ τοῦ ἵλημι. διὰ δὲ τὸ μέτρον ἐκτέταται ἡ παραλήγουσα, ὡς ἐν τῷ δίδωθι κτλ. ὑγιῶς οὖν Καλλ. ἔκλινεν,

ἵλαθί μοι φαλαρῖτι, πυλαιμάχε

635 Scholia to Homer, *Iliad*

Enter the wall . . . so that you may save the Trojans: the wall is the city. Callimachus,

> The Locrian[1] is here, defender of the Italic wall

[1] See *Fr. Inc. Sed.* 669, where Locrian is synonymous with Italian. Perhaps of a Locrian hero such as Euthymus of Locri, (*Aet.* 98–99b).

636 Scholia to Homer, *Iliad*

I wish that you had been killed . . . instead of Hector: also Callimachus,

> I wish that you may not come any more into one
>   another's sight

637 Scholia to Homer, *Odyssey*

From my father I will suffer evils, and the god will give others: from my father . . . refers to Odysseus. For [Telemachus] does not recognize him, since [Homer] says, "seeing his noble father in his mind" (*Od.* 1.115). Otherwise in Callimachus,

> terrible is the wrath of the terrestial gods

638 Scholia to Homer, *Odyssey*

(h)ilēthi (be gracious): from (h)ilēmi. [The long vowel] is placed next to last on account of the meter, as in didōthi, etc. Callimachus inflects it correctly,

> Be gracious ([h]ilāthi) to me Athena, Warrior at the
>   Gate[1]

[1] Epithet of Athena (Ar. *Eq.* 1172).

639 Pf. = *Hec.* 47.6

640 Schol. BHMPT ad Hom. *Od.* 7.107

καιροσέων δ᾽ ὀθονέων· . . . καῖρος ἡ διαπλοκὴ τοῦ
διάσματος, ἐν ᾗ οἱ στήμονες καθίενται. ἔνθεν καὶ αἱ
καιρωτίδες καιρωστρίδες παρὰ Καλλιμάχῳ.

641 Schol. (s³, Tzetzes) ad Lyc. *Alex.* 42

Κρόνου παρ᾽ αἰπὺν ὄχθον· τόπος ἐστὶν ἐν Ὀλυμπίᾳ
Κρόνου λόφος καλούμενος, οὗ μέμηται καὶ Καλλίμα-
χος.

642 Schol. (s⁴, Tzetzes) ad Lyc. *Alex.* 139

ψαλάξεις ἐς κενὸν νευρᾶς κτύπον, ἄσιτα κἀδώρητα
φορμίζων μέλη· λέγεται δὲ ἀπὸ προιμίας κιθαριστῶν
ἀσίτως καὶ ἀδώρως κιθαριζόντων, ἥτις ἐστὶν αὕτη·
"εἰς κενὸν κρούεις τὰς χορδάς." ἔθος εἶχον οἱ παλαιοί,
ὡς καὶ Καλλίμαχος ἱστορεῖ, μετὰ κιθάρας περὶ τοὺς
ἅλας ἰέναι καὶ ἀνυμνεῖν καὶ ἐγκωμιάζειν.

643 Schol. (s⁴, Tzetzes) ad Lyc. *Alex.* 207

ᾧ ποτ᾽ ἐν μυχοῖς Δελφινίου . . . Ταύρῳ κρυφαίας χέρ-
νιβας κατάρξεται· ἐτιμᾶτο δὲ καὶ Διόνυσος ἐν Δελ-

639 Pf. = *Hecale* 47.6

640 Scholia to Homer, *Odyssey*

kairoseōn d' othoneōn (weaving cloth): . . . the ravel (*kairos*) is the interconnection of the warp [and the frame], in which the threads are lowered, and from this the words *kairōtides* and *kairōtstrides* (weavers) in Callimachus [are derived].[1]

[1] Cf. *Fr. Inc. Sed.* 547.

641 Tzetzes on Lycophron, *Alexandra*

beside the steep hill of Cronus: there is a place in Olympia called the Hill of Cronus,[1] which Callimachus mentions.

[1] The father of Zeus (Hes. *Theog.* 453–58), who gave his name to a hill adjacent to the sanctuary of Zeus at Olympia (Pind. *Ol.* 1.111, 6.64, 8.17, 9.3; *Nem.* 11.25).

642 Tzetzes on Lycophron, *Alexandra*

You will twang the strings [to produce] a fruitless sound playing songs without food or fee: in the prologue cithara players are mentioned who play without food or fee, which is the same thing: "you strike the strings for nothing." The ancients had a custom, as Callimachus says, to go with the cithara to the sea and to sing hymns and songs of praise.

643 Tzetzes on Lycophron, *Alexandra*

To the Bull god once in the innermost sanctum of Apollo Delphinius . . . he will commence secret rites; and even

φοῖς σὺν Ἀπόλλωνι οὑτωσί· οἱ Τιτᾶνες τὰ Διονύσου
μέλη σπαράξαντες Ἀπόλλωνι, ἀδελφῷ ὄντι αὐτοῦ,
παρέθεντο ἐμβαλόντες λέβητι· ὁ δὲ παρὰ τῷ τρίποδι
ἀπέθετο, ὥς φησι Καλλίμαχος καὶ Εὐφορίων.

644 Schol. (ss³, Tzetzes) ad Lyc. *Alex.* 249

ὀρχηστὴς Ἄρης στρόμβῳ τὸν αἱμάτηρον ἐξάρχων
νόμον· ἐπειδὴ ἐπετήδευον πάλαι μέλη τινὰ πρός τὸ
παροξῦναί τε καὶ εἰς ἀνδρείαν κινῆσαι τοὺς ἀκούο-
ντας. καὶ Καλλίμαχος,

νόμον δ' ἤειδεν Ἄρηος

645 Schol. (s) ad Lyc. *Alex.* 351

εἰς ἀνώροφον στέγην εἱρκτῆς ἁλιβδύσασα λυγαίας
δέμας· κυρίως δὲ ἁλιβδῦσαί ἐστι τὸ ἐν θαλάσσῃ δι-
αφθαρῆναι ἤγουν ἁλὶ δῦσαι. καὶ Καλλίμαχος,

†αἱ νῆσαι ἁλιδύουσαι†

646 Schol. (ss³s⁴, Tzetzes) ad Lyc. *Alex.* 409

ὅσην Ἄρατθος· Ἄρατθος ποταμὸς Ἠπείρου οὗ καὶ
Καλλ. μέμνηται·

αἱ δὲ βοοκρήμνοιο παρ' ἀγκύλον ἴχνος Ἀράτθου

Dionysus was honored in this way in Delphi with Apollo. The Titans, after they pulled apart the limbs of Dionysus, offered them to Apollo, his own brother, putting them in a cauldron. And he placed it beside his tripod, as Callimachus says, and Euphorion.[1]

[1] Fr. 14 Lightfoot.

644 Tzetzes on Lycophron, *Alexandra*

Ares the dancer leading the bloody song with his conch shell: since long ago they practiced certain songs to stimulate those hearing (them) and spur them to manliness, and Callimachus,

> he sang the strain of Ares

645 Scholia to Lycophron, *Alexandra*

on the uncovered roof of the gloomy prison, having hidden ([h]*alibdusasa*) my body: properly (h)*alibdusai* is to perish in the sea or rather to sink in the sea. Also Callimachus,

> †the ships sinking†

646 Tzetzes on Lycophron, *Alexandra*

as much as Aratthus: Aratthus is a river in Epirus, which Callimachus mentions,

> which beside the winding track of steep-banked
> Aratthus

647 Schol. (s³s⁴s⁶, Tzetzes) ad Lyc. *Alex*. 598

ῥάμφεσσι· ῥάμφος καλεῖται τὸ ἐπικαμπὲς χεῖλος τῶν
ὀρνέων, ὡς καὶ Καλλίμαχος,

ῥάμφεϊ †καθνώδει τόργος ἔκοπτε νέκυν

648 Schol. (ss³s⁴, Tzetzes) ad Lyc. *Alex*. 647

καὶ χεῦμα Θερμώδοντος Ὑψάρνου θ᾽ ὕδωρ· Θερμώδων
ἐστὶ μὲν ἕτερος ποταμὸς Παφλαγονίας περὶ Σινώπην,
ὅπου ἦσαν αἱ Ἀμαζόνες· ὁ δὲ νῦν κείμενος Θερμώδων
καὶ Ὕψαρνος ποταμοὶ Βοιωτίας. καὶ Καλλ.,

ἂψ ἐπὶ Θερμώδοντος ὁδεύετον

649 Schol. (s³) ad Lyc. *Alex*. 678

βρύξουσιν· φάγονται. τὸ θέμα παρὰ Καλλιμάχῳ
βρύχω.

650 Schol. (ss³s⁴, Tzetzes) ad Lyc. *Alex*. 771

μύκλοις γυναικόκλωψιν· μύκλος καλεῖται ἡ ἐν τῷ τρα-
χήλῳ τῶν ὄνων ὑποδίπλωσις. μύκλους δὲ εἶπεν ἐν-
ταῦθα τοὺς μνηστῆρας διὰ τὸ ἀδηφάγον καὶ κατω-
φερές· ὡς καὶ Καλλ.,

ἔστιν μοι Μάγνης ἐννεάμυκλος ὄνος

647 Tzetzes on Lycophron, *Alexandra*

with their beaks: a bird's curved lip is called a beak, as Callimachus,

> with his beak the vulture pecked at the corpse

648 Tzetzes on Lycophron, *Alexandra*

and the flood of Thermodon and the water of Hypsarnus: Thermodon is another river of Paphlagonia near Sinope, where the Amazons were. The rivers Thermodon and Hypsarnus are now in Boeotia. Also Callimachus,

> again the two traveled on the Thermodon

649 Scholia on Lycophron, *Alexandra*

bruxousin (they will devour): they will eat. The base form in Callimachus is *bruchō*.

650 Tzetzes on Lycophron, *Alexandra*

lustful (*muklois*) wifestealers: the skinfold in the neck of asses is called *myklos*. He said then that the suitors were *muklos* on account of being greedy and lewd. As Callimachus also says,

> my Magnesian ass is nine years old[1]

---

[1] That is, he has nine skin folds. Alternatively, he is very strong.

651 Schol. (ss³s⁴, Tzetzes) ad Lyc. *Alex.* 817

μεσσαβοῦν· . . . ἀντὶ τοῦ ζευγνύειν. μέσσαβα γὰρ
λέγονται αἱ τοῦ ζυγοῦ γλυφαί, ἔνθα οἱ αὐχένες τῶν
βοῶν δέδενται. καὶ Καλλίμαχος,

μέσσαβα βοῦς ὑποδύς

652 Schol. (ss³s⁴, Tzetzes) ad Lyc. *Alex.* 1225

Ὀγκαίου· . . . τοῦ τῆς Δήμητρος τουτέστι τοῦ ἐρινυώ-
δους, παρ' ὅσον Ὄγκαις τῆς Ἀρκαδίας Ἐρινὺς Δη-
μήτηρ τιμᾶται, ὡς καὶ Καλλίμαχος,

τὴν μὲν ὅ γ' ἐσπέρμηνεν Ἐρινύι Τιλφωσαίῃ

653 Schol. (ss⁶, Tzetzes) ad Lyc. *Alex.* 1316

ἐρράου σκύλος· ἐρράου τοῦ κριοῦ, ὁ δὲ Καλλίμαχος
τοῦ κάπρου.

654 Schol. ad Nic. *Ther.* 35

θιβρὴν δ' ἐξελάσεις ὀφίων ἐπιλωβέα κῆρα· θιβρὴν δὲ
τὴν θερμὴν καὶ ὀξεῖαν διὰ τὰς ἐξ αὐτῆς γινομένας
φλεγμονάς. Καλλίμαχος,

θιβρῆς Κύπριδος ἁρμονίης

651 Tzetzes on Lycophron, *Alexandra*

messaboun (to yoke): . . . instead of to harness. The openings in the yoke are called *messaba* where the necks of the cattle are fastened. Also Callimachus,

> the cattle put under the yokes

652 Tzetzes on Lycophron, *Alexandra*

of the Oncaean: . . . that is of Demeter Erinys, since in Oncae of Arcadia Demeter Erinys is honored, as also Callimachus,

> the girl he engendered with the Erinys of Tilphosa[1]

[1] The daughter, Despoina, was worshipped in Arcadia as the water nymph Telphousa (Paus. 8.25.4, 8.42.1).

653 Tzetzes on Lycophron, *Alexandra*

the hide of a ram (*erraou*): of the ram (*kriou*), but Callimachus [uses it] of a boar.

654 Scholia to Nicander, *Theriaca*

you will drive out the hot (*thibēn*) and deadly doom of the serpents: *thibēn* means hot and sharp on account of the heat coming from it. Callimachus,

> of the coupling[1] of hot Aphrodite

[1] *Harmonia*, which could also be a proper name, the wife of Cadmus, who was the daughter of Ares and Aphrodite (Hes. *Theog.* 933–37).

655 Schol. ad Nic. *Alex.* 101

τῶν ἄλλων ἱστορούντων τὴν περσείαν καταφυτεῦσαι
τὸν Περσέα ἐν Αἰγύπτῳ, ὡς καὶ Καλλ.,

> καὶ τριτάτη Περσῆος ἐπώνυμος, ἧς ὁρόδαμνον
> Αἰγύπτῳ κατέπηξεν

656 Schol. ad Nic. *Alex.* 185

κηκὰς ἀλώπηξ· κηκὰς δ' ἡ ἀλώπηξ, ἤτοι κακωτική,
κακοποιός, κακοῦργος, ἢ χλευαστική. Καλλ.,

> κηκάδι σὺν γλώσσῃ

657 Schol. ad Nic. *Alex.* 433

μήκωνος κεβληγόνου· τῆς ἐν τῇ κεφαλῇ τὸν γόνον
ἐχούσης, ὅ ἐστι τὸ σπέρμα· συγγενὲς γὰρ τὸ β̄ τῷ φ̄·
καὶ Καλλ.,

> ἀμφί τε κεβλήν
> εἱρμένον[1] ἀγλίθων οὖλον ἔχει στέφανον

[1] εἱρμένον Bergk: εἱρμένος codd.

658 Schol. ad Nic. *Alex.* 450

Δηοῖ πολυωπέας ἤνυσαν ὄμπας πολυωπέας· πολλὰς
ὀπὰς ἐχούσας· τοιαῦτα γὰρ τὰ κηρία. ὄμπαι οἱ μέλιτι
δεδευμένοι πυροί, καὶ Καλλίμαχος,

> ἐν δὲ θεοῖσιν ἐπὶ φλογὶ καιέμεν ὄμπας

655 Scholia to Nicander, *Alexipharmaca*

according to other historians Perseus planted the *persea*
in Egypt, as also in Callimachus,

> and the third named for Perseus,[1] from which he
> planted a cutting in Egypt

[1] The persea tree, of the variety *mimusops*.

656 Scholia to Nicander, *Alexipharmaca*

the mischievous fox: the fox is mischievous or noxious, an
evilmaker, an evildoer, or a scornful jester. Callimachus,

> with a mischievous tongue

657 Scholia to Nicander, *Alexipharmaca*

of the poppy with its seed in its head (*keblēgonou*): having
its procreative power in its head, which is the seed. The
beta in *keblēgonou* is akin to a phi. Also Callimachus,

> around the head
> he has a thick crown intertwined with garlic cloves ·

658 Scholia to Nicander, *Alexipharmaca*

for Demeter [the bees] made honey cakes (*ompas*) with
many holes (*poluōpeas*): *poluōpeas* means having many
holes, like honeycombs. *Ompai* are cakes of wheat
drenched with honey, also Callimachus,

> to burn cakes on the fire for the gods

659 Schol. ad Nic. *Alex.* 611

μὴ μὲν δὴ σμῖλον σὺ κακὴν ἐλατηΐδα μάρψαις Ὀι-
ταίην, θανάτοιο πολυκλαύτοιο δότειραν· . . . περὶ δὲ
τῆς σμίλου φησὶν Ἀνδρέας περὶ Αἰτωλίαν πληθύνειν,
καὶ τοὺς ἐγκοιμηθέντας αὐτῷ ἀποθνήσκειν, ὁ δὲ Θεό-
φαστος περὶ μὲν τῶν ἀνθρώπων οὐδὲν εἴρηκεν, αὐτὸ
δὲ μόνον, ὅτι τὰ λόφουρα τῶν ζῴων γευσάμενα ἀπο-
θνήσκει. λόφουρα δέ εἰσι βόες, ἡμίονοι. Καλλίμαχος,

ἑρπετὰ τῶν αἰεὶ τετρίφαται λοφιαί

660 Schol. ad Opp. *Hal.* 4.556–60

δουριφάτους· δοριφονεύτους ἐξανελόντες. Καλλίμα-
χος ἄπελος τὸ ἕλκος λέγει ἀπὸ τοῦ ᾱ στερητικοῦ
μορίου καὶ τοῦ πελῶ τοῦ πλησιάζω, τὸ ἑλκυσθὲν καὶ
διακριθὲν κατὰ διέχειαν σῶμα. τὰ γὰρ ἕλκεα πολλὰ
καὶ αἰόλα ἐν τοῖς σώμασι τῶν νεκρῶν.

661 Schol. (Bb) ad Ov. *Ib.* 351

quaeque sui venerem iunxit cum fratre mariti Locris,
in ancillae dissimulata nece: Callimachus dicit Hyper-
mestram quondam in adulterio deprehensam cum fratre
mariti sui profugisse auxilio tenebrarum; deinde servum
suum Pavonem et Locrin ancillam necavit, ut illa Locris
diceretur deprehensa.

659 Scholia to Nicander, *Alexipharmaca*

You should not take hold of the harmful pine-like yew of Oeta, the giver of much-lamented death: . . . and about the yew Andreas says it is abundant around Aetolia and that those who have slept on it perish, but Theophrastus says nothing about men, but this only, that pack animals tasting it while living die. The animals are cows and mules. Callimachus,

> beasts, whose manes are always rubbed away

660 Scholia to Oppian, *Halieutica*

slain by a spear: taking up the dead. For *elkos* (wound) Callimachus says *apelos* [which is formed] from an alpha privative prefix and *pelō*, from *plēsiazō* (to approach). The body was dragged and torn into pieces. For there are many and bright wounds in the bodies of the dead.

661 Scholia to Ovid, *Ibis*

Some Locrian woman[1] had sex with her husband's brother, hidden by the death of her slave: Callimachus says that Hypermestra,[2] once caught in adultery with her brother-in-law, fled under cover of darkness, then killed her slave Pavo and her attendant Locris so that it could be said that Locris had been caught.

[1] Possibly Arsinoe II, whose second husband was her half brother (Ptolemy Ceraunus), and whose third, her full brother (Ptolemy Philadelphus). Following the death in battle of her first husband, Lysimachus, she escaped from the mob in Ephesus by exchanging clothes with her slave, who was murdered in her place (Polyaenus, *Strat*. 8.57). [2] The scholiast relates Ovid's cryptic reference to another story.

662 Schol. (Bab) ad Ov. *Ib.* 379

ut qui Bistoniae templo cecidere Minervae, propter quod
facies nunc quoque tecta deae est: Thracia a Bistonia pa-
lude vel flumine dicta est, et ibi auctore Callimacho in
oppido Seris nomine Lemnii a Lacedaemoniis interfecti
sunt in templo Minervae; quod ne videret, Minerva fertur
sua lumina operuisse ("ex quo nunc etiam est") in templo
vultu retorto, ut d(icit) Callimachus.

663 Schol. (BPb) ad Ovid *Ib.* 451

vulnera totque feras quot dicitur ille tulisse, cuius ab infe-
riis culter abesse solet: Callimachus dicit in Creta Mene-
demo heroi sacra fieri, et non ferro, quia in Troiano bello
plurimis vulneribus cultorum interiit.

664 Schol. (Bpab) ad Ov. *Ib.* 477

praedaque sis illis quibus est Latonia Delos ante diem
rapto non adeunda Thaso: Sacerdos Apollinis Delii Anius
fuit, ad quem cum venisset per noctem filius eius Thasus
a canibus laniatus est, unde Delon nullus canis accedit
auctore Callimacho.

---

[1] Of Apollo, son of Leto. Delos was his birthplace and one of
his principal shrines (*Hymn* 4).　　[2] On Thasus and Anius in
the *Aetia*, see Harder vol. 2, 261.

662 Scholia to Ovid, *Ibis*

as those who perished in the temple of Bistonian Minerva[1]
on account of which the face of the goddess is covered:
Thrace is meant from the wetlands or river Bistonia, and
there, on the authority of Callimachus, in the town named
Siris, Lemnians were killed by Lacedaemonians in the
temple of Minerva; in order not to see this, Minerva, it is
said, covered her eyes, ("hence it is thus even now") in the
temple her face is turned away, as Callimachus says.[2]

[1] Athena.   [2] For other explanations, see Lyc. *Alex*. 984–
92; Strabo 6.1.14; *Aet*. 35.

663 Scholia to Ovid, *Ibis*

May you sustain as many wounds as they say he suffered,
whose rites are usually performed without knives: Callim-
achus says that in Crete,[1] rites are held for the hero Me-
nedemus without iron implements because in the Trojan
War he perished from a great many knife wounds.

[1] Apparently, the scholiast confuses Crete with Cythnos, the
Cycladic island associated with Menedemus.

664 Scholia to Ovid, *Ibis*

May you be prey for those who may not approach Lato-
nian[1] Delos because Thasus was killed before his time:
Anius[2] was a priest of Apollo at Delos, and when his son
Thasus came to him in the night, he was torn apart by
dogs. Whence no dog may approach Delos, on the author-
ity of Callimachus.

665 Schol. (Bb) ad Ov. *Ib.* 501

feta tibi occurrat patrio popularis in arvo sitque Phalaecae
causa laena necis: Pegasus Epirotes, cum circumsideret
Ambraciam, exivit venatum et leaenae catulum nactus sus-
tulit; quem consecuta leaena laniavit, auctore Callimacho.

666 Schol. Paus. 6.13.1

περὶ Ἀστύλου, οὗ καὶ Καλλίμαχος μέμνηται . . .
Ἀστύλος δὲ Κροτωνιάτης Πυθαγόρου μέν ἐστιν ἔρ-
γον, τρεῖς δὲ ἐφεξῆς Ὀλυμπίασι σταδίου τε καὶ δι-
αύλου νίκας ἔσχεν. ὅτι δὲ ἐν δύο ταῖς ὑστέραις ἐς
χάριν τὴν Ἱέρωνος τοῦ Δεινομένους ἀνηγόρευσεν αὐ-
τὸν Συρακούσιον, τούτων ἕνεκα οἱ Κροτωνιᾶται τὴν
οἰκίαν αὐτοῦ δεσωτήριον εἶναι κατέγνωσαν καὶ τὴν
εἰκόνα καθεῖλον παρὰ τῇ Ἥρᾳ τῇ Λακινίᾳ κειμένην.

667 Pf. = *Aet.* 190c

665 Scholia to Ovid, *Ibis*

May a local lioness who has just given birth meet you in a
native field and be the cause of death like that of Phalae-
cus:[1] Pegasus Epirotes, when he was beseiging Ambracia,
went out to the hunt and, getting hold of a lioness' cub,
carried it off; the lioness followed him and tore him apart,
on the authority of Callimachus.

[1] Tyrant of Ambracia. The story with variations is in Antoninus
Liberalis 4.5b.

666 Scholia to Pausanias, *Description of Greece*

About Astylus, whom Callimachus mentions . . . [The
statue of] Astylus[1] of Croton is the work of Pythagoras. He
had three successive victories at Olympia in the stadion
and the *diaulos*.[2] Because in the last two he declared that
he was a Syracusan in gratitude to Hieron[3] the son of
Dinomenes, the Crotonites condemned his house to be a
prison and took down his statue, which had been located
beside the temple[4] of Lacinian[5] Hera.

[1] A famous athlete celebrated by Simonides (*PMG* 506).
[2] The stadion (ca. 190 meters, introduced in 776 BC) and
diaulos (ca. 400 m., introduced in 724 BC) were Olympic compe-
titions for running.   [3] Hieron I, Tyrant of Syracuse in Sicily
(ca. 475–467 BC; Polyb. 1.8–9). He won victories at Delphi in 470
(Pind. *Pyth.* 1) and at Olympia in 476 (Pind. *Ol.* 1; *P.Oxy.* 222).
[4] On the temple, see Strabo 6.1.11.   [5] Lacinius was slain
by Heracles (Diod. Sic. 4.24.7).

667 Pf. = *Aetia* 190c

668 Schol. (BCDEQ) ad Pind. *Ol*. 4.32a

Λαμνιάδων· καὶ ὁ Καλλίμαχος,

    Ἐργῖνος †Κλυμένου† ἔξοχος ἐν σταδίῳ

669 Schol. (A) ad Pind. *Ol*. 10.18b

νέμει γὰρ ἀτρέκεια πόλιν Λοκρῶν Ζεφυρίων, μέλει τέ
σφισι Καλλιόπα· οὐκ ἀπὸ σκοποῦ τούτους εἶπε τοὺς
Λοκροὺς μουσικούς, ἀλλ᾽ ὅτι ἔστι τις ἁρμονία Λοκρι-
στὶ προσαγορευομένη, ἣν ξυναρμόσαι φασὶ Ξενόκρι-
τον τὸν Λοκρόν. Καλλίμαχος,

    ὃς <   > Ἰταλὴν ἐφράσαθ᾽ ἁρμονίην

670 Schol. (B) ad Pind. *Ol*. 13.27a

τίς γὰρ ἱππείοις ἐν ἔντεσσιν μέτρα . . . ἐπέθηκ; του-
τέστι τὰ ἵππεια μέτρα τοῦ χαλινοῦ . . . Δίδυμος δέ
φησι μήτε τοὺς ἱππικοὺς δρόμους . . . μήτε τὸν χα-
λινὸν διὰ τούτων δηλοῦσθαι, ἀλλὰ τὸν κεραμεικὸν

668 Scholia to Pindar, *Olympian Odes*

Lamniadōn (of the Lemnians): also Callimachus,

> Erginus,[1] son of Clymenus, outstanding in the stadion

[1] One of the Argonauts who won the stadion on Lemnos, despite his gray hair (Pind. *Ol.* 4.19–27). The Argonauts are treated in *Aet.* 7c–21d and the anchor of the Argo at *Aet.* 108–9a.

669 Scholia to Pindar, *Olympian Odes*

Strictness[1] rules the city of the Epizephyrian Locrians, and Calliope[2] is a care to them: he did not say from this perspective that the Locrians were musical, but that there is a certain (musical) scale that is called Locrian, which they say Xenocritus[3] the Locrian put together. Callimachus,

> who . . . invented the Italian[4] scale

[1] A reference to the law code of Zaleucus (mid-7th c. BC), a Pythagorean philosopher in Epizephyrian Locri (Pind. *Ol.* 10.13–14; Strabo 6.1.8).   [2] A Muse.   [3] Musician and lyric poet ([Plut.] *Mus.* 9).   [4] Epizephyrian Locri was a colony of the Opuntian Locrians at the toe of the boot that is the Italian peninsula.

670 Scholia to Pindar, *Olympian Odes*

Who added restraints . . . to the horses' gear?: that is to say, the restraints of the horses' bit . . . Didymus[1] says neither horse tracks . . . nor the horse's bit is meant by this, but the potters' wheel, and the metaphor works in two

[1] Alexandrian grammarian (1st c. BC).

τροχόν, ἐκ μεταφορᾶς διχόθεν μετενηνεγμένης, τοῦτο
μὲν ὅτι ἵπποις οἰκεῖος ὁ τροχός, τοῦτο δὲ ὅτι ἑκατέρω-
θεν ἐλαύνεται ὑπὸ ποδὸς πτέρνης. Καλλίμαχος,

> πτέρνῃ θ' ἵππος ἐλαυνόμενος

671 Schol. (BDEGQ) ad Pind. *Pyth.* 4.107a

Δελφίδος αὐτομάτῳ κελάδῳ· ἤτοι αὐτοκελεύστῳ· οὐ
γὰρ κατὰ ἐπίταγμα τῶν χρησῳδουμένων ἡ προφῆτις
τοὺς χρησμοὺς ἐκφέρει, ἀλλ' ἐπινοίᾳ· ἢ τῷ μὴ ἐκ συν-
τάξεως φερομένῳ, ἀλλ' ἀπαυτοματιζομένῳ· καὶ ἰδίως·
οὐκ ἐρωτηθεῖσ' ὑπὸ τοῦ Βάττου περὶ τῆς ἀποικίας,
ἀλλὰ περὶ τῆς φωνῆς. ἔνθεν δὴ καὶ αὐτώρης ὁ τρί-
πους. Καλλίμαχος,

> αὐτώρης ὅτε τοῖσιν ἐπέφραδε

672 Schol. (BDEGQ) ad Pind. *Pyth.* 4.377

κελαινώπεσσι Κόλχοισιν· . . . οἱ δὲ ὅτι Αἰγυπτίων
ἄποικοί εἰσιν οἱ Σκύθαι, διὰ τοῦτο καὶ μελανόχροας
αὐτοὺς εἶναι λέγουσιν. δοκοῦσι δὲ καὶ Αἰγυπτίων εἶ-
ναι ἄποικοι. ἔχουσι δὲ καὶ λινουργοῦσι τὴν καλάμην,
ὥσπερ Αἰγύπτιοι. Καλλίμαχος,

> Κολχίδος ἐκ καλάμης

ways, first because the wheel (*trochos*) is properly a horse-track and then because it is driven by the heel (*pternē*) of the foot on both sides. Callimachus,

> the horse driven by the heel

671 Scholia to Pindar, *Pythian Odes*

by the spontaneous voice of the Delphic tripod: or unbidden. The prophet brings forth the oracles not on command of the oracles' attendants but by inspiration. Nor is it produced by an order, but of its own accord and spontaneously. Not asked by Battus[1] about the colony, but about his voice; and then the tripod [spoke] spontaneously. Callimachus,

> when of its own accord it made a pronouncement to them

[1] The founder of the Greek colony of Cyrene in North Africa who came to Delphi to inquire about his stuttering (Hdt. 4.155).

672 Scholia to Pindar, *Pythian Odes*

by the dark-faced Colchians: . . . they say that the Scythians are colonists of the Egyptians on account of this and that they are dark skinned. They seem to be colonists of the Egyptians. The have flax and make it into linen like the Egyptians. Callimachus,

> from the flax of Colchis[1]

[1] City on the Black Sea visited by the Argonauts, where Medea's father, Aeëtes, was king and kept the Golden Fleece, the object of their quest (Ap. Rhod. 2.1277–78).

673 Schol. (BDEGQ) ad Pind. *Pyth*. 5.31

Κυράνα γλυκὺν ἀμφὶ κᾶπον Ἀφροδίτας· κῆπον Ἀφρο-
δίτης τὴν Κυρήνη ὠνόμασεν ὡς καλλίκαρπον καὶ διὰ
τοῦτο ἐράσμιον καὶ ἐπαφρόδιτον· εἰ μὴ ἄρα τὸν τῶν
Χαρίτων λόφον ὠνόμασεν οὕτως. Καλλίμαχος,

    ἢ ὑπὲρ αὐσταλέον Χαρίτων λόφον

674 Schol. (DEGQ) ad Pind. *Pyth*. 5.44b

ποδαρκέων δωδεκαδρόμων τέμενος· ὅτι δὲ δωδεκάκις
τρέχουσι, μαρτυρεῖ καὶ Καλλίμαχος,

    δωδεκάκις περὶ δίφρον ἐπήγαγεν ὄμματα
    †δίφρου†

675 Schol. ad Pind. fr. 59 S.-M. nt. 3

Σελλοι· Καλλίμαχ[ος,

    ].ἔδρανον Ἑλλ.[
    Τ]μαρίοις[

676 Schol. (Arethas) ad Pl. *Lys*. 206e

ἀστραγαλίζοντας· ἀστραγαλίζειν τὸ ἀστραγάλοις
παίζειν, ὅπερ καὶ ἀστρίζειν ἔλεγον, ἐπεὶ καὶ τοὺς
ἀστραγάλους ἄστριας ἐκάλουν. Καλλίμαχος,

673 Scholia to Pindar, *Pythian Odes*

At Cyrene around the sweet garden of Aphrodite: he called Cyrene the garden of Aphrodite because it has beautiful fruit and is lovely and charming; would that he had not named the hill of the Graces in this way. Callimachus,

> above the arid hill of the Graces.[1]

[1] Described by Hdt. 4.175 as thickly wooded.

674 Scholia to Pindar, *Pythian Odes*

of the twelve swift-footed races in the precinct: because they run twelve times [around the turning post, as] Callimachus also attests,

> twelve times around eyes urged on the chariot

675 Scholia to Pindar (unattributed fragment)

Selloi: Callimachus,

> the seat of the Helli[1] on Mt. Tmarus[2]

[1] Helli and Selli are alternative spellings of the name of the priests at the oracle of Zeus at Dodona (Hom. *Il*. 16.234). In *Aet*. 23.3 Callimachus uses the singular Sellos.   [2] Near Dodona in Epirus (Strabo 7.7.11).

676 Scholia to Plato, *Lysis*

playing with knucklebones: *astragalizein* is to play with knucklebones, which he also says is *astrizein* since knucklebones are also called *astriai*. Callimachus,

225

ζορκός τοι, φίλε κοῦρε, Λιβυστίδος αὐτίκα δώσω
πέντε νεοσμήκτους ἄστριας

677 Pf. = *Aet.* 60a

678 Schol. L. ad Soph. *Ant.* 711

ἀλλ' ἄνδρα, κεἴ τις ᾖ σοφός, τὸ μανθάνειν πόλλ' αἰσ-
χρὸν οὐδὲν καὶ τὸ μὴ τείνειν ἄγαν· μὴ αὐθάδη εἶναι
ἀντιτείνοντα τοῖς συμβουλεύουσιν· τοῦτο δὲ παρὰ
τὸ Σόλωνος, "γηράσκω δ' αἰεὶ πάντα διδασκόμενος."
Καλλίμαχος,

679 Schol. Laur. ad Soph. *Trach.* 308

ἄνανδρος ἢ τεκνοῦσα· τέκνα ἔχουσα ὅπερ Καλλίμα-
χός φησι παιδοῦσα.

680 Pf. = *Hec.* 171

681 Schol. Laur. ad Soph. *OC* 489

ἄπυστα φωνῶν· ἀνήκουστα . . . τοῦτο ἀπὸ τῆς δρω-
μένης θυσίας ταῖς Εὐμενίσι φησί· μετὰ γὰρ ἡσυχίας
τὰ ἱερὰ δρῶσι καὶ διὰ τοῦτο οἱ ἀπὸ ἡσύχου θύουσιν
αὐταῖς καθάπερ Πολέμων ἐν τοῖς Πρὸς Ἐρατοσθένην

I will at once give you, dear boy, five newly-cleaned
knucklebones of a Libyan gazelle[1]

[1] Perhaps Aphrodite bribing her son Eros.

677 Pf. = *Aetia* 60a

678 Scholia to Sophocles, *Antigone*

But for a man, even if someone is wise, it is not shameful
to learn many things, and not to hold on to anything very
tightly:[1] that he not be stubborn resisting his advisors; this
is opposed to the [words] of Solon "I will grow old forever
learning everything."[2] Callimachus,[3]

[1] Haemon to his father Creon.   [2] Fr. 18 West.
[3] The quotation is missing.

679 Laurentian Scholia to Sophocles, *Trachiniae*

without a husband or giving birth (*teknousa*): having chil-
dren, which Callimachus calls *paidousa*.

680 Pf. = *Hecale* 171

681 Laurentian Scholia to Sophocles, *Oedipus at Colo-
nus*

saying things unheard: whispered . . . they say this of the
woman making sacrifices for the Eumenides; for they per-
form the rites in quiet and for that reason they sacrifice to
them in stillness, as Polemon says in his *Against Eratos-*

φησὶν οὕτω· . . . καὶ Ἀπολλόδωρος δὲ ἐν τῇ Περὶ
Θεῶν ιζ περὶ τοῦ τῶν Ἡσυχιδῶν γένους καὶ ἱερᾶς
φησί· καὶ Καλλίμαχος,

> νηφάλιαι καὶ τῇσιν ἀεὶ μελιηδέας ὄμπας
> λήτειραι καίειν ἔλλαχον Ἡσυχίδες

682 Pf. = *Hec.* 158

683 Schol. ad Stat. *Theb.* 2.258

Arcados Euhippi spolium, cadit aereus orbis: Euhippus
rex Argivorum mirae felicitatis fuit; cuius clipeum qui
apud Argos nobiliter rem gessisset, accipiebat, ut illo per
urbem incedens honestaretur. unde proverbium apud illos
tale est, cum alicuius ignaviam irriderent, ut Callimachus
ait,

> ὡς τὴν ἀσπίδα †ατον† ἑλών (?)

684 Pf. = *Hec.* 175

685 Schol. (KUEAG) ad Theoc. *Id.* 2.17

ἴυγξ· ὄρνεον Ἀφροδίτης ὃ αἱ φαρμακίδες συνεργὸν
ἔχουσι πρὸς τὰς μαγείας . . . ἢ τὴν Ἴυγγα, ὥς φησι
Καλλίμαχος Ἠχοῦς θυγατέρα φαρμακεύειν δὲ τὸν

thenes . . . and Apollodorus says in *On the Gods* Book 17[1] concerning the family of the Hesychidae and the rites, also Callimachus,

> for them the priestesses, sober descendants of Hesychus (Quiet),[2] are allotted always to burn sweet cakes

[1] *BNJ* 244 F 101.   [2] Hereditary priestesses of the Eumenides. Since they are chthonic deities, their sacrifices do not include wine.

682 Pf. = *Hecale* 158

683 Scholia to Statius, *Thebaid*

spoil of Arcadian Euhippus,[1] the bronze orb falls: Euhippus, king of the Argives, had amazing good luck; he who had wielded his shield nobly among the Argives carried it as he went through the city as an adornment. From this a similar proverb is current among them when they laugh at someone's worthlessness, as Callimachus says,

> like [someone] who has taken up the shield

[1] Otherwise unknown.

684 Pf. = *Hecale* 175

685 Scholia to Theocritus, *Idylls*

the wryneck (*iunx*): the bird of Aphrodite which sorceresses have as collaborators in their magic . . . or as Callimachus says, the *iygx*, daughter of Echo, bewitched Zeus so

CALLIMACHUS

Δία, ὅπως ἂν †αὑτῷ† μιχθῇ· ὅθεν ὑπὸ Ἥρας εἰς ὀρ-
νιθάριον αὐτὴν μεταβληθῆναι καὶ συνεργεῖν ταῖς
φαρμακείαις.

686 Schol. (GUE) ad Theoc. Id. 4.62–63d

εὖ γ᾿, ὤνθρωπε φιλοῖφα. τό τοι γένος ἢ Σατυρίσκοις
ἐγγύθεν ἢ Πάνεσσι κακοκνήμοισιν ἐρίσδει· τοὺς Πᾶ-
νας πλείους φησὶν ὡς καὶ τοὺς Σειληνοὺς καὶ τοὺς
Σατύρους, ὡς Αἰσχύλος μὲν ἐν Γλαύκῳ, Σοφοκλῆς δὲ
ἐν Ἀνδρομέδᾳ. ὅτι οἱ Σάτυροι καὶ οἱ Πᾶνες εὐεπίφοροι
πρὸς τὰς συνουσίας λάγνοι ὄντες, καὶ Καλλίμαχός
φησιν,

　　†εἴ τί φημι ἄμωρος ἐρημώθη δύνατο ἐν πείρᾳ†

687 Pf. = Hec. 176

688 Schol. (K.) ad Theoc. Id. 7.70c

τρύγα δὲ τὸν νέον οἶνον. Καλλίμαχος,

　　　　　　　ἐπὶ τρύγα δ᾿ εἶχεν ἐδωδῇ

689 Schol. (LUEAT) ad Theoc. Id. 7.103a

τόν μοι Πάν· ἐπικαλεῖται τὸν Πᾶνα <ὡς παιδερα-
στήν>, ἐπεὶ καὶ αὐτὸς τοιοῦτός ἐστιν. καὶ Καλλίμα-
χος,

　　Πὰν ὁ Μαλειήτης τρύπανον αἰπολικόν

230

that she could have sex with him. From this she was changed into a little bird by Hera and became a collaborator with witches.

686 Scholia to Theocritus, *Idylls*

well done, my good lecher. Your race rivals closely the Satyrs and bandy-legged Pans: He says that Pans are for the most part like the Sileni and the Satyrs, as Aeschylus [says] in the *Glaucus* and Sophocles in the *Andromeda*. He says the Satyrs and the Pans are lustful and prone to intercourse and Callimachus says,

[corrupt line][1]

[1] Pfeiffer offers various possibilities for emendation (vol. 1, 449 Pf.).

687 Pf. = *Hecale* 176

688 Scholia to Theocritus, *Idylls*

truga is new wine. Callimachus,

he had new wine with his dinner

689 Scholia to Theocritus, *Idylls*

by me, Pan: he is called Pan [as a pederast], since he is one himself. Also Callimachus,

Pan of Malea,[1] the borer of goatherds

[1] A mountain in southeast Laconia (Hdt. 4.179) or a town in Arcadia near Mt. Psophis (Glauc. *Anth. Pal.* 9.341).

690 Schol. (K) ad Theoc. *Id.* 8.30a

ἰυγκτά· κράκτα· τοῦτο γὰρ δηλοῖ τὸ ἰύζειν. Καλλίμα-
χος,

ἰύζων δ᾽ ἀν᾽ ὄρος

691 Schol. (K) ad Theoc. *Id.* 8.86a

οἱ μὲν χρώματος εἶδος τὴν μυτάλην, οἱ δὲ ὄνομα
ἤκουσαν, οἱ δὲ τελευταίαν. Καλλ.,

θήκατο †μὴ εἰς† αἷμα πιεῖν μύταλον

692 Schol. (K) ad Theoc. *Id.* 13.56a

Ἀμφιτρυωνιάδας . . . ᾤχετο, Μαιωτιστὶ λαβὼν εὐκα-
μπέα τόξα· ἀντὶ τοῦ Σκυθιστί· Μαιῶται γὰρ ἔθνος
Σκυθικὸν παροικοῦν τὴν Μαιῶτιν λίμνην, τοξικώτα-
τον. Σκυθικοῖς δὲ ὅπλοις ἐχρήσατο Ἡρακλῆς, ὥς φα-
σιν Ἡρόδωρος καὶ Καλλίμαχος.

693 Schol. (K) Theoc. *Id.* 13.25a

ἆμος δ᾽ ἀντέλλοντι Πελειάδες· αἱ Πλειάδες. φησὶ
Καλλίμαχος ὅτι τῆς βασιλίσσης τῶν Ἀμαζόνων
ἦσαν θυγατέρες αἱ Πλειάδες, αἱ Πελειάδες προσηγο-
ρεύθησαν. πρῶτον δ᾽ αὗται χορείαν καὶ παννυχίδα
συνεστήσαντο παρθενεύουσαι. ὁ δὲ νοῦς . . . τὰ
ὀνόματα τῶν Πλειάδων· Κοκκυμώ, Γλαυκία, Πρῶτις,
Παρθενία, Μαῖα, Στονυχία, Λαμπαδώ.

690 Scholia to Theocritus, *Idylls*

iygkta (crier): a bawler; This means *iydzein* (to cry out). Callimachus,

> crying out on the mountain

691 Scholia to Theocritus, *Idylls*

Some have said that the goat is called *mytala* on account of the appearance of its skin, some, that it is a proper name, and others, that it is the last born. Callimachus,

> It was ordained not to drink the blood of a *mytala*.

692 Scholia to Theocritus, *Idylls*

the son of Amphytrion[1] . . . went forth, after taking up his bow, curved in the Maeotian style: instead of the Scythian. The Maeotae were a Scythian tribe living by the Maeotian marsh, very skilled with the bow. Heracles used Scythian armor, as Herodorus[2] says and Callimachus.[3]

[1] Heracles (Apollod. *Bibl.* 2.4.8). [2] Herodorus (5th c. BC; *BNJ* 31 F 18), mytho-historian. [3] No quote follows.

693 Scholia to Theocritus, *Idylls*

When the Peleiades rise: the Pleiades. Callimachus says that the Pleiades were the daughters of the queen of the Amazons, who were called Peleiades. As maidens, they first organized the choral dance and the all-night festival. The meaning of . . . the names of the Pleiades: Coccymo, Glaukia, Protis, Parthenia, Maia, Stonychia, Lampado.

694 Schol. ad Thuc. 2.17.1 (*P.Oxy.* 853 col. x, 34)

καὶ τ[ὰ] ἡρῷα πάντα· . . . λέγουσι δὲ ἡρώων μὲ[ν τοὺς]
σηκούς, θεῶν δὲ ναούς· Καλλ[ίμαχος,]

ἀεὶ δ᾽ ἔχον ἔντομα σηκοί

695 Schol. (ABFMC₂) ad Thuc. 7.57.9

Μαντινῆς δὲ καὶ ἄλλοι Ἀκάδων . . . τοὺς μετὰ Κοριν-
θίων ἐλθόντας Ἀρκάδας οὐδὲν ἧσσον διὰ κέρδος
ἡγούμενοι πολεμίους· ἡ παροιμία. "πιπρήσκει—ἀργύ-
ριον" τοῦ Καλλιμάχου,

πιπρήσκει δ᾽ ὁ καλὸς πάντα πρὸς ἀργύριον

696 Pf. = *Aet.* 2b.1–2, 2f.20–40

697 Serv. ad Verg. *Aen.* 3.16

litore curvo moenia prima: . . . Aenum significat, ut Sallus-
tius . . . quamquam Homerus dicat inde auxilia ad Troiam
venisse; ergo iam fuerat. Euphorion et Callimachus hoc
dicunt etiam, quod Aenum dicatur a socio Ulixis illic se-
pulto eo tempore quo missus est ad frumenta portanda.

694 Scholia to Thucydides, *History of the Peloponnesian War* (Oxyrhynchus papyrus)

and all the shrines of heroes: . . . they call them *sēkoi* of the heroes and temples (*naoi*) of the gods. Callimachus,

> always the shrines had sacrificial victims

695 Scholia to Thucydides, *History of the Peloponnesian War*

The Mantineans and other Arcadians . . . induced by profit and thinking that the Arcadians who had come with the Corinthians were nothing less than enemies: the proverb of Callimachus,

> the beautiful boy sells everything for money

696 Pf. = *Aetia* 2b.1–2, 2f.20–40

697 Servius, *Commentary on Virgil*

on the curved shore first city walls: . . . he means Aenus, as Sallustius[1] [says] . . . although Homer says that auxiliary troops had come from there to Troy; and therefore it had existed already. Euphorion[2] and Callimachus say this, that Aenus[3] takes its name from a companion of Odysseus who was buried there at the time when he was sent to carry back grain.

---

[1] Sallustius (ca. 4th–5th c. AD), commentator on Callimachus' *Hecale* and *Hymns* cited in the *Etymologicum Genuinum*.
[2] Fr. 88 Lightfoot. [3] On Aenus in Thrace, *Ia*. 197–197a.

698 Anon. brev. exp. in Verg. *G.* 1.502 (Append. Serv. 3.2, p. 278 Hagen)

satis iam pridem sanguine nostro Laomedonteae luimus periuria Troiae: . . . tam longe petit bellorum civilium causas et pluraliter "periuria" dicit semel adversus Herculem gesta, semel adversus Apollinem et Neptunum, ut Callimachus docet, propter pollicitam Hesionem, Apollini et Neptuno propter muros constructos.

699 [Probus] in Verg. *Ecl.* 6.82

Eurotas: amnis, ut ait Callimachus, in flumina serpit per Laconum fines. fontes agit ex monte Maenalio confunditur Alpheo rursusque discedit.

700 Commentarius (?) anonym. (*P.Oxy.* 2259 fr. 1 col. II, 4–11)

-ί]δακρυς δὲ διττο[-ίδα]κρυς δὲ παρ' ἐνίοις. Ὁ] μὲν
γὰρ Καλλίμα[χος],

  ἡ δ' ἔτι καὶ λίην ἀριδ[ά]κρυος

698 Scholia to Virgil, *Georgics*

Long since we have atoned enough with our blood for Laomedon's perjuries at Troy: . . . so long he seeks the causes of the civil wars and he says "perjuries" in the plural, once carried out against Hercules, once against Apollo and Neptune, as Callimachus teaches, on account of Hesione's having been promised, and on account of the walls built by Apollo and Neptune.[1]

[1] Poseidon was angry with Laomedon, king of Troy, for building walls around the city and sent a sea monster to afflict it. On Apollo's orders, the king offered to sacrifice his daughter Hesione to save the city from the monster, but she was rescued by Heracles (Diod. Sic. 4.42).

699 Pseudo-Probus, *Commentary on Virgil*

Eurotas:[1] the river, as Callimachus says, spreads into streams through the territory of Laconia. It takes its source from Mt. Maenalus,[2] mingles with the Alpheus, and again separates.

[1] On the Eurotas, see *Hec.* 47.6 and Hollis (191–92).
[2] In Arcadia, sacred to Pan (Paus. 8.36.8).

700 Anonymous commentary? (Oxyrhynchus papyrus)

]-tearful twice, but [-tear]ful in some authors. For Callimachus says,

she still is too given to tears

701 Steph. Byz. a 116 Billerbeck s.v. Αἴδηψος

Αἴδηψος· πόλις Εὐβοίας . . . ἦν δὲ καὶ σιδηρᾶ καὶ
χαλκᾶ μέταλλα κατ᾽ Εὔβοιαν. Καλλίμαχος,

δέδαεν δὲ λαχαινέμεν ἔργα σιδήρου

702 Steph. Byz. a 125 Billerbeck s.v. Αἰθόπιον

Αἰθόπιον· χωρίον Λυδίας παρὰ Ὕλλῳ πλησίον τοῦ
Εὐρίπου ἀφ᾽ οὗ ἡ Ἄρτεμις Αἰθοπία. οἱ δὲ ὅτι παρὰ
τοῖς Αἰθίοψι διάγουσαν Ἀπόλλων ἤγαγεν αὐτήν (?)·
οἱ δὲ τὴν αὐτὴν τῇ Σελήνῃ παρὰ τὸ αἴθειν ὡς Καλ-
λίμαχος.

703 Steph. Byz. a 206 Billerbeck s.v. Ἁλικαρνασσός

Ἁλικαρνασσός· πόλις Καρίας. †Ἄνθης φησίν† ἀπὸ
τοῦ ἁλὶ περιέχεσθαι τὴν Καρίαν· αὐτὸς δ᾽ ὁ Ἄνθης ἐκ
Τροιζῆνος μετῴκησε, λαβὼν τὴν Δύμαιναν φυλήν, ὡς
Καλλίμαχος.

704 Pf. = *Hec.* 170

705 Pf. = *Hec.* 174

706 Steph. Byz. a 544 Billerbeck s.v. Αὔσιγδα

Αὔσιγδα· πόλις Λιβύης, οὐδετέρως, ὡς Καλλίμαχος.

701 Stephanus of Byzantium

Aedepsus: a city of Euboea . . . There were both iron and
bronze metal in Euboea. Callimachus,

> they knew how to dig iron mines

702 Stephanus of Byzantium

Aethopion: A place in Lydia beside the Hyllus[1] near the
Euripus, from which Artemis is called Aethopia. Others
[derive the name] from the fact that Apollo carried her (?)
off while she was spending time with the Ethiopians; and
still others, like Callimachus, [say] that she shines (*aithein*).

[1] River in Asia Minor (Hom. *Il*. 20.392).

703 Stephanus of Byzantium

Halicarnassus: a city of Caria. Anthes named it from Caria
being surrounded by the sea. Anthes himself settled it
from Troezen after defeating the Dymaean tribe, as Cal-
limachus says.[1]

[1] On Anthes' settlement of Halicarnassus, see Strabo 8.6.14,
14.2.16.

704 Pf. = *Hecale* 170

705 Pf. = *Hecale* 174

706 Stephanus of Byzantium

Ausigda: city of Libya, a neuter [noun], as in Callimachus.

707 Steph. Byz. δ 82 Billerbeck s.v. Δίκτη

Δίκτη· ὄρος Κρήτης. Καλλίμαχος . . . τὸ ἐθνικὸν
Δικταῖος καὶ Δικταία.

708 Steph. Byz. δ 82 Billerbeck s.v. Μαγνησία

Μαγνησία· πόλις παρὰ τῷ Μαιάνδρῳ καὶ χώρα, ἀπὸ
Μάγνητος. . . . τὸ θηλυκὸν Μάγνησσα παρὰ Καλ-
λιμάχῳ καὶ Μαγνησὶς παρὰ Παρθενίῳ καὶ Μαγνῆτις
παρὰ Σοφοκλεῖ.

709 Steph. Byz. μ 224 Billerbeck s.v. Μοψοπία

Μοψοπία· ἡ Ἀττική ἀπὸ μόψοπος. Καλλίμαχος. ἄρ-
ρητος ἡ Μοψοψ εὐθεῖα.

710 Steph. Byz. π 56 Billerbeck s.v. Πάρος

Πάρος· νῆσος . . . ᾠκεῖτο δὲ τὸ μὲν πρῶτον ὑπὸ Κρη-
τῶν καί τινων Ἀρκάδων ὀλίγων. τοὔνομα μὲν λέγεται
ἀπὸ Πάρου τοῦ Παρρασίου ἀνδρὸς Ἀρκάδος ἔχειν, ὡς
Καλλίμαχος.

711 Steph. Byz. τ 17 Billerbeck s.v. Τάναγρα

Τάναγρα· πόλις Βοιωτίας, ἣν Ὅμηρος 'Γραῖαν' καλεῖ
διὰ τὸ πλησίον εἶναι. ἐκαλεῖτο δὲ πρότερον Ποιμαν-
δρία . . . Γραῖαν ἔνοι λέγεσθαι τὸ νῦν τῆς Θηβαϊκῆς
καλούμενον ἕδος, τινὲς δὲ τὴν Ταναγραίαν ὧν εἷς ἐστι
καὶ Καλλίμαχος.

707 Stephanus of Byzantium

Dicte: mountain of Crete. Callimachus . . . adjectival forms are Dictaeus and Dictaea.

708 Stephanus of Byzantium

Magnesia: city beside the Maeander and its territory, from *Magnēs*. . . . The feminine is *Magnēssa* according to Callimachus, *Magnēsis* in Parthenius,[1] and *Magnētis* in Sophocles.[2]

[1] Fr. 46 Lightfoot. [2] Fr. 1066 Radt.

709 Stephanus of Byzantium

Mopsopia: Attica, from *Mopsops*. Callimachus. The nominative is unpronounceable.

710 Stephanus of Byzantium

Paros: an island . . . settled at first by Cretans and a few Arcadians. It is said to be named from Paros the son of Parrhasius, an Arcadian man, as Callimachus [says].

711 Stephanus of Byzantium

Tanagra: a city of Boeotia, which Homer calls Graea on account of its being nearby.[1] At first it was called Poemandria. . . . Some say that the area that now is part of Thebes was called Graea, and some, Tanagraea; Callimachus is one of them.

[1] *Il.* 2.498.

712 Steph. Byz. υ 27 Billerbeck s.v. Ὑλλεῖς

Ὑλλεῖς· ἔθνος Ἰλλυρικόν, ἀπὸ Ὑλλου τοῦ Ἡρακλέους
καὶ Μελίτης τῆς Αἰγαίου τοῦ ποταμοῦ, ὡς Ἀπολ-
λώνιος δ' Ἀργοναυτικῶν. ἔστι καὶ πόλις Ὑλλη. τὸ
ἐθνικὸν Ὑλλεύς καὶ θηλυκὸν Ὑλληίς, ὡς ⟨ὁ⟩ αὐτός
φησι καὶ παρὰ Καλλιμάχῳ Ὑλλίς Ὑλλίδος ἀπὸ Αἰ-
γείας μιᾶς τῶν νυμφῶν.

713 Stob. *Flor.* 4.17.10

Περὶ ναυτιλίας καὶ ναυαγίας, Καλλιμάχου,

   ἔνθ' ἀνέμων μεγάλων κῦμα διωλύγιον

714 Stob. *Flor.* 4.48b.24

Περὶ παρηγορίας, Καλλιμάχου,

   κουφοτέρως τότε φῶτα διαθλίβουσιν ἀνῖαι,
      ἐκ δὲ τριηκόντων μοῖραν ἀφεῖλε μίαν,
   ἢ φίλον ἢ ὅτ' ἐς ἄνδρα συνέμπορον ἢ ὅτε κωφαῖς
      ἄλγεα μαψαύραις ἔσχατον ἐξερύγῃ

715 Strabo 17.1.28

(ἡ τοῦ Ἡλίου πόλις) . . . τῆς δὲ κατασκευῆς τῶν
ἱερῶν ἡ διάθεσις τοιαύτη· κατὰ τὴν εἰσβολὴν τὴν εἰς
τὸ τέμενος λιθόστρωτόν ἐστιν ἔδαφος, πλάτος μὲν

FRAGMENTS OF UNCERTAIN LOCATION

712 Stephanus of Byzantium

Hylleis: An Illyrian[1] tribe, from Hyllus, the son of Heracles and Melites [daughter] of the river Aegaeus,[2] per Apollonius in Book 4 of the *Argonautica*.[3] There is also a city Hylle. The ethnic name is *Hylleus* and the feminine *Hylleis*, as he himself says[4] and in Callimachus, *Hyllis*, *Hyllidos* from Aegeia, one of the nymphs.

[1] On settlements around the Illyrian Sea, see *Aet.* 11.
[2] On the nymphs, daughters of the Aegaeus, see Ap. Rhod. 4.1149.   [3] Ap. Rhod. 4.537–43.   [4] Ap. Rhod. 4.524, 4.527, 4.535, 4.562.

713 Stobaeus, *Anthology*

On Sailing and Shipwrecks, from Callimachus,

> When an enormous wave by great winds

714 Stobaeus, *Anthology*

On Consolation, from Callimachus,

> then troubles more lightly distress a man and it
> takes away one part from thirty when to a friend or
> a fellow traveler or finally to deaf breezes he belches
> out his pain

715 Strabo, *Geography*

(The city of Helios)[1] . . . The plan of the construction of the temples is like this: at the entrance into the precinct there is a floor paved with stones, with a breadth of about

[1] Heliopolis, City of the Sun, now a suburb of Cairo.

ὅσον πλεθριαῖον ἢ καὶ ἔλαττον, μῆκος δὲ καὶ τριπλά-
σιον καὶ τετραπλάσιον, ἔστιν ὅπου καὶ μεῖζον· καλεῖ-
ται δὲ τοῦτο δρόμος, καθάπερ Καλλίμαχος εἴρηκεν,

ὁ δρόμος ἱερὸς οὗτος Ἀνούβιδος

716 Strabo 17.3.20

τῆς δὲ Κυρήνης . . . πόλεως μεγάλης . . . ἔστι δὲ Θη-
ραίων κτίσμα, Λακωνικῆς νήσου, ἣν καὶ Καλλίστην
ὠνόμαζον τὸ παλαιόν, ὥς φησι καὶ Καλλίμαχος,

καλλίστη τὸ πάροιθε, τὸ δ' ὕστερον οὔνομα
Θήρη,
μήτηρ εὐίππου πατρίδος ἡμετέρης

717 (717 Pf. + SH 298) Suda a 495 s.v. ἀδμωλία[1] + P.Ant.
2.60 (ed. J. W. B. Barnes)

```
      ]            ·μ[
4   ] αναγνοντες [
    ]χος αδμωλη[

    ]νοιαν παραμε[
8   ]ως αναγινωσκ[
```

[1] ἡ ἄγνοια παρὰ Καλλιμάχῳ

718 *Suda* a 3071

ἀπεστώ· ὡς Σαπφώ. παρὰ Καλλιμάχῳ ἡ ἀποδημία.

a plethrum[2] or less and a length either three or four times
that size, or in some places more; this is called the *dromos*,
as Callimachus says,

> this is the holy course (*dromos*) of Anubis[3]

[2] About 100 feet (*OCD*[4]).   [3] Greek name of the Egyptian god of Death, often depicted as a man with the head of a jackal.

716 Strabo, *Geography*

from Cyrene . . . a great city . . . the colony of Thera, a
Laconian island which in antiquity was called Calliste, as
Callimachus says,

> formerly Calliste, later the name was Thera,
>   Mother of our fatherland,[1] rich in horses

[1] Cyrene, Callimachus' native city, was colonized from Thera,
which had been settled by Sparta. Thera's original name was Calliste (Pind. *Pyth.* 4.258; Hdt. 4.147; Ap. Rhod. 4.1757–64). On the
foundation of Cyrene in Callimachus, see *Hymn* 2.65–96.

717 (717 Pf. + *SH* 298) *Suda* entry under *admōlia*[1] and
an Antinoöpolis papyrus

> knowing well . . . ignorance . . . he knew well

[1] "Ignorance," according to Callimachus.

718 *Suda*

let him be gone: like Sappho. According to Callimachus,
absence.

719 Suda ε 786

Ἐλελεῦ· ἐπίφθεγμα πολεμικὸν τὸ ἐλελελεῦ. οἱ γὰρ
προσιόντες εἰς πόλεμον τὸ ἐλελεῦ ἐφώνουν μετά τινος
ἐμμελοῦς κινήσεως, καθὸ καὶ Ἀχαιὸς Ἐρετριεὺς ἐν
τῷ Φιλοκτήτῃ ποιεῖ τὸν Ἀγαμέμνονα παραγγέλλοντα
τοῖς Ἀχαιοῖς . . . μήποτε καὶ τὸ Καλλιμάχειον,

> θεῷ τ᾽ ἀλάλαγμα νόμαιον
δοῦναι

720 Theodos. *Can. isagog. de flex. nom.*

Περὶ κλίσεως τῶν εἰς ὦν βαρυτόνων. τὰ εἰς δῶν λή-
γοντα βαρύτονα δισύλλαβα διὰ τοῦ ω κλίνονται, εἰ
μὴ μετοχικὴν κλίσιν ἀναδέξονται . . . τὸ γὰρ Νέδων
ὁ μὲν Καλλίμαχος τῷ λόγῳ τῶν μετοχικῶν διὰ τοῦ
ντ κλίνει Νέδων Νέδοντος.

721 Pf. = *Hec.* 162

722 Varro, *Ling.* 5.113

lana Graecum, ut Polybius et Callimachus scribunt.

719 *Suda*

Eleleleu: the *eleleleu* is the refrain of war. Those going into battle cry out *eleleu* along with some rhythmic movement, like Achaeus[1] of Eretria in his *Philoctetes* makes Agamemnon command the Acheans . . . perhaps this phrase from Callimachus is of this kind,

> to give the customary *alalagma* to the god

[1] Greek tragic poet (5th c. BC; *Suda* α 4683).

720 Theodosius, *Introductory Canons for the Inflection of Nouns*

On the inflection of enclitics in *-ōn*: Dissyllabic enclitics ending in *-dōn* are inflected with an omega so that they are not inflected like participles. . . . but in the case of *Nedōn* Callimachus declines it like a participle with *-nt*: *Nedōn*, *Nedontos*.[1]

[1] On the Neleidae (rulers of Messenia), the river Nedon, and Athena Nedusia, see Strabo 8.4.1–4.

721 Pf. = *Hecale* 162

722 Varro, *On the Latin Language*

Greek wool,[1] as Polybius[2] and Callimachus write.

[1] Scaliger suggests a woolen fillet (*Coni. in Varr.* 1.1, 1565).
[2] *Fr. inc.* 57 Büttner-Wobst.

CALLIMACHUS

723

a Varro, *Ling* 7.34

hinc Casmilus nominatur Samothrace<s> mysteris dius
quidam amminister diis magnis. verbum esse graecum
arbitror, quod apud Callimachum in poematibus, eius in-
veni.

b Stat. Tull. ap. Serv. Dan. ad Verg. *Aen.* 11.543; Macrob.
Sat. 3.8.6

Statius Tullianus *De vocabulis rerum* libro primo ait
dixisse Callimachum Tuscos Camillum apellare Mercu-
rium, quo vocabulo significant praeministrum deorum.'

724 Zen. vulg. 5.66

πτωχοῦ πήρα οὐ πίμπλαται· τοῦτο παρὰ Καλλιμάχῳ
ἐπὶ τῶν ἀπλήστων εἴρηται,

πτωχῶν οὐλὰς ἀεὶ κενεή

725 Pf. = *Hec.* 178

725a (*SH* 300) Hdn. *De pros. cath.* fr. 46 Hunger

μέντοι τινὲς παρὰ τῷ Κυρηναίῳ προπαροξύνουσιν τό,

†ἀφελὲς οὖλοον ἄστρον

FRAGMENTS OF UNCERTAIN LOCATION

723

a Varro, *On the Latin Language*

From this a certain god is called Casmilus in the mysteries of Samothrace, since he is a servant to the Great Gods. I think the word is Greek because I found it in the poems of Callimachus.

b Statius Tullianus in Servius Danielis, *Commmentary on Virgil*; Macrobius, *Saturnalia*

Statius Tullianus in the first book of *On Vocabulary* says that Callimachus said that the Etruscans call Mercury Camillus,[1] and signify by this word that he is a servant of the gods.

[1] Possibly in *Ia.*199.

724 Zenobius

The pouch of a beggar is not full: This is said by Callimachus about those who are greedy,

the wallet of beggars is always empty

725 Pf. = *Hecale* 178

725a (*SH* 300) Herodian, *General Prosody*

Some including the Cyrenean (Callimachus) put the acute accent on the antepenult,

a destructive star

725b (*SH* 301) Ammon. *Diff.* 5.15 app. (p. 35 Nickau)

διαβόητος καὶ ἐπιβόητος διαφέρει. διαβόητος μὲν
γάρ ἐστιν ὁ ἐπ' ἀρετῇ ἐγνωσμένος. ἐπιβόητος δὲ ὁ
μοχθηρὰν ἔχων φήμην. τοῦτον δ' ἔνιοι τῶν ποιητῶν
ἐπίφατον καλοῦσι. Καλλίμαχος ἐπὶ Ἀκοντίου[1] τέταχε,
Θουκυδίδης δὲ ἐπίρρητον εἶπεν ἐν τῇ τρίτῃ.

    ἐπίφατον

  [1] Ἀκοντίου Nickau: ἀκοστίου cod.

725c (*SH* 302) *Et. Gen.* s.v. λαῖφος

λαῖφος· λινοειδές· βέλτιον λινουφές. τὸ ἄρμενον.

    λαῖφος

725d (*SH* 303) Hsch. μ 12.1273 (vol. 2, p. 664 Latte)

μήτειρα· φρονίμη· καὶ ἡ μήτηρ ‹ὡς παρὰ Καλλι-
μάχῳ.›

    μήτειρα(ν)

725e (*SH* 304)[1] *Et. Gen.* AB s.v. ὄβδην

ὄβδην· ἐπίρρημά ἐστι μεσότητος ἀπὸ τοῦ ὦμμαι
ὄβδην, ὡς ἀπὸ τοῦ ἔστηκα στάδην. συνέστειλε τὸ ω
εἰς ο.

  [1] Olim 218 Pf. sed hexametrus non iambus

725b (*SH* 301) Ammonius, *On the Differences of Synonymous Expressions*

Diaboētos is different from *epiboētos*. *Diaboētos* is being known for excellence. *Epiboētos* is having a bad reputation. Some of the poets call this notorious. Callimachus applies this to Acontius;[1] Thucydides says infamous in Book 3.[2]

> notorious

[1] The lover in *Aet.* 67–75e.   [2] Perhaps in reference to *epiboētos* (notorious) at Thuc. 6.16.1.

725c (*SH* 302) *Etymologicum Genuinum*

rag:[1] like linen; better, weaving. A sail.[2]

> rag

[1] *Hec.* 28.   [2] *Epig.* 5.4.

725d (*SH* 303) Heschyius

mēteira (intelligence): cleverness; also mother [as in Callimachus.]

> mother

725e (*SH* 304) *Etymologicum Genuinum*

obdēn (into the sight): the abverb is formed from *ōmmai obdēn* (coming into the sight), like *stadēn* from *estēka*. The omega becomes an omicron.

Μούσῃσι[2] γὰρ ἦλθεν ἐς ὄβδην

2 Μούσῃσι Jacques: Μούσῃ Et. Mag. 612.54

725f (*SH* 305) Hdn. *De pros. cath.* fr. 47 Hunger

τὸ λίχνος· βαρύνουσι γὰρ αὐτό· οὕτως παρὰ τῷ Κυρηναίῳ ἀναγιγνώσκουσιν,

†ὁρᾷς ἀμφίς, ὡς λίχνον ὀμμάτιον λέπει

725g (*SH* 306) Hdn. *De pros. cath.* fr. 48 Hunger

νήδυιος· Καλλίμαχος,

τοὔνομα νήδυιος

725h (*SH* 307) Phld. *Piet.* (*P.Herc.* 243 col. II, ed. Henrichs)

```
        ] Καλλιμ[αχ
       ]κυφους Πάν-
   [δρο]σον δὲ καὶ λί-
   [θον]    διότι τὴν ἀ-
5  [δελ]φὴν Περσην
   ['Ωκ]υρόη καταυτω
                 κατ᾽᾽
   [...]αλαβων καιτ ..
   [...]ις ὑπομενον
   [...σ]υνεχεσθαι[.]ε[
10     ].ωνα.[.]σκαιυ
       ]ανπ[α]ντ.[.]ιν[
```

they came into the sight of the Muses[1]

[1] For an almost identical lemma, but no useful context, see *Ia*. 216.

725f (*SH* 305) Herodian, *General Prosody*

lichnos (curious): they pronounce it without an accent on the final syllable; so, in the Cyrenean (Callimachus) they read,

round about, as he peels his curious little eyes

725g (*SH* 306) Herodian, *General Prosody*

nēduios (not knowing): Callimachus,

I do not know the word

725h (*SH* 307) Philodemus, *On Piety* (Herculaneum papyrus)

Callimachus . . . Pandrosos[1] and a stone[2] . . . [5] since the sister Perse[3] . . . Ocyroe[4] . . . staying behind . . . to be

[1] One of the three daughters of Cecrops who opened the chest containing Erichthonius contrary to Athena's instructions (Apollod. *Bibl.* 3.14.6). In other versions, her two sisters Aglaurus and Herse are also implicated, and various punishments are alleged.
[2] In Ovid's version, Mercury turns Aglaurus to stone (*Met.* 2.819–32).   [3] Perhaps an error for Herse, rather than the Oceanid Perse.   [4] A prophetess, daughter Chiron, who was turned into a horse (Ov. *Met.* 2.633–79).

```
      ]αι πασων των[
      ]των[.]..σθ
      ]της [...].οδ.[
15    ]καθευδοντα[
      ]δ᾽ Ἥφαιστον ου[
      ]ο τῆς πηρώσε[ως
      σ]ωφρονι[.].[
      ]και ῾τῆς᾽ αφ
20    ]τακαιτησα[
      ]καιτ[...]ρ[
      κ]αὶ τῆς θει[
      ]δ᾽ Ἡσίοδον καὶ
      [τ]ῶν Μελάνων
25    [καὶ τ]ῶν Αἰθι[όπ]ω[ν]
      [καὶ τ]ῶν Κατουδαί-
      [ων κ]αὶ τῶν Πυγμαι-
```

725i (*SH* 308) Phld. *Piet.* (*P.Herc.* 243 col. VII, ed. Henrichs)

```
            ]ωικεναυτην
            ].ν ἐξ ἄλλων
            ]φιλεῖν μακα
            ]Κα[.]᾽λλ᾽ ἱμαχος
5           ]αι[...]νστρει
               ]εραστρι
               ]δε
               ]μ[
```

hunched over . . . of all . . . [15] sleeping . . . Hephaestus . . . of his disabling . . . with moderation . . . Hesiod and the black men [25] and the Aethiopians and those who live underground and the pygmies[5]

[5] Hes. fr. 150.17–19 M.-W. (99 Most).

725i (*SH* 308) Philodemus, *On Piety* (Herculaneum papyrus)

. . . from others . . . to love . . . Callimachus . . .

UNATTRIBUTED FRAGMENTS

FRAGMENTA INCERTI
AUCTORIS

726 Ap. Dysc. *Adv.* (*Gramm. Gr.* vol. 1.1, p. 154.25
Schneider)

τῷ ἔμπης παράκειται τὸ ἔμπα,

   ἔμπα γε μὴν ἴθι δεῦρο

727 Ap. Dysc. *Adv.* (*Gramm. Gr.* vol. 1.1, p. 185.20
Schneider)

καθάπερ καὶ ἐπ' ὀνομάτων ἔσθ' ὅτε παραγωγαὶ γίνον-
ται κατὰ τῶν αὐτῶν σημαινομένων, ὡς τὸ ἀναγκαίη
καὶ τὸ εὐναίας ἐβάλοντο.

   εὐναίας τ' ἐβάλοντο

728 Ap. Dysc. *Coni.* (*Gramm. Gr.* vol. 1.1, p. 250.8
Schneider)

δεδείξεται οὖν ὡς οὐ πάντοτε πλεονάζουσι οἱ παρα-
πληρωματικοί, ἀλλὰ καί ποτε τόπον ἴσχουσι τὸν ση-
μαίνοντά τι . . . καὶ ἐν τῷ 'τοῦτό—χάρισαι' . . . ἔμ-
φασις ἱκανὴ μειότητος.

   τοῦτό γέ μοι χάρισαι

258

UNATTRIBUTED FRAGMENTS

726 Apollonius Dyscolus, *On Adverbs*

empes (in any case) is parallel to *empa*,

> in any case, do come here!

727 Apollonius Dyscolus, *On Adverbs*

Just as it is for nouns when parallel forms exist with the same meanings, as with *anagkaiē*[1] and the casting of *eunaias*.[2]

> they cast down the anchors

[1] *Od.* 19.73, with the same meaning as *anagkē* (necessity).
[2] Sing. *eunaia*, with the same meaning as *eunē* (anchor), *Il.* 1.436.

728 Apollonius Dyscolus, *On Conjunctions*

It has been demonstrated, therefore, how words completing the sense or meter do not always have additional syllables, but sometimes occupy a meaningful position, and in this example the appearance of minimization is sufficient.

> gratify me in this

729 Ap. Dysc. *Constr.* (*Gramm. Gr.* vol. 2.2, p. 493.1 Uhlig)

παρὰ δὴ τὸ ἀφανής ὄνομα ἀπετελεῖτό τι θηλυκὸν κατὰ παρώνυμον σχηματισμόν ἀφανία καὶ ἀφάνεια. δισσὰ γὰρ τὰ τοιαῦτα, εὐσεβής-εὐσέβεια, ἀφ' οὗ πάλιν τὸ,

εὐσεβίη τέθνηκεν

730 Ap. Dysc. *Constr.* (*Gramm. Gr.* vol. 2.2, p. 493.6 Uhlig)

ἀδρανίη †τοδεπολλον†

731 *Et. Gen.* B s.v. θεῦν

θεῦν· σημαίνει τὴν θεόν, οἷον

τὴν θεῦν Ἄρτεμιν οἳ ἔπαθεν

732 Pf. = *Hec.* 165

733 Clem. Alex. *Protr.* 2.40.2

ἔστι μὲν ἐφευρεῖν καὶ ἀναφανδὸν οὕτω κατὰ πόλεις δαίμονας ἐπιχωρίους τιμὴν ἐπιδρεπομένους, παρὰ Κυθνίοις Μενέδημον, παρὰ Τηνίοις Καλλισταγόραν, κατὰ Δηλίοις Ἄνιον, παρὰ Λάκωσιν Ἀστράβακον· τιμᾶται δέ τις καὶ Φαληροῖ κατὰ πρύμναν ἥρως.

729 Apollonius Dyscolus, *On Syntax*

Besides the noun *aphanēs* (unseen) a feminine is created according to a derivative formation, *aphania* and *aphaneia*. Two such types are *eusebēs* and *eusebeia*, from which again comes,

> pious she died

730 Apollonius Dyscolus, *On Syntax*

> weakness

731 *Etymologicum Genuinum*

theun: it means *tēn theon* (the goddess), for instance,

> he [called on] the goddess Artemis, for what he suffered

732 Pf. = *Hecale* 165

733 Clement of Alexandria, *Protrepticus*

It is possible to find public compilations, city by city, of local deities who receive honor: among the Cythnians, Menedemus;[1] among the Tenians, Callistagora; among the Delians, Anius,[2] among the Laconians, Astrabacus.[3] And a certain hero below the stern is honored at Phalerum.[4]

---

[1] On Menedemus, see *Fr. Inc. Sed.* 663.   [2] King of Delos and priest of Apollo. On his son Thasus, attacked by dogs, see *Fr. Inc. Sed.* 664, and in the *Aetia*, Harder vol. 2, 261.

[3] Hdt. 6.69.   [4] Androgeus, a son of Midas (*Aet.* 103–103a), whose monument was at Phalerum, the old harbor at Athens (Paus. 1.1.4).

CALLIMACHUS

734 *Epimer. Hom.* λ 37 (vol. 2, p. 471 Dyck)

λοιγός· τὰ εἰς γος δισύλλαβα φύσει μακρᾷ παραλη-
γόμενα ὀξύνονται· φηγός, πηγός . . . ἓν ἀντιπίπτει·
τὸ Λᾶγος, ἐπὶ τοῦ κυρίου, ὃ †εἴδη† εἴρηται καὶ τρισυλ-
λάβως, Λάαγος,

Λάαγου φίλος υἱὸς ἀρίζηλος Πτολεμαῖος

735 *Epimer. Hom.* μ 70 (vol. 2, p. 503 Dyck)

μέτασσαι· ὥσπερ παρὰ τὴν ἐπί γίνεται ἔπισσα, ση-
μαίνει δὲ τὴν νεωτάτην, τὴν ἐπὶ πᾶσι γεγενημένην,
οἷον

Μνημοσύνης ἠδ᾽ (?) ὧδε γόνου χαρίεντος ἔπισσα

736 *Et. Gen.* B et *Et. Gen.* par. s.v. ἀλυκρόν

ἀλυκρόν· ἀντὶ τοῦ θαλυκρόν, οἷον

ἃ πάντη πάντα θαλυκρὸς ἐγώ

737 *Et. Gen.* AB s.v. ἁμαρτῇ

ἁμαρτῇ· . . . εἰσὶ δέ τινα εἰς ῃ λήγοντα [sc. ἐπιρ-
ρήματα] μὴ ἔχοντα τὸ ι προσγεγραμμένον. εἰσὶν δὲ
ταῦτα· ἤ . . . φή· οἷον,

φὴ νέος οὐκ ἀπάλαμνος

734 *Epimerismi Homerici*

loigos (ruin): disyllabic words ending in *-gos*, with a naturally long penult have an acute accent: *phēgos*, *pēgos* . . . one is irregular: *lāgos* [which has a cirumflex], a proper name, also written trisyllabically, *Laägos*.

> Ptolemy[1] the widely-honored dear son of Lagus

[1] Ptolemy I Soter, associate of Alexander the Great who ruled Egypt, 323–283 BC.

735 *Epimerismi Homerici*

metassai (thereafter): so it is parallel to being born after; it means the youngest, the one born later than all, for example,

> so the last of the charming offspring of Mnemosyne[1]

[1] Mother of the Muses (Hes. *Theog.* 53–67). The youngest Muse is perhaps Calliope, whom Hesiod names last (*Theog.* 77–79).

736 *Etymologicum Genuinum*; *Etymologicum Genuinum Parvum*

alykron (lukewarm): instead of *thalykron* (hot), for example,

> Ah! I am altogether hot in every way

737 *Etymologicum Genuinum*

(*h*)*amartēi* (altogether): . . . there are some [adverbs] ending in eta and without an iota subscript . . . such as *phē*; for example,

> like a youth who is not helpless

738 *Et. Gen.* AB s.v. ἀμίσαλλος

ἀμίσαλλος· οἷον,

> ἀμίσαλλοί τε γέροντες

739 *Et. Gen.* AB s.v. Ἀμφιτρύων

Ἀμφιτρύων· ὁ ἥρως. παρὰ τὸ τρύος, ὅ ἐστι πόνος, οἷον καὶ

> πολὺ τρύος ἤλασεν ἔξω

740 *Et. Gen.* B. s.v. Ἀργαφίης

Ἀργαφίης· οἷον,

> νιψάμεναι κρήνης ἔδραμον Ἀργαφίης

741 Pf. = *Hec.* 165

742 *Et. Gen.* B s.v. ἀχρὴς

ἀχρὴς· οἷον,

> ἀχρὴς δ᾽ ἀνέπαλτο

743 *Et. Gen.* B s.v. Βασσαρίδες

Βασσαρίδες· αἱ Βάκχαι, οἷον,

> κέντορι Βασσαρίδων

738 *Etymologicum Genuinum*

amisallos (unsociable): for example,

> unsociable old men

739 *Etymologicum Genuinum*

Amphitryon: the hero.[1] Labor is parallel to toil, for example,

> much toil drove [him] out

[1] The human father of Heracles (Theoc. *Id.* 24).

740 *Etymologicum Genuinum*

Argaphiēs: for example,

> after washing they ran from the spring of Argaphia[1]

[1] A river sacred to the Graces, sometimes called Acidalia (Verg. *Aen.* 1.720), near Orchomenus in Boeotia.

741 Pf. = *Hecale* 165

742 *Etymologicum Genuinum*

achrēs (pale): for example,

> pale, he shook

743 *Etymologicum Genuinum*

Bassarides: the Bacchae, for example,

> by the goader of the Bassarides[1]

[1] Thracian bacchants who wore garments made of fox skin (*bassaris*). Their "goader" is likely Dionysus.

CALLIMACHUS

744 *Et. Gen.* AB s.v. βούθοια

βούθοια· πόλις τῆς Ἰλλυρίδος. Σοφοκλῆς . . . οἷον,

ὀνομακλεῖ†

Βουθούη Δρίλωνος ἐπὶ προχοῇσιν ἐνάσθη

745 *Et. Gen.* B s.v. Βύνη

Βύνη· ἡ Λευκοθέα, ἡ Ἰνώ· οἷον,

Βύνης καταλέκτριαι αὐδηέσσης

746 *Et. Gen.* s.v. δέχνυμι

δέχνυμι· ἐκ τοῦ δέχω—οὗ τὸ παθητικὸν δέχομαι—γί-
νεται δεχύω, καὶ πλεονασμῷ τοῦ ν̄ δεχνύω . . . καὶ
ὑπερθέσει τοῦ ν̄ δεχνύω· ἀφ' οὗ δέχνυμι τετάρτης συ-
ζυγίας τῶν εἰς μῑ . . . ἐξ οὗ τὸ

δέχνυσο μῆτερ

747 *Et. Gen.* B s.v. Διάσια

Διάσια· ἑορτὴ ἐπιτελουμένη Ἀθήνησι τῷ Διΐ· παρὰ
τὰς ἄσας τὰς ἀνίας· οἷον

μή μιν ἔδουσιν ἄσαι;

744 *Etymologicum Genuinum*

Buthoea: city of Illyria. Sophocles . . . for example,

> Buthoue was situated at the mouth of the Drilon[1]

[1] On the river Drilon (now the Drin), see Strabo 7.5.7.

745 *Etymologicum Genuinum*

Bynē: Leukothea, Ino.[1] For example,

> the attendants of articulate Byne

[1] Melicertes was the son of Ino and Athamas, king of Orchomenos. When Ino leaped into the sea with Melicertes, she became the Nereid Leucothea, and he became the sea-god Palaemon. Sisyphus founded the Isthmian games in his honor (*Aet.* 91–92a).

746 *Etymologicum Genuinum*

dechnymi (I accept): from *dechō*—of which the passive form is *dechomai*—and also *dechyō* is created, and with the addition of nu, *dechnyō* . . . and with the transposition of the nu, *dechnyō*, from which comes *dechnymi*, of the fourth conjugation of verbs ending in *-mi*, from which comes

> welcome, mother

747 *Etymologicum Genuinum*

Diasia: a festival celebrated for Zeus at Athens; *asa* is parallel to *ania* (grief), for example,

> do sorrows not eat him up?

CALLIMACHUS

748 *Et. Gen.* B s.v. ἐλειήτης

ἐλειήτης· ὁ λέων,

  ἐσχατίην ὑπὸ πέζαν ἐλειήταο Λέοντος

749 *Et. Gen.* B s.v. ἠγαλέην—ἀειρομένη

ἠγαλέην—ἀειρομένη· τὴν κατεαγεῖσαν ἢ κολοβωθεῖ-
σαν, ἢ κοιλωθεῖσαν. παρὰ τὸ ἄγος, ὃ σημαίνει τὸ
ῥῆγμα,

  ἠγαλέην κάλπιν ἀειρομένη

750 *Et. Gud.* s.v. θειλόπεδον

θειλόπεδον· διὰ τοῦ εῖ, περισσὸν τὸ θ̄ . . . (σημαίνει
τὸν τόπον ἔνθα τίθενται αἱ σταφυλαὶ ζηρανθησόμε-
ναι)· τὴν μέντοι τῶν σύκων ψύξιν τρασιὰν λέγουσι,

  τρασιῆς ψευδόμενον φύλακα

751 *Et. Gen.* B s.v. Κιδαλία

Κιδαλία· ἡ γὰρ λίμνη Ἀκιδαλία ἐκαλεῖτο· οἷον,

  Κιδαλίης κρηνῖδος

UNATTRIBUTED FRAGMENTS

748 *Etymologicum Genuinum*

eleiētēs (blistering): the Lion,

> under the furthest foot of savage Leo[1]

[1] This refers to the constellation Leo and the position of another celestial object in reference to it.

749 *Etymologicum Genuinum*

ēgaleēn: broken or docked, or hollowed out. From *agos* meaning break:

> she, lifting up the broken pitcher

750 *Etymologicum Gudianum*

theilopedon (a sunny spot): on account of the *ei*, the theta is superfluous . . . (it means the place where the grapes are set out to be dried); a drying rack for figs, they say,

> a false guardian of the drying rack

751 *Etymologicum Genuinum*

Cidalia: the marsh was called Acidalia,[1] for example,

> Of the spring Cidalia

[1] Spring of the Melas River, associated with the Charites in Orchomenus (Boeotia). Cf. Verg. *Aen.* 1.720, with Servius' commentary.

752 *Et. Gen.* B s.v. κόρση

κόρση· ἡ κεφαλή, ὡς μὲν Ἀπολλόδωρος ἀπὸ τοῦ κο-
ρυφοῦσθαι . . . ὅθεν καὶ κορσωτήρ, ὁ τὰς τρίχας τίλ-
λων καὶ κουρεύων· οἷον,

> ὡς δ᾽ ἐνὶ κορσωτῆρος ὑπὸ τρίχα καλλύνονται

753 *Et. Gen.* AB s.v. κόχλος

κόχλος· . . . ὡς παρὰ τὸ ἱερὸς γίνεται ἱέραξ, . . . καὶ
μύρμος μύρμαξ, οἷον,

> αὐτίκα <—> μύρμων πλείονες ἢ ψιάδων

754 *Et. Gen.* AB s.v. λοῖσθος καὶ λοίσθιος

λοῖσθος καὶ λοίσθιος· οἱ μὲν παρὰ τὸ ὄλισθος καθ᾽
ὑπερβιβασμὸν τοῦ λ̄, λοῖσθος καὶ λοίσθιος,

> ὅτε γλώσσῃ πλεῖστος ὄλισθος ἔνι

755 *Et. Gen.* A s.v. λοφνίδας

λοφνίδας· τὰς λαμπάδας. κυρίως μὲν λοφνίδες λέγον-
ται αἱ μονόξυλοι λαμπάδες καὶ δαλῷ παραπλήσιοι
δᾷδες μετὰ κατασκευῆς τινος καὶ κόσμου γεγονυῖαι.
λαμπάδες δὲ αἱ ὁπωσδήποτε κατεσκευασμέναι καὶ ἂν
ἀκόσμως δεδεμέναι ὦσιν.

> σὺ †δ᾽ οὔτι† τεὰς ἀνὰ λοφνίδας ἴσχων

752 *Etymologicum Genuinum*

korsē (temple): the head, per Apollodorus[1] from *kory-phousthai* (to bring to a head); . . . from which [they say] *korsōtēr* (barber), the one plucking hairs and *koureuōn* (getting a haircut), for example,

in the barbershop their hair is beautified

[1] Apollodorus of Athens (2nd c. BC; *BNJ* 244 F 256).

753 *Etymologicum Genuinum*

kochlos (shellfish): . . . as *(h)ierax* (a hawk) is generated from *(h)ieros*, . . . and *murmax* (ant) from *murmos*, for example,

at once . . . more ants than raindrops

754 *Etymologicum Genuinum*

loisthos and *loisthios* (last): they are derived from *olisthos* by transposition of the lambda,

what is most slippery on the tongue

755 *Etymologicum Genuinum*

lophnidas (torches): *lophnidas* are properly torches made from a single block of wood and resembling torches like a firebrand, created with a certain construction and order, whereas *lampades* are torches constructed any which way, and may be bound in a disorderly fashion.

you, not holding up your torches

271

756 Pf. = *Hec.* 166

757 *Et. Gen.* AB s.v. πλειότερος

πλειότερος· . . . πλεῖος οὖν πλειότερος, οἷον

> φθέγγεο κυδίστη πλειοτέρῃ φάρυγι

758 *Et. Gen.* B s.v. Σπαρτιάτης

Σπαρτιάτης· ἀπὸ τοῦ Σπάρτη Σπαρτίτης, καὶ πλεο-
νασμῷ τοῦ ᾱ Σπαρτιάτης. ὅμοιόν ἐστι καὶ τὸ Κροτω-
νιάτης,

> οὐδὲ Κροτωνίτης ἐξεκάθαιρε Μίλων

759 *Et. Sym.* s.v. ὥς (cod. V. Gaisford; *Et. Mag.*, p. 824.14)

ὥς· . . . τὸ ὥς μόριον τοῦ οὕτως ὁλοκλήρου ἐπιρρήμα-
τος λείψανον εἶναι θέλουσιν. διὰ τοῦτο γοῦν ἐνίοτε
σὺν τῷ ᾱ ἐκφέρεται, οἷον

> τὼς δ᾽ ἐφθέγξατο Καλλιόπεια

756 Pf. = *Hecale* 166

757 *Etymologicum Genuinum*

pleioteros: . . . *pleios* (full) therefore *pleioteros* (fuller), for example,

> you were speaking most nobly with a fuller throat

758 *Etymologicum Genuinum*

Spartiatēs (a Spartan): from *Spartē*, *Spartitēs*, and adding an alpha, Spartiates. It is like *Crotōniatēs* (a person from Croton),

> nor did Milo[1] the Crotonite purge

[1] Milo, son of Diotimus of Croton, was a victor in wrestling multiple times at Olympia and famous for his feats of strength (Paus. 6.14.5–8). Here he may be compared with Heracles, who purged the stables of Augeas.

759 *Etymologicum Symeonis*

(*h*)*ōs* (thus): . . . they want (*h*)*ōs* to be a remnant, part of the complete adverb (*h*)*outōs*. On account of this at least sometimes it is formed with a tau, for example,

> Calliopeia[1] spoke in this way

[1] The Muse Calliope. She speaks at *Aet.* 7c.4 and probably elsewhere in the *Aetia*.

760 Hephaest. *Ench. de Met.* 1.3 (p. 2.8 Consbruch)

θέσει μακραὶ . . . γίνεται δὲ τοῦτο κατὰ πέντε τρό-
πους· ἤτοι γὰρ λήξει εἰς δύο σύμφωνα οἷον,

Τίρυνς οὐδέ τι τεῖχος ἐπήρκεσε

761 Hephaest. *Ench. de Met.* 12.3 (p. 39.1 Consbruch)

τὸ ἀπ᾽ ἐλάσσονος ἰωνικόν . . . τὸ τετράμετρον κατα-
ληκτικόν . . . τοῦτο μέντοι καὶ γαλλιαμβικὸν καὶ μη-
τρωακὸν καλεῖται . . . διὰ τὸ πολλὰ τοὺς νεωτέρους
εἰς τὴν μητέρα τῶν θεῶν γράψαι τούτῳ τῷ μέτρῳ ὡς
καὶ τὰ πολυθρύλητα ταῦτα παραδείγματα δηλοῖ,

Γάλλαι μητρὸς ὀρείης φιλόθυρσοι δρομάδες,
αἷς ἔντεα παταγεῖται καὶ χάλκεα κρόταλα

762 Hdn. Περὶ μονήρους λέξεως 2 (*Gramm. Gr.* vol. 2,
p. 934.22 Lentz)

τὸ ῥῆμα . . . εἰς ἑαυτὸ παράγεται, ὡς παρὰ τὸ ἀθλῶ
τὸ ἀθλεύω . . . ἢ εἰς ὄνομα . . . ἢ εἰς ἐπίρρημα, ὡς
ἀπὸ τοῦ ὄπτω ὄβδην, πλέκω πλέγδην,

μέσφα περιπλέγδην

760 Hephaestion, *Handbook on Meter*

A syllable long by position . . . happens in five ways. Either it will terminate in two consonants such as

> the wall of Tiryns[1] was not strong enough to prevent anything

[1] Mycenean city later associated with Heracles (Apollod. *Bibl.* 2.5.1).

761 Hephaestion, *Handbook on Meter*

an Ionic *a minore* (meter) . . . the tetrameter catalectic . . . this is called the galliambic and the metroiacon on account of younger poets writing many things in this meter for the Mother of the Gods, as these well-known examples show,

> the Galli[1] of the Mountain Mother, loving the
> thyrsus, running,
> for whom instruments clash and the bronze castanets

[1] Attendants of Cybele, the Mountain Mother (cf. Catull. 63, in the same meter).

762 Herodian, *On Peculiar Words*

The verb . . . is derived from itself, as *athleuō* (contend) from *athlō* (contend) . . . or a noun . . . or an adverb as *obdēn* (sight) from *optō* (see), *plegdēn* (entwined) from *plekō* (twine),

> until closely entwined

763 Hdn. Περὶ διχρόνων 2 (*Gramm. Gr.* vol. 3.2, p. 18.9 Lentz)

de verbis in -ίω . . . τὸ δὲ κηκίω ἐκ διπλασιασμοῦ,

πολιὴ δ᾽ ἀνεκήκιεν ἅλμη

764 Hsch. s.v. γάζης κεκορεσμένος (nil nisi lemma)

γάζης κεκορεσμένος

765 Hsch. s.v. ἐννύχιον κρύπτεις

ἐννύχιον κρύπτεις· σκοτεινῶς καὶ δολίως. τινὲς δὲ ἐμμύξιον, ἐν τῷ μυχῷ.

ἐννύχιον κρύπτεις

766 Hsch. s.v. ἑσπέριον ξένον

ἑσπέριον ξένον· τὸν ἑσπέρας ἥκοντα

ἑσπέριον ξένον

767 Hsch. s.v. ἤβολον ἦμαρ

ἤβολον ἦμαρ· . . . ἢ εὔκαιρον, ἱερόν

ἤβολον ἦμαρ

763 Herodian, *On Disyllabic Words*

concerning verbs in -*iō* . . . *kēkiō* (gush) from reduplication,

> the gray sea gushed up

764 Hesychius

> satiated with treasure

765 Hesychius

ennychion krypteis (you hide by night): darkly and deceitfully. Some [say] *emmychion*, in the innermost part of the house,

> you hide by night

766 Hesychius

(*h*)*esperion xenon* (the evening guest):the coming of evening

> the evening guest

767 Hesychius

ēbolon ēmar (a favorable day): . . . or opportune, sacred.

> a favorable day

768 Hsch. s.v. ἠκαλέον γελόωσα

ἠκαλέον γελόωσα· πρᾴως, οὐκ ἐσκυθρωπακυῖα

ἠκαλέον γελόωσα

769 Hsch. s.v. Ἰὼ Καλλιθύεσσα

Ἰὼ Καλλιθύεσσα· Καλλιθύεσσα ἐκαλεῖτο ἡ πρώτη
ἱέρεια τῆς Ἀθηνᾶς.

Ἰὼ Καλλιθύεσσα

770 Hsch. s.v. Κλειτόεν ὕδωρ

Κλειτόεν ὕδωρ· ποταμὸς Ἀρκαδίας. Κλείταιόν φασιν
εἶναι οἱ Κρῆτες.

Κλειτόεν ὕδωρ

771 Hsch. s.v. κλεψίρρυτον ὕδωρ

κλεψίρρυτον ὕδωρ· τὸ τῆς Κλεψύδρας. αὕτη δέ ἐστιν
κρήνη Ἀθήνησιν, ἀπὸ τῆς Ἀκοπόλεως ἐπὶ σταδίους
εἴκοσιν ὑπὸ γῆν φερομένη, εἰς ἣν τὰ ἐμβαλλόμενα
πάλιν θεωρεῖται ἀρχομένων τῶν ἐτησίων.

κλεψίρρυτον ὕδωρ

768 Hesychius

ēkaleon geloōsa (a woman laughing quietly): gently, not scornfully,

    a woman laughing quietly

769 Hesychius

Io Callithyessa: the first festival of Athens was called Callithyessa.[1]

       Io Callithyessa

  [1] Both Io and Callithyessa (or Callithyia) are usually associated with Argive Hera (Plut. in Euseb. *Praep. evang.* 3.8.1).

770 Hesychius

Kleitoen (h)ydōr (Clitoan water): a river of Arcadia. The Cretans say it is Clitaeon.

          Clitoan water

771 Hesychius

klepsirryton (h)ydōr (secretly flowing water): the [well] of Clepsydra. It is a spring at Athens running underground for twenty stadia from the Acropolis; at the beginning of each year, things that were cast in can be seen again.

      secretly flowing water

772 Hsch. s.v. κουρὶξ αἰνυμένους

κουρὶξ αἰνυμένους· τῆς κόμης λαμβανομένους

κουρὶξ αἰνυμένους

773 Hsch. s.v. κυλικήρυτον αἷμα

κυλικήρυτον αἷμα· ὡς τὸ κοτυλήρυτον, οἷον πολύ

κυλικήρυτον αἷμα

774 Hsch. s.v. Λευκοῦ πεδίου

Λευκοῦ πεδίου· τοῦ Μεγαρικοῦ χωρίου.

Λευκοῦ πεδίου

775 Hsch. s.v. οὐδ᾽ ἐπινυκτίδ⟨ι⟩ος

οὐδ᾽ ἐπινυκτίδ⟨ι⟩ος· οὐδὲ ἐπὶ μιᾶς νυκτός, οὐδὲ πρὸς
μίαν νύκτα ἐπὶ νυκτίδος.

οὐδ᾽ ἐπινυκτίδιος

776 Hsch. s.v. οὔθατα βόσκει

οὔθατα βόσκει· αἶγας βόσκει.

οὔθατα βόσκει

772 Hesychius

kourix ainymenous (taking by the hair): grasping the hair (*komēs*),

> taking by the hair

773 Hesychius

kylikēryton (h)aima (abundant blood): like blood drawn in cups, for instance, a lot

> abundant blood

774 Hesychius

Leukou pediou (the White Plain): a place in Megara.

> from the White Plain

775 Heschyius

oud' epinyktidios (not by night): neither on one night, nor about one night, but at night.

> not by night

776 Heschyius

outhata boskei (he feeds the udders): he feeds the [breeding] goats.

> he feeds the udders

777 Hsch. s.v. Προσεληνίδες

Προσεληνίδες· αἱ Ἀρκαδικαὶ νύμφαι.

778 Ioann. Philop. *Tonika paragelmata* (p. 18.5 Dindorf)

ὑπάται ὑπατῶν, νέαται νεατῶν· ἐπὶ τῶν χορδῶν περι-
σπῶμεν. κύρια γάρ εἰσιν αὐτῶν ὀνόματα καὶ διὰ
τοῦτο μονογενῆ.

    κοῦραι πετράων ἤριπον ἐξ ὑπάτων

779 Ioann. Philop. *Tonika paragelmata* (p. 27.22 Dindorf)

εἰ μέντοι ἐν τέλει στίχου εἴη ἢ ἁπλῶς ἐν τέλει ὀνόμα-
τος μεθ᾽ ἣν τίθεται στιγμή ἀναστρέφεται πάντως,
οἷον ἐστι τὸ,

        πάντων δ᾽ ἔπτυσε πουλὺ κάτα

780 Ioann. Philop. *Tonika paragelmata* (p. 29.7 Dindorf)

⟨περὶ ἐπιρρημάτων⟩ ἀπὸ τοῦ ἐτεόν ὀξυτόνου· ἀλλ᾽ . . .
ἐτεά. καὶ ἀπὸ τοῦ ἐτός πάλιν ὀξυτόνου ἐτά ὀξυτόνως·

   ὡς ἐτὰ Τημενίδος χρύσεον γένος

UNATTRIBUTED FRAGMENTS

777 Heschyius

Proselēnides (women older than the moon):[1] Arcadian nymphs.

[1] Cf. *Ia.* 191.56, where Amphacles, the son of Arcadian Bathycles, is called the "Pre-moon Man."

778 John Philoponus

hypatai, hypatōn (the highest), *neatai, neatōn* (the lowest): we write the (musical) notes with a circumflex. These are proper names and on account of this have only one gender.

> the girls threw from the highest rocks

779 John Philoponus

If [a preposition] is at the end of a line or simply at the end of a noun after which a period is placed, the accent is brought forward. This is an example,

> he spat a lot at all [the people]

780 John Philoponus

(*On adverbs*), from *eteon* (truly) with an acute accent, but . . . *etea*. And again from *etos* with an acute accent comes *eta* with an acute accent:

> how truly the golden race of the Temenidae[1]

[1] Sons of Temenus, the royal house of Macedonia. They were the subject of Euripides in his lost tragedies *Temenus* and *Temenidae*.

781 Ioann. Philop. *Tonika paragelmata* (p. 29, 35 Dindorf)

(περὶ ἐπιρρημάτων), καὶ τὸ πρῴην δὲ παρ' αἰτιατικὴν σχηματίζουσιν . . . καὶ τὸ "ἀκὴν ἐγένοντο σιωπῇ" καὶ,

ἀκμήν τοι βρύα τῆμος ἐπὶ στήθεσσι κέχυνται

782 *Metr. anon. Oxy.* (*P.Oxy.* 220 col. XI, 15)

ἀπό[κο]πτε τοῦ Κυρηναϊκοῦ [τὸ]ν πρῶτον τρισύλλαβον [π]όδα, καὶ τὸ καταλειπό[μ]ενον προφερόμενος [πο]ιήσεις τόδε τὸ μ[έτρο]ν οὕτως,

∪ ∪ – ∪ ∪ παρθένον κόρην

783 Phld. *Piet.* (*P.Herc.* 433 col. IIa)

<pre>
13   Ὅ]μηρος
            ]νθαι υ
            ]ονεα
            ]τεκεῖν
17   Κ]αλλιμ¹
     χ.......] Τάραντι
            κ]αταλαβών
</pre>

¹ Suppl. Gomperz (*Herkulanische Studien* 2 [1866]: p. 29)

UNATTRIBUTED FRAGMENTS

781 John Philoponus

(*On adverbs*), and they form *prōiēn* (just now) from the accusative . . . and "they became hushed (*akēn*) in silence"[1] and,

> still for you today algae are poured on your breast[2]

[1] Hom. *Il.* 3.95.   [2] Possibly about Melicertes the sea god, whom Callimachus treats in *Aet.* 91–92a.

782 Anonymous metrician (Oxyrhynchus papyrus)

Cut off the first trisyllabic foot of the Cyrenaic[1] and bringing forward the remaining part, you will make the meter in this way,

> ∪ ∪ – ∪ ∪ the virgin girl

[1] The choriambic Cyrenaic meter is likely Callimachean (West 1982, 152).

783 Philodemus, *On Piety*

> Ho]mer . . . .
> C]allim[achus
>]Tarantine[1]
>]after seizing

[1] From Tarentum, a colony of Sparta in Apulia, Italy. It was associated with Poseidon, whose son Taras was the founder (Paus. 10.10.6–8).

CALLIMACHUS

784 Plut. *De inimic. utilit.* 890c

ἡ δὲ σιγὴ πανταχοῦ μὲν ἀνυπεύθυνον (οὐ μόνον ἄδι-
ψον, ὥς φησιν Ἱπποκράτης) ἐν δὲ λοιδορίαις σεμνὸν
καὶ Σωκρατικόν, μᾶλλον δ' Ἡράκλειον, εἴ γε κἀκεῖ-
νος,

> οὐδ' ὅσσον μυίης στυγερῶν ἐμπάζετο μύθων

785 Schol. (V Ald.) ad Ar. *Pax* 637

δικροῖς ἐώθουν τὴν θεὸν κεκράγμασιν· δικράνοις,

> †δίκρανον ἤρυγε φιτρὸν ἐπαιρόμενος

786 Schol. (B)T ad Hom. *Il.* 19.1

ἀπ' Ὠκεανοῖο ῥοάων· Βοιώτιος ἡ φωνή· καὶ ἀπὸ τῶν
εἰς ες ἀρσενικῶν,

> Ἄρτεμι Κρητάων (?) πότνια τοξοφόρων

787 Schol. A ad Hom. *Il.* 3.182

ὀλβιόδαιμον· προπαροξυτόνως· ἔστι γὰρ σύνθετον,

> ψευδόμενοί σε Παλαῖμον

788 Schol. A ad Hom. *Il.* 23.254

ἑανῷ λικὶ κάλυψεν· λιτί ὡς φωτί. οὕτως καὶ Ἀρίσταρ-
χος. πᾶσα γὰρ δοτικὴ δισύλλαβος ἐπ' ὀνομάτων εἰς

784 Plutarch, *How to Profit by One's Enemies*

Silence is utterly beyond criticism (not just an antidote for thirst, as Hippocrates says), but in abuse it is holy and Socratic, or rather Heraclean, if indeed that one,

> not as much as a fly took heed of angry words

785 Scholia to Aristophanes, *Peace*

they thrust out the goddess with forked cries: pitchforks,

> he bellowed lifting up a wooden pitchfork

786 Scholia to Homer, *Iliad*

from the streams of Ocean: the Boeotian form; and of masculines ending in epsilon + sigma,

> O Artemis, mistress of Cretan (?) bowmen

787 Scholia to Homer, *Iliad*

with good fortune: with an acute accent on the antepenult,

> the ones deceiving you, Palaemon[1]

[1] Melicertes (see *Fr. Inc. Auct.* 781; *Aet.* 91–92a).

788 Scholia to Homer, *Iliad*

they covered it with soft linen: *līti* (linen) like *phōti* (mortal). So too Aristarchus. Every disyllabic dative in nouns

287

τῖ λήγεται ὀξύνεται, χρωτί δαιτί Κρητί. οὕτως οὖν καὶ
λιτί. τούτῳ γὰρ τῷ λόγῳ καὶ βλητί ὀφείλομεν κατ'
ὀξεῖαν τάσιν ἀναγιγνώσκειν,

νύμφα φίλη, καὶ βλητὶ λίθῳ ἐνὶ δάκρυον ἧκας

789 Schol. (BGCb) ad Ov. *Ib.* 285

utque dedit saltus a summa Thessalus Ossa, tu quoque
saxoso praecipitere loco": Ionus rex Thessaliae, filius †Per-
peti Agrintantini† ultra modum potus de Ossa monte
praecipitatus est, ut ait Gallus

790 Schol. (BGCDb) ad Ov. *Ib.* 287

aut, velut Eurylochi, qui sceptrum cepit ab illo, sint artus
avidis anguibus esca tui: Eurylochus Ioni filius quia filiam
stuprare voluit, a serpentibus consumptus est, quod idem
Gallus tangit.

791 Schol. (BGC) ad Ov. *Ib.* 323

quosque putas fidos, ut Larisaeus Alevas vulnere non fidos
experiare tuo: Alevas Therodomantis filius, fuit de Larissa
civitate, quem sui interfecerunt. Unde Gallus: "Therodo-
mantiades, etc."

---

[1] In Thessaly, on the Peneius River (Strabo 7.15a).

ending in tau + iota is accented with an acute: *chrōti, daiti, Krēti*. And so also *līti*. In this word and in *blēti* we must read the acute pitch,

> dear bride, with a thrown rock you inspired tears

789 Scholia to Ovid, *Ibis*

Just as Thessalus leaped down from the height of Ossa,[1] may you also be thrown from a rocky place: Ionus king of Thessaly, son of (?) drinking beyond moderation, was hurled from Mt. Ossa, as Gallus[2] says

[1] Mountain in Thessaly, known in myth for the attempt of Otus and Ephialtes to put Mt. Ossa on Olympus and Mt. Pelion on Ossa in order to ascend to the heavens (Apollod. *Bibl.* 1.7.4).

[2] In some manuscripts the name Gallus is mistakenly substituted for Callimachus.

790 Scholia to Ovid, *Ibis*

Or, like Eurylochus, who took the scepter from him, may your limbs be food for greedy snakes: Eurylochus, the son of Ionus, because he wished to ravish his daughter, was eaten by snakes. Gallus touches on the same tale.[1]

[1] The story is not known from other sources.

791 Scholia to Ovid, *Ibis*

Like Aleus of Larissa, may you by your own wound find that those whom you think are trustworthy are not: Aleus, the son of Therodomantes of the state of Larissa,[1] whom his relatives killed. From this Gallus says, "The sons of Therodomantes, etc."

792 Schol. (BGCb) ad Ov. *Ib.* 325

utque Milo, sub quo cruciata est Pisa tyranno, vivus in
occulatas praecipiteris aquas: Milonem sui in mare proie-
cerunt. Unde Gallus: "Dives erat Milo, etc.—pelagus."

793 Schol. (BGC) ad Ov. *Ib.* 327

quaeque in Adimantum Phliasia regna tenentem a Iove
venerunt, te quoque tela petant": Adimantus rex Philiasiae
indignans superis oboedire et etiam Iovi, a Iovi fulminatus
est. unde idem: "Philacides, etc."

794 Schol. (BGC) ad Ov. *Ib.* 363

infamemque locum sceleris quae nomine fecit, pressit et
inductis membra paterna rotis: Servius Tullius habuit fi-
liam, quae quia adulterari noluit equis alligatum tam diu
traxit, donec dilaceratus est; qui locus Athenis sceleratus
dicitur. unde Gallus: "noluit etc."

795 Schol. (CD) ad Ov. *Ib.* 383

Therodamanteos ut qui sensere leones: Therodomantus
(sic) rex Meneleam quandam leonibus suis obiecit; quem

792 Scholia to Ovid, *Ibis*

And like Milo, under whose tyranny Pisa was tormented, may you be thrown alive into the waters that keep secrets: his relatives threw Milo into the sea. From this Gallus says, "Milo was rich, etc.—the sea."

793 Scholia to Ovid, *Ibis*

May the spears also seek you out, which came from Jupiter against Adimantus, who held the kingdom of Phliasia: Adimantus, king of Phliasia, who distained to obey the gods and even Jupiter, was struck by Jupiter's lightning bolt. From this, the same author:[1] "Philacides, etc."

---

[1] Gallus, i.e., Callimachus.

794 Scholia to Ovid, *Ibis*

Or she[1] who made the place infamous by the name of her crime, and crushed her father's limbs under the driving wheels: Servius Tullius had a daughter who, because he was unwilling to commit incest, dragged him, tied to horses, for such a long time that he was torn limb for limb; which at Athens is called the place of crime. From this, Gallus [says] "he was unwilling, etc."

---

[1] This story is also told of Tullia, the wife of Tarquinius Superbus (Livy 1.48).

795 Scholia to Ovid, *Ibis*

Like those who felt the lions of Therodomanteus: king Therodomantus (sic) threw a certain Meneleas to his lions;

filia eius Messagete occidit, cum ipse vellet adulterari cum
ea ut testatur Darius.

796 Schol. (CD) ad Ov. *Ib*. 517

quodque ferunt Brotean fecisse cupidine mortis; des tua
succensae membra cremanda pyrae: Broteas Iovis filius
excaecatus est a Iove quia nequissimus erat, et ideo proie-
cit se in pyram ardentem odio habens vitam suam, ut ait
Darius.

797 Schol. (CD) ad Ov. *Ib*. 531

utque coturnatum periisse Lycophrona narrant, haereat in
fibris fixa sagitta tuis: Lycophron quidam poeta fuit qui
dum comoediam suam in scena recitabat puras, i.e. nudas,
puerorum et puellarum cohortes repraesentabat et quen-
dam nimis acriter reprehendebat, qui eum in ipsa recita-
tione cum sagitta in manu dextra vulneravit: unde sic emit-
tendo sanguinem periit, teste Gallo.

whom his daughter Messagete[1] killed when he wished to commit incest with her, as Darius[2] testifies.

[1] Apparently, a Libyan tale. Others treated by Callimachus include *Aet.* 37; *Fr. Inc. Sed.* 484, 584, 673, 706; and *Fr. Inc. Auct.* 810.   [2] Understood as another alias of Callimachus (see Pfeiffer's note); cf. *Hec.* fr. 95c.

796 Scholia to Ovid, *Ibis*

And what they say Broteas did in his longing for death, may you give your limbs to be cremated on the kindled pyre: Broteas the son of Jupiter was blinded by Jupiter because he was completely worthless, and on account of this he threw himself onto a burning pyre in hatred of his life, as Darius says.

797 Scholia to Ovid, *Ibis*

And as they say Lycophron the actor perished, may an arrow be fixed in your guts: A certain Lycophron was a poet who, while he performed his comedy on the stage, was displaying groups of naked boys and girls and was criticizing someone very vehemently, who wounded him in the midst of his performance with an arrow to his right hand: from this he died from spurting blood, as Gallus testifies.[1]

[1] Perhaps Lycophron of Chalcis, author of the *Alexandra* and near contemporary of Callimachus. The story is not recorded elsewhere, though it would be consistent with the tradition of bizarre deaths in the biographies of poets.

798 (falsum) Schol. (CD) ad Ov. *Ib.* 569

utque loquax in equo est elisus guttur acerno, sic tibi clau-
datur pollice vocis iter: Agenor turpia locutus fuit in Dia-
nam, unde irata fecit ut dum equum currere faceret, equo
labente et pollice sub gula opposito, dum pronus caderet
iugulatus est teste Gallo.

799 Schol. (KUEAT) ad Theoc. *Id.* 7.155

βωμῷ πὰρ Δάματρος ἁλωίδος· ἇς ἐπὶ σωρῷ αὖτις
ἐγὼ πάξαιμι μέγα πτύον· ὅταν δὲ λικμῶντες σωρεύ-
ωσι τὸν πυρόν, κατὰ μέσον πηγνύουσι τὸ πτύον, καὶ,

  τὴν θρινάκην κατέθεντο

800 Steph. Byz. θ 9 Billerbeck s.v. θαυμακία

θαυμακία· πόλις Μαγνησίας . . . δευτέρα πόλις κατὰ
τὸν Μαλιακὸν κόλπον. οἱ ἔνοικοι Θαυμακοί. και,

  Θαυμακίης ἱερὸν Ἀρτέμιδος

798 (incorrect) Scholia to Ovid, *Ibis*

As the talkative throat was crushed in the maple horse, so may the pathway of your voice be closed by a thumb: Agenor said base things against Diana, and angry, she brought it about that while he made his horse run, it slipped and a thumb was placed under his throat; as he fell forward he was strangled, according to the testimony of Gallus.[1]

[1] The scholiast has misunderstood Ovid's reference to Anticlus, who was with the other Greek warriors inside the Trojan Horse when he began to answer Helen, who was imitating the voices of their wives; Odysseus stopped him by choking him with his hand (Hom. *Od.* 4.271–89).

799 Scholia to Theocritus, *Idylls*

By the altar of Demeter of the threshing floor; in her heap of grain may I again plant my great winnowing shovel: whenever winnowing, they heap up the wheat and stick the winnowing shovel in the middle and,

> they lay down the three-pronged fork

800 Stephanus of Byzantium

Thaumacia: a city of Magnesia . . . the second city on the Malian Gulf. The inhabitants [are called] Thaumaci. And,

> the temple of Artemis of Thaumacia[1]

[1] Cf. Hom. *Il.* 2.716; Strabo 9.5.16.

295

801 Steph. Byz. θ 56 Billerbeck s.v. Θράκη

Θράκη· . . . τὸ δὲ Θραΐκιος λέγεται καὶ διὰ μακροῦ
τοῦ ῑ.

> ἀνέρα δὲ Τροίη Θρηΐκιον οὔτι φορήσει

802 Steph. Byz. π 58 Billerbeck s.v. Παρρασία

Παρρασία· πόλις Ἀρκαδίας . . . ὁ πολίτης Παρράσιος
καὶ Παρρασιεύς καὶ Παρρασίς,

> δέξονται Φολόης οὔρεα Παρρασίδος

803 Steph. Byz. π 85 Billerbeck s.v. Πειραιός

Πειραιός· οὕτως ἐκαλεῖτο ὁ λιμὴν τῆς Ἀττικῆς . . .
ἔστι καὶ τῆς Κορινθίας λιμήν. λέγεται δὲ καί,

> Πειρήτιδος ἱερὸς ὄρνις

804 Tert. *De cor.* 7

Heracles nunc populum capite praefert, nunc oleastrum,
nunc apium.

805 Theodos. Περι κλίσεως τῶν εἰς ῶν βαρυτόων exc.
Hdn. (p. 19.23 Hilgard)

τὰ ὑπὲρ δύο συλλαβὰς βαρύτονα διὰ τοῦ ῶ κλίνεσθαι
θέλουσιν, οἷον . . . τὸ ὀλίζων ὀλίζονος διὰ του ō,

> ἐς ὀλίζονας ἀστέρας ἄρκτου

801 Stephanus of Byzantium

Thrace: ... *Thraïkios* (Thracian) is written with a long iota.

> Troy will not bear a Thracian man[1]

1 Perhaps a quotation from an oracle.

802 Stephanus of Byzantium

Parrhasia: a city of Arcadia . . . a citizen [is called] Parrhasius and Parrhasieus and Parrhasis,

> they will occupy the hills of Pholoe of Parrhasia[1]

1 Arcadia and a city in southern Arcadia (Hom. *Il.* 2.608).

803 Stephanus of Byzantium

Peiraeus: the name of the harbor of Attica . . . it is also the harbor of Corinth. And one reads,

> the sacred bird of Piraeus

804 Tertullian, *On the Crown*

Heracles now wore a poplar [wreath] on his head, now oleaster, now parsley.

805 Theodosius in Herodian, *On the Declension of Words with Unaccented Final Syllables Ending in Omega-Nu*

They want words with unaccented final syllables that have more than two syllables to be declined with omega, such as . . . and *olizōn*, *olizonos* with an omicron,

> into the smaller stars of the bear[1]

1 The constellation Ursa Major or, more likely, Ursa Minor (*Ia.* 191.54–55).

806 Zonaras s.v. λίστρον (p. 1312 Tittmann)

λίστρον· τὸ ξύστρον,

λίστροισιν ἐοικότα

DUBIA

807 *Et. Gen.* B s.v. λίς

λίς· ὁ λέων . . . ἔδει μέντοι περισπᾶσθαι, ὡς μῦς μῦν.
Ἀριστάρχῳ δὲ ἐπείσθη ἡ παράδοσις ὀξύνοντι. τὸ δὲ
πληθυντικὸν παρὰ Καλλιμάχῳ,

λῖες μέντοι† λίεσσι

808 *Et. Gen.* AB s.v. ἄωρος

ἄωρος· . . . Καλλίμαχος δὲ κατὰ μετάληψιν τοὺς
ἀγρίους. ἄωρον γὰρ τὸ ὠμόν.

809 Schol. AD ad Hom. *Il.* 3.1

αὐτὰρ ἐπεὶ κόσμηθεν· . . . διαφέρει δὲ ὁ αὐτάρ τοῦ δέ
καθὸ ὁ μὲν αὐτάρ προτάσσεται, ὁ δὲ δέ ὑποτάσσεται.
ζητεῖται δὲ πῶς δεῖ τὸν αὐτάρ σύνδεσμον προφέρε-
σθαι, πότερον ὀξυτόνως ἢ βαρυτόνως. οἱ μὲν οὖν ὀξυ-
τόνως ἀνεγνώκασιν, ὡς Καλλίμαχος, οἱ δὲ βαρυτόνως
λόγῳ τῷδε.

UNATTRIBUTED FRAGMENTS

806 Zonaras, *Lexicon*

listron (spade): a scythe,

> like spades

DUBIA

807 *Etymologicum Genuinum*

līs: lion . . . it must have a circumflex accent like *mūs, mūn* (mouse). In Aristarchus it is transmitted with an acute accent. An expanded form is in Callimachus,

> but lions (*līes*) to the lions (*līessi*)

808 *Etymologicum Genuinum*

aōros (unripe): . . . Callimachus by transference, wild fruits. *Aōros* means raw.

809 Scholia to Homer, *Iliad*

but when it was arranged: . . . *autar* (but) differs from *de* (but) in that *autar* is placed before the phrase and *de* is postpositive. We must investigate how it is necessary for the conjunction to be pronounced, whether with an accute accent or a circumflex. Some read it with an acute, like Callimachus, some with a circumflex.

810 Ioann. Malalas 7 (*Chronicon Paschale*, p. 207.1 Dindorf)

τὸν δὲ αὐτὸν ἱππικὸν ἀγῶνα ὁ Ἐννάλιος ἅρμασι δι-
πώλοις ἐφεῦρε, καθὼς ταῦτα συνγράψατο Καλλίμα-
χος ὁ σοφὸς ἐν τοῖς Αἰτίοις αὐτοῦ.

811 Ioann. Tortellii *De orth.* s.v. Osiris

Osiris . . . sed tandem teste Callimacho Aegyptio historico,
quem secutus est Seneca in libro, quem de sacris Aegyp-
tiorum composuit cum Osiris a Aegyptio vel ut ait Servius
super VI Aeneid. a Typhone fratre occulte occisus et
laniatus fuisset et ab uxore Iside diu eius membra quae-
rerentur nec inveniri possent, . . .

812 Tzetz. *Chil.* 4.390–93

καὶ τί φημί σοι τὰ φυτά; Ῥόδιόν ἐστιν ὄρος
τὴν κλῆσιν Ἀταβύριον, χαλκᾶς πρὶν ἔχον βόας
αἲ μυκηθμὸν ἐξέπεμπον, χωρούσης Ῥόδῳ
βλάβης·
Πίνδαρος καὶ Καλλίμαχος γράφει τὴν ἱστορίαν.

UNATTRIBUTED FRAGMENTS

810 John Malalas

Enyalius won the same equestrian contest in the two-horse chariots, as learned Callimachus wrote in his *Aetia*.

811 John Tortellii, *On Spelling*

Osiris . . . but finally with Callimachus the Aegyptian historian as a witness,[1] whom Seneca followed in the book he composed on the sacred rites of the Egyptians, when Osiris was secretly killed by an Egyptian or as Servius says in his commentary on Book 6 of the *Aeneid*,[2] by his brother Typhon, and had been torn apart, and his wife Isis searched for his limbs for a long time and they could not be found . . .

[1] It is not known in which of his works Callimachus told this tale.   [2] Serv. ad. Verg. *Aen*. 6.154.

812 Tzetzes, *Chiliads*

And what do I say to you about these creatures?
    There is a Rhodian hill,
Atabyrion by name; which once had bronze bulls,
that bellowed when harm was coming to Rhodes.
Pindar and Callimachus wrote the tale.[1]

[1] In *Ol.* 7.87 Pindar mentions Atabyrion, without the bulls (cf. Schol. A ad loc.). It is not clear where Callimachus might have discussed them.

813 Ap. Dysc. *Constr.* (*Gramm. Gr.* vol. 2.2, p. 192.7 Uhlig)

ἐν προτάξει . . . αἱ ἀντωνυμίαι . . . ἔχονται τοῦ ὀρθοῦ τόνου . . . εἰ μέντοι τὰ τῆς συντάξεως ἀναστραφείη, οἷόν τέ ἐστιν καὶ ἐγκλίνεσθαι τὴν ἀντωνυμίαν,

> αὐτόν με πρώτιστα συνοικιστῆρα †γαίας†
> ἔσδεξαι τεμενοῦχον

814 Scholia (s) ad Lyc. *Alex.* 1352

χρυσεργὰ Πακτωλοῦ ποτά· Πακτωλὸς ποταμὸς Λυδίας χρυσοῦ ψήγματα ἔχων, ὥς φησι,

> Πακτωλοῦ χρυσέοισιν ἐπ' ἀνδήροισι θάασσον

813 Apollonius Dyscolus, *On Syntax*

In a command . . . the pronouns . . . have a real accent . . . and if they are subject to anastrophe, for example, the pronoun is declined . . .[1]

> you, who have a sacred precinct,[2] accept me myself
> first of all as a fellow settler of this earth

[1] Examples from Homer are given (*Il.* 9.249, 9.680), followed by our quotation.   [2] An epithet of several gods.

814 Scholia to Lycophron, *Alexandra*

the gold-producing water of Pactolus: Pactolus is a river of Lydia which has gold dust, as they say,

> they were sitting on the golden banks of the Pactolus[1]

[1] A river near Sardis associated with Dionysus and King Midas (Ov. *Met.* 11.87–88).

TESTIMONIA

TESTIMONIA

DE VITA

1 *Suda* κ 227

Καλλίμαχος· υἱὸς Βάττου καὶ Μεσάτμας, Κυρηναῖος, γραμματικός, μαθητὴς Ἑρμοκράτους τοῦ Ἰασέως, γραμματικοῦ· γαμετὴν ἐσχηκὼς τὴν Εὐφράτου τοῦ Συρακουσίου θυγατέρα. ἀδελφῆς δὲ αὐτοῦ παῖς ἦν ὁ νέος Καλλίμαχος, ὁ γράψας περὶ νήσων δι' ἐπῶν. οὕτω δὲ γέγονεν ἐπιμελέστατος, ὡς γράψαι μὲν ποιήματα εἰς πᾶν μέτρον, συντάξαι δὲ καὶ καταλογάδην πλεῖστα. καί ἐστιν αὐτῷ τὰ γεγραμμένα βιβλία ὑπὲρ τὰ ὀκτακόσια· ἐπὶ δὲ τῶν χρόνων ἦν Πτολεμαίου τοῦ Φιλαδέλφου. πρὶν δὲ συσταθῆναι τῷ βασιλεῖ, γράμματα ἐδίδασκεν ἐν Ἐλευσῖνι, κωμυδρίῳ τῆς Ἀλεξανδρείας. καὶ παρέτεινε μέχρι τοῦ Εὐεργέτου κληθέντος Πτολεμαίου, ὀλυμπιάδος δὲ †ρκζ', ἧς κατὰ τὸ δεύτερον ἔτος ὁ Εὐεργέτης Πτολεμαῖος ἤρξατο τῆς βασιλείας.

Τῶν δὲ αὐτοῦ βιβλίων ἐστὶ καὶ ταῦτα· Ἰοῦς ἄφιξις, Σεμέλη, Ἄργους οἰκισμός, Ἀρκαδία, Γλαῦκος, Ἐλπίδες, σατυρικὰ δράματα, τραγῳδίαι, κωμῳδίαι, μέλη,

TESTIMONIA

ON HIS LIFE

1 *Suda*

Callimachus: son of Battus and Mesatma, of Cyrene. A grammarian. A student of Hermocrates of Iasus, a grammarian. He married the daughter of Euphrates of Syracuse. Callimachus the younger was the son of his sister who wrote *On Islands* in epic meters. He was so industrious that he wrote poems in every meter and composed much prose. And he wrote more than eight hundred books. He lived at the time of Ptolemy Philadelphus and before he was associated with the king he taught grammar in Eleusis, a neighborhood of Alexandria. His life extended until the time of Ptolemy called Euergetes, in the 127th Olympiad (272–269 BC),[1] in the second year of which Ptolemy Euergetes began his reign.

And these are his books: the *Arrival of Io*, *Semele*, the *Foundation of Argos*, *Arcadia*, *Glaucus*, *Hopes*, satyric dramas, tragedies, comedies, lyric poems, the *Ibis* (which aims at obscurity and abuse against a certain Ibis who was

---

[1] An error. Ptolemy Euergetes began his reign in 246 BC, and Callimachus lived into the 230s.

Ἶβος (ἔστι δὲ ποίημα ἐπιτετηδευμένον εἰς ἀσάφειαν
καὶ λοιδορίαν, εἴς τινα Ἶβιν, γενόμενον ἐχθρὸν τοῦ
Καλλιμάχου· ἦν δὲ οὗτος Ἀπολλώνιος, ὁ γράψας τὰ
Ἀργοναυτικά)· Μουσεῖον, Πίνακες τῶν ἐν πάσῃ παι-
δείᾳ διαλαμψάντων, καὶ ὧν συνέγραψαν, ἐν βιβλίοις
κ΄ καὶ ρ΄, Πίναξ καὶ ἀναγραφὴ τῶν κατὰ χρόνους καὶ
ἀπ᾽ ἀρχῆς γενομένων διδασκάλων, Πίναξ τῶν Δημο-
κρίτου γλωσσῶν καὶ συνταγμάτων, Μηνῶν προση-
γορίαι κατὰ ἔθνος καὶ πόλεις, Κτίσεις νήσων καὶ
πόλεων καὶ μετονομασίαι, Περὶ τῶν ἐν Εὐρώπῃ πο-
ταμῶν, Περὶ τῶν ἐν Πελοποννήσῳ καὶ Ἰταλίᾳ θαυμα-
σίων καὶ παραδόξων, Περὶ μετονομασίας ἰχθύων,
Περὶ ἀνέμων, Περὶ ὀρνέων, Περὶ τῶν ἐν τῇ οἰκουμένῃ
ποταμῶν, Θαυμάτων τῶν εἰς ἅπασαν τὴν γῆν κατὰ
τόπους ὄντων συναγωγή.

2 De patre Batto v. *Epig.* 35.

3 De avo Callimacho v. *Epig.* 21.

4 Strabo 17.8.3.21–22

λέγεται δὲ ἡ Κυρήνη κτίσμα Βάττου· πρόγονον δὲ τοῦ-
τον ἑαυτοῦ φάσκει Καλλίμαχος.

5 Schol. ad *Hymn* 2.65

λέγεται ὅτι ὁ Βάττος οὗτος ἄφωνος ἦν. ἀπῆλθεν οὖν
εἰς τὸ τοῦ Ἀπόλλωνος ἱερὸν ἐπὶ τῷ τὸν θεὸν ἐρωτῆσαι

an enemy of Callimachus. This was Apollonius of Rhodes who wrote the *Argonautica*), the *Museum*, the *Index of All Those Preeminent in Literature and of Their Writings in 120 Books*; a list and a chronological register of all those from the beginning who were teachers, and an *Index of the Glosses and Writings of Democritus*, and the *Names of the Months by Tribes and Cities*, the *Foundations of Islands and Cities and Their Changes of Name*, *On the Rivers of Europe*, *On Wondrous and Paradoxical things on the Peloponnese and in Italy*, *On Changes in the Names of Fish*, *On Winds*, *On Birds*, *On Rivers of the Inhabited World*, *Collection of Marvels throughout the World by Location*.

2 On his father, Battus, see *Epigram* 35.

3 On his grandfather Callimachus, see *Epigram* 21.

4 Strabo, *Geography*

Cyrene is called the foundation of Battus. Callimachus says that he is his forefather.

5 Scholia to Callimachus, *Hymn to Apollo*[1]

It is said that this Battus was mute. Therefore he went to the oracle of Apollo to ask about his voice. The god did not respond to him then about his voice, but about migration.

[1] Cf. T 87.

περὶ τῆς φωνῆς. ὁ δὲ ἔχρησεν αὐτῷ οὐκέτι περὶ φωνῆς
ἀλλὰ περὶ μετοικίας. καὶ ὁ Βάττος πεισθεὶς τῷ
χρησμῷ ἦλθεν εἰς τὴν Λιβύην. λέγεται δὲ εἶναι πολ-
λοὺς λέοντας ἐν τῇ χώρᾳ ταύτῃ. ἐπιδημήσας οὖν ὁ
Βάττος, καὶ λέοντα αἰφνηδὸν θεασάμενος τῇ τοῦ φό-
βου ἀνάγκῃ βιασθεὶς φλέγξασθαι διέρρηξε τὴν
φλέβα, ἥτις τὴν ἐκείνου φωνὴν ἐπεῖχε, καὶ οὕτω φω-
νήεις ἐγένετο καὶ τὴν Κυρήνην ἔκτισεν, ὅθεν ἐστὶν ὁ
Καλλίμαχος.

6 Solin. 27.44

maior Syrtis ostentat oppidum—Cyrenas vocant—quod
Battus . . . condidit: quae domus Callimacho poetae fuit
patria.

7 Antig. Car. *Hist. mir.* 45

Καλλίμαχος ὁ ἐκ τῆς Αἰγύτου.

8 Gell. *NA* 17.21.41

Anno . . . bellum adversus Poenos primum coeptum est,
neque diu post Callimachus, poeta Cyrenensis, Alexandriae
apud Ptolemaeum regem celebratus est.

And persuaded by the oracle Battus went into Libya. It was said that there were many lions in the land. After he was settled there, Battus saw a lion unexpectedly, and forced to burst out by the necessity of his fear he broke through the blood vessel which had held back his voice and thus he became articulate and founded Cyrene, the homeland of Callimachus.

6 Gaius Iulius Solinus, *Collection of Memorable Things*

The Greater Syrtis exposes the city to view—they call it Cyrene—that Battus . . . founded: which was the homeland of the poet Callimachus.

7 Antigonus Carystius, *Collection of Miraculous Histories*

Callimachus who was from Egypt.[1]

[1] Cf. *Fr. Inc. Sed.* 469, and also T 85 and T 90, where Callimachus is called "the Libyan."

8 Gellius, *Attic Nights*

In that year (264 BC) . . . The first Punic War began, and not long afterward Callimachus, the poet from Cyrene, was celebrated in Alexandria at the court of king Ptolemy.

9 *Vit. Theoc.* b (p. 2.1 Wendel)

ἰστέον ὅτι ὁ Θεόκριτος ἐγένετο ἰσόχρονος τοῦ τε
Ἀράτου καὶ τοῦ Καλλιμάχος καὶ τοῦ Νικάνδρου. ἐγέ-
νετο δὲ ἐπὶ τῶν χρόνων Πτολεμαίου τοῦ Φιλαδέλφου.

10

a *Vit. Arat.* IV (Martin 1974, 19)

Ἄρατος . . . ἦν δὲ ἐπὶ Πτολεμαίου τοῦ Φιλαδέλφου
. . . συνήκμασε δὲ Ἀλεξάνδρῳ τῷ Αἰτωλῷ καὶ Καλ-
λιμάχῳ καὶ †Μελανδρίῳ[1] καὶ Φιλίτᾳ . . . γηραιῷ δὲ
τῷ Κυρηναίῳ ἐπεβάλετο.

[1] Μελανδρίῳ A: Μελανχρίῳ M: Μενάνδρῳ VP[2]: Λεανδρίῳ
Wendel

b Theo. Alex. *Vit. Arat.* III (Martin 1974, 17–18)

ὁ Καλλίμαχος συνεγγίζων αὐτῷ κατὰ τοὺς χρόνους.

c [Ach. Tat.] *Vit. Arat.* I (Martin 1974, 9)

μέμηται γοῦν αὐτοῦ καὶ Καλλίμαχος ὡς πρεσβυτέ-
ρου.

d *Vit. Arat. Lat.* III (Martin 1974, 16)

Callimachus adsistens ei (sc. Arato) ab infantia propter
Praxiphanem Mytilenum (sic).

9 *Life of Theocritus*

It is clear that Theocritus was a contemporary of Aratus and Callimachus and Nicander (*BNJ* 271 T4). He lived at the time of Ptolemy Philadelphus.

10

a *Life of Aratus*

Aratus . . . lived at the time of Ptolemy Philadelphus . . . He flourished together with Alexander the Aetolian and Callimachus and Menander[1] and Philitas . . . and spent his old age in Cyrene.[2]

[1] The name is uncertain.   [2] Cf. *Epig.* 27.

b Theon of Alexandria, *Life of Aratus*

Callimachus was with him throughout that time.

c Pseudo-Achilles Tatius, *Life of Aratus*

Callimachus recalls him as an old man.[1]

[1] Cf. *Fr. Doct.* 460.

d Latin *Life of Aratus*

Callimachus defended him (sc. Aratus) from [the charge of] ineloquence made by Praxiphanes of Mytilene.[1]

[1] Cf. *Fr. Doct.* 460.

11

a Schol. ad Vit. Ap. Rhod. a (p. 1.7 Wendel)

Ἀπολλώνιος . . . ἐγένετο δὲ ἐπὶ τῶν Πτολεμαίων,
Καλλιμάχου μαθητής. τὸ μὲν πρῶτον συνὼν Καλλι-
μάχῳ τῷ ἰδίῳ διδασκάλῳ < . . . > ὀψὲ δὲ ἐπὶ τὸ ποιεῖν
ποιήματα ἐτράπετο.

b Vit. Ap. Rhod. b (p. 2.5 Wendel)

οὗτος ἐμαθήτευσε Καλλιμάχῳ ἐν Ἀλεξανδρείᾳ ὄντι
γραμματικῷ . . . τινὲς δέ φασιν, ὅτι ἐπανῆλθεν ἐν
Ἀλεξανδρείᾳ καὶ αὖθις ἐκεῖσε ἐπιδειξάμενος εἰς ἄκρον
εὐδοκίμησεν, ὡς καὶ τῶν βιβλιοθηκῶν τοῦ Μουσείου
ἀξιωθῆναι αὐτὸν καὶ ταφῆναι δὲ σὺν αὐτῷ τῷ Καλ-
λιμάχῳ.

12 Suda a 3419

Ἀπολλώνιος· Ἀλεξανδρεὺς . . . μαθητὴς Καλλιμάχου,
σύγχρονος Ἐρατοσθένους καὶ Εὐφορίωνος καὶ Τι-
μάρχου, ἐπὶ Πτολεμαίου τοῦ Εὐεργέτου ἐπικληθέντος,
καὶ διάδοχος Ἐρατοσθένους γενόμενος ἐν τῇ προστα-
σίᾳ τῆς ἐν Ἀλεξανδρείᾳ βιβλιοθήκης.

13 Index praefectorum bibliothecae Alexandrinae
(P.Oxy. 1241 col. II, 1)

Ἀπολλώ]ν[ι]ος Σιλλέως Ἀλεξανδρεὺς ὁ [κ]αλούμενος
Ῥόδιος, Καλλ[ι]μάχου γνώριμος· οὗτος ἐγένετο καὶ

11

a Scholia to *Life of Apollonius of Rhodes*

Apollonius . . . lived at the time of the Ptolemies, a student of Callimachus. First associating with Callimachus as a private teacher . . . then later he turned to writing poems.

b *Life of Apollonius of Rhodes*

This man studied in Alexandria with Callimachus, who was a grammarian . . . Some say that he returned to Alexandria and after making a presentation there again was highly esteemed and was deemed worthy of the Libraries of the Museum; and that he was buried with Callimachus himself.

12 *Suda*

Apollonius: an Alexandrian . . . student of Callimachus, contemporary of Eratosthenes and Euphorion and Timarchus, in the reign of Ptolemy called Euergetes; Eratosthenes was his successor in the directorship of the Library in Alexandria.

13 List of the Heads of the Library of Alexandria (Oxyrhynchus papyrus)

Apollonius son of Silleus the Alexandrian, called Rhodius, a pupil of Callimachus. This man lived at the time of the

διδάσκαλος τοῦ τρίτου βασιλέως· τοῦτον διεδέξατο
Ἐρατοσθένης· μεθ᾽ ὃν Ἀριστοφάνης Ἀπελλοῦ Βυ-
ζάντιος.

14

a Tzetz. *De com. Gr.*, prooem. II (Koster, *Scholia in
Aristophanem*, pars 1 [1975], pp. 31–32)

ὁ Πτολεμαῖος φιλολογώτατος ὢν . . . τὰς βίβλους εἰς
Ἀλεξάνδρειαν συνήθροισεν καὶ δυσὶ βιβλιοθήκαις
ταύτας ἀπέθετο· ὧν τῆς ἐκτὸς μὲν ἀριθμὸς τετρακισ-
μύριαι δισχίλιαι ὀκτακόσιαι, τῆς δὲ τῶν ἀνακτόρων
ἐντὸς συμμιγῶν μὲν βίβλων ἀριθμὸς τεσσαράκοντα
μυριάδες, ἀμιγῶν δὲ καὶ ἁπλῶν μυριάδες ἐννέα·
ὧν τοὺς πίνακας ὕστερον Καλλίμαχος ἀπεγράψατο.
Ἐρατοσθένει δὲ ἡλικιώτῃ Καλλιμάχου παρὰ τοῦ
βασιλέως τὸ τοιοῦτον ἐνεπιστεύθη βιβλιοφυλάκιον.

b Tzetz. *De com. Gr.*, prooem. I (Koster, *Scholia in
Aristophanem*, pars 1 [1975], pp. 22–23)

Ἀλέξανδρος ὁ Αἰτωλὸς καὶ Λυκόφρων ὁ Χαλκιδεὺς
. . . τὰς σκηνικὰς διωρθώσαντο βίβλους . . . συμ-
παρόντος αὐτοῖς καὶ συνανορθοῦντος καὶ τοῦ βιβλιο-
φύλακος τῆς τοσαύτης βιβλιοθήκης Ἐρατοσθένους·
ὧν βίβλων τοὺς πίνακας Καλλίμαχος ἀπεγρά-
ψατο. . . . νεανίαι ἦσαν Καλλίμαχος καὶ Ἐρατοσθέ-
νης.

third Ptolemy and was his teacher. Eratosthenes succeeded him; and after him Aristophanes of Byzantium the son of Apelles.

14

a Tzetzes, *On Comedy*

Ptolemy, the greatest bibliophile . . . brought the books into Alexandria and placed them in two libraries; of these 42,800 were in the outer library and of those inside the palaces the number was 400,000 mixed volumes and 90,000 unmixed, single volumes. Later, Callimachus made indexes of these. The Library was entrusted by the king to Eratosthenes, a contemporary of Callimachus.

b Tzetzes, *On Comedy*

Alexander the Aetolian and Lycophron of Chalchis . . . corrected the books of the dramatists . . . and being present with them and assisting in the correction was Eratosthenes the director of the Library. Callimachus wrote indexes of these books . . . Callimachus and Eratosthenes were young men.

c Tzetz. *De com. Gr.*, prooem. II (Koster, *Scholia in Aristophanem*, pars 1 [1975], p. 32)

ὁ Καλλίμαχος νεανίσκος ὢν τῆς αὐλῆς ὑστέρως μετὰ τὴν ἀνόρθωσιν τοὺς πίνακας αὐτῶν ἀπεγράψατο. Ἐρατοσθένης δὲ ὁ ἡλικιώτης αὐτοῦ παρὰ τοῦ βασιλέως τὸ τοσοῦτον ἐνεπιστεύθη βιβλιοφυλάκιον. ἀλλὰ τὰ Καλλιμάχου καὶ τοῦ Ἐρατοσθένους μετὰ βραχύν τινα χρόνον ἐγένετο τῆς συναγωγῆς τῶν βίβλων, ὡς ἔφην, καὶ διορθώσεως, κἂν ἐπ᾽ αὐτοῦ τοῦ Πτολεμαίου τοῦ Φιλαδέλφου.

d Scholium q.d. Plautinum (ed. F. Ritschl, *Opuscula* I 5)

sicuti refert Callimachus aulicus regius bibliothecarius, qui etiam singulis voluminibus titulos inscripsit. fuit praeterea qui idem asseveret Eratosthenes non ita multo post eiusdem custos bibliothecae.

15 *Suda* ε 2898

Ἐρατοσθένης· . . . Κυρηναῖος, μαθητὴς φιλοσόφου Ἀρίστωνος Χίου, γραμματικοῦ δὲ Λυσανίου τοῦ Κυρηναίου καὶ Καλλιμάχου τοῦ ποιητοῦ. μετεπέμφθη δὲ ἐξ Ἀθηνῶν ὑπὸ τοῦ τρίτου Πτολεμαίου καὶ διέτριψε μέχρι τοῦ πέμπτου . . . ἐτέχθη δὲ ρκζ' ὀλυμπιάδι καὶ ἐτελεύτησεν π' ἐτῶν γεγονώς . . . μαθητὴν ἐπίσημον καταλιπὼν Ἀριστοφάνην τὸν Βυζάντιον.

c Tzetzes, *On Comedy*

Callimachus, being a young man of the court, next, after the correction [of the books], made indexes of these. Eratosthenes, his contemporary, was appointed Librarian by the king. But the work of Callimachus and of Eratosthenes took place a short time after the gathering of the books and their correction, as I said, if it was under the same Ptolemy Philadelphus.

d So-called *Scholium Plautinum*

So reports Callimachus, the Librarian of the royal court, who wrote labels for the single volumes. It was Eratosthenes in particular (keeper of the very same Library not long afterward) who insists on this.

15 *Suda*

Eratosthenes: . . . of Cyrene, A pupil of the philosopher Ariston of Chios, the grammarian Lysanias of Cyrene, and Callimachus the poet. He was summoned from Athens by Ptolemy III (246–221 BC) and he lived until Ptolemy V (205/4–181/0 BC) . . . He was born in the 126th Olympiad (276/3 BC) and died aged eighty . . . He left a distinguished pupil, Aristophanes of Byzantium.

16 Strabo 17.3.22

Κυρηναῖος δέ ἐστι καὶ Καλλίμαχος καὶ Ἐρατοσθένης,
ἀμφότεροι τετιμημένοι παρὰ τοῖς Αἰγυπτίων βασι-
λεῦσιν, ὁ μὲν ποιητὴς ἅμα καὶ περὶ γραμματικὴν
ἐσπουδακώς, ὁ δὲ καὶ ταῦτα καὶ περὶ φιλοσοφίαν καὶ
μαθήματα, εἴ τις ἄλλος, διαφέρων.

17 *Suda* a 3933

Ἀριστοφάνης· Βυζάντιος, γραμματικός . . . μαθητὴς
Καλλιμάχου καὶ Ζηνοδότου· ἀλλὰ τοῦ μὲν νέος, τοῦ
δὲ παῖς ἤκουσε . . . γέγονε δὲ κατὰ τὴν ρμδ΄ Ὀλυμ-
πιάδα.

18 *Suda* ι 706

Ἴστρος· . . . Κυρηναῖος ἢ Μακεδών, συγγραφεύς,
Καλλιμάχου δοῦλος καὶ γνώριμος.

19 Ath. 8.331d

Φιλοστέφανος [*FHG* vol. 3, p. 32, fr. 20] δ᾽ ὁ Κυρηναῖος
μὲν γένος, Καλλιμάχου δὲ γνώριμος.

19a Ath. 2.58f, 5.213f, 15.696f

Ἕρμιππος ὁ Καλλιμάχειος.

16 Strabo, *Geography*

Callimachus also was a Cyrenean, and Eratosthenes, both of whom were honored by the Egyptian kings, the former being a poet and at the same time an enthusiast for the study of letters, and the latter being superior, not only in respect to these, but also in philosophy and in mathematics, if ever anyone was.

17 *Suda*

Aristophanes: of Byzantium, a grammarian . . . student of Callimachus and of Zenodotus; he studied under the former as a young man, the latter as a youth. He lived in the 144th Olympiad.

18 *Suda*

Istrus: . . . from Cyrene or Macedon, historian, slave and pupil of Callimachus.

19 Athenaeus, *The Learned Banqueters*

Philostephanus [*FHG* vol. 3, p. 32, fr. 20], Cyrenean by birth and pupil of Callimachus.

19a Athenaeus, *The Learned Banqueters*

Hermippus the Callimachean.[1]

---

[1] Cf. Pfeiffer on *Fr. Doct.* 453.

20 Strabo 14.2.16

Ἁλικαρνασός . . . ἄνδρες δὲ γεγόνασιν ἐξ αὐτῆς . . .
Ἡράκλειτος ὁ ποιητής, ὁ Καλλιμάχου ἑταῖρος.

21 *Dieg.* 9.27 ad *Ia.* 202

Τοῦτο γέγραπται εἰς ἕβδομα θυγατρίου γεννηθέντος
Λέοντι γνωρίμῳ τοῦ ποιητοῦ.

22 Nomina adversariorum (Telchinum); *PSI* fr. 1.1–15 =
Aet. 1b (Schol. Flor. ad *Aet.* 1.1–15)

πολλάκι μοι Τελχῖνες ἐπιτρύζουσιν ἀοιδῇ

[   ]τει δ[. . .]. [. .].
            ]. Διονυσίοις δυ[σ]ί, τῷ . .
         ]νι κ(αὶ) τῷ ἴλειονι κ(αὶ) Ἀσκλη-
5 [πιάδη τῷ Σικε]λίδη κ(αὶ) Ποσειδίππῳ τῷ ονο
         ]υρίππῳ τῷ ῥήτορι κ(αὶ) Ανα
[   ]βῳ κ(αὶ) Πραξιφάνη τῳ Μιτυ-
[ληναίῳ, τοῖς με]μφομ(έν) ο[ι]ς αὐτοῦ τὸ κάτισ-
[χνον τ(ῶν) ποιη]μάτ(ων) κ(αὶ) ὅτι οὐχὶ μῆκος ηρα
10 [. . . . . . .]. . [. . . . .] ουμ(εν)ο.[.] οι .[. .].
. . .]. ων λου.[.]ο.[.] πα..[. . . .]
[παρα]τίθεταί τε ἐν σ(υγ)κρίσει τὰ ὀλίγων στί-
[χ(ων) ὄν]τ(α) ποιήματα Μιμνέρμου τοῦ Κο-
λοφω]νίου κ(αὶ) Φιλίτα τοῦ Κώιου βελτίονα
15 [τ(ῶν) πολ]υστίχων αὐτ(ων) φάσκων εἶναι [. . . .

20 Strabo, *Geography*

Halicarnasus . . . men who were born there . . . the poet
Heraclitus, a friend of Callimachus.[1]

  [1] Cf. *Epig.* 2.

21 *Diegeseis*

This (*Ia*. 202) was written for Leon, a friend of the poet,
on the occasion of the seventh-day celebration of his
daughter's birth.

22 List of Adversaries (Telchines); papyrus fragment

  Often the Telchines grumble at my poem

. . .

[3] . . . two Dionysioi. . .
[5] . . . and Asclepiades (Sicelides) and Posidippus;
the rhetor . . .
[7] and Praxiphanes of Mytilene.
and those blaming the excessive thinness of his poems
and because [he writes] nothing long

. . .
. . .

[12] He compares the short poems of Mimnermus of
Colophon and Philitas of Cos, saying that they are better
than their poems of many lines.

DE CARMINIBUS

23 Epigr. adesp.

Ὑμνῶ τὸν ὑψίζυγον ἐν πρώτοις Δία,
Φοῖβον δ' ἔπειτα, καὶ τρίτην τὴν Ἄρτεμιν,
Δῆλον τετάρτην, εἶτα Λουτρὰ Παλλάδος,
ἕκτην δὲ τὴν Δήμητρα τὴν παλαιτέραν.
5 μέλπω δὲ γραὸς τῆς φιλοξένου τρόπους
καὶ τὴν τελευτήν, Θησέως τε τὴν ἄγραν·
καὶ τῶν μεγίστων Αἰτίων τὴν τετράδα.
σκώπτω δ' ἐπαραῖς ἶβιν Ἀπολλώνιον·
καὶ τὴν Ἀθηνᾶν ὕστατον μέλπω πάλιν
10 γρίφῳ βαθίστῳ καὶ δυσευρέτοις λόγοις.

24 *Suda* μ 194

Μαριανός· . . . πατρίκιος γεγονώς, . . . κατὰ τὸν βα-
σιλέα Ἀναστάσιον. ἔγραψε βιβλία τοσαῦτα· . . . Με-
τάφρασιν Καλλιμάχου Ἑκάλης, Ὕμνων καὶ τῶν Αἰ-
τίων καὶ ἐπιγραμμάτων ἐν ἰάμβοις ϛωι'.

Aetia

25 [Ap. gramm.] *Anth. Pal.* 11.275

Καλλίμαχος τὸ κάθαρμα, τὸ παίγνιον, ὁ ξύλινος
νοῦς,
αἴτιος ὁ γράψας "Αἴτια Καλλιμάχου."

ON HIS POEMS

23 Anonymous epigram (6th c. AD or later)[1]

Among the first I sing of high-throned Zeus, then Phoebus, and third Artemis, fourth Delos, then the Bath of Pallas, and the sixth is ancient Demeter. [5] I sing of the character of the hospitable old woman and her death, and the hunt of Theseus, and the four books of the masterpiece, the *Aetia*. I mock with curses the Apollonian Ibis.

And again I sing of Athena last in the most impenetrable [10] riddles and words that are hard to decipher.

[1] Found among the manuscripts of the *Hymns*; see Pfeiffer's Introduction, p. lv.

24 *Suda*

Marianus: . . . born a [Roman] patrician . . . by the favor of the King Anastasius (AD 491–518). He wrote many books . . . a paraphrase of Callimachus' *Hecale*, *Hymns*, *Aetia*, and *Epigrams* in 6,810 iambics.

Aetia[1]

25 Pseudo-Apollonius the Grammarian

Callimachus the Waste, the Trifle, the Blockhead, the Culprit behind the "*Aetia* of Callimachus."

[1] Cf. T 23, T 24.

25a Mart. 10.4.9–12

Non hic Centauros, non Gorgonas Harpyiasque
    invenies: hominem pagina nostra sapit.
sed non vis, Mamurra, tuos cognoscere mores
    nec te scire: legas Aetia Callimachi.

26 Clem. Alex. *Strom.* 5.8.50 (vol. 2, p. 360.27 Stählin)

καὶ μυρία ἐπὶ μυρίοις εὔροιμεν ἂν ὑπό τε φιλοσόφων
ὑπό τε ποιητῶν αἰνιγματωδῶς εἰρημένα . . . Εὐφορίων
γὰρ ὁ ποιητὴς καὶ τὰ Καλλιμάχου Αἴτια καὶ ἡ Λυ-
κόφρονος Ἀλεξάνδρα καὶ τὰ τοιούτοις παραπλήσια
γυμνάσιον εἰς ἐξήγησιν γραμματικῶν ἔκκειται παι-
σίν.

27 De somnio (in *Aet.* Lib. 1 initio)

a *Aet.* 2d (*PSI* 1219 fr. 1, p. 71 Mass)

ὡς κ]ατ᾽ ὄναρ σ(υμ)μείξας ταῖς Μούσ[αις ἐν
    Ἑλι]κῶνι
εἰλήφοι π(αρ᾽ α)ὐτ(ῶν) τ(ὴν) τ(ῶν) αἰτίων [ἐξήγησιν
ἀ]ρτιγένειος ὤν, ὑ(π)έμνησε
....ἀ]π᾽ αὐτ(ῶν) ἀρχῃ[ν] λαβὼν ἑ᾽ος᾽α [......
       ] λόγου

b Prop. 2.34.31–32

Tu satius Musam leviorem imitere Philitae
    et non inflati somnia Callimachi.

25a Martial, *Epigrams*

You won't find Centaurs here or Gorgons or Harpies: my page has a human flavor. But you don't want to recognize your own behavior, Mamurra, or to know yourself: you should read the *Aetia* of Callimachus.

26 Clement of Alexandria, *Stromata*

And we would find numberless enigmatic sayings by philosophers and poets . . . Euphorion the poet and the *Aetia* of Callimachus and the *Alexandra* of Lycophron and parallels to these, set as an exercise in interpretation for the students of the grammarians.

27 On the Dream (at the Beginning of *Aetia*, Book 1)

a Scholia to Callimachus, *Aetia*

How in a dream he met with the Muses on Helicon and received from them the explanation of the causes of things when he was a young man, newly bearded, and he recalled them . . . and after learning from them about the origin . . . of the tale.

b Propertius, *Elegies*

It is better that you imitate the lighter Muse of Philitas and the slender dreams of Callimachus.

c Epigr. adesp. *Anth. Pal.* 7.42

Ἆ μέγα Βαττιάδαο σοφοῦ περίπυστον ὄνειαρ,
    ἦ ῥ᾽ ἐτεὸν κεράων οὐδ᾽ ἐλέφαντος ἔης.
τοῖα γὰρ ἄμμιν ἔφηνας, ἅτ᾽ οὐ πάρος ἀνέρες ἴδμεν
    ἀμφί τε ἀθανάτους ἀμφί τε ἡμιθέους,
5 εὖτέ μιν ἐκ Λιβύης ἀναείρας εἰς Ἑλικῶνα
    ἤγαγες ἐν μέσσαις Πιερίδεσσι φέρων·
αἱ δέ οἱ εἰρομένῳ ἀμφ᾽ ὠγυγίων ἡρώων
    Αἴτια καὶ μακάρων εἷρον ἀμειβόμεναι.

d v. etiam infra T 65 de Cydippe.

Hecale

28 Crinag. *Anth. Pal.* 9.545 (11 G.-P.)

Καλλιμάχου τὸ τορευτὸν ἔπος τόδε· δὴ γὰρ ἐπ᾽
    αὐτῷ
ὡνὴρ τοὺς Μουσέων πάντας ἔσεισε κάλους.
ἀείδει δ᾽ Ἑκάλης τε φιλοξείνοιο καλιὴν
    καὶ Θησεῖ Μαραθὼν οὓς ἐπέθηκε πόνους·
5 τοῦ σοὶ καὶ νεαρὸν χειρῶν σθένος εἴη ἀρέσθαι,
    Μάρκελλε, κλεινοῦ τ᾽ αἶνον ἴσον βιότου.

29 Ovid *Rem. am.* 747–48

cur nemo est Hecalen, nulla est quae ceperit Iron?
    nempe quod alter egens, altera pauper erat.

c Anonymous epigram

O great and renowned dream of the skilled son of Battus, truly you were of horn and not of ivory. For you revealed to us such things that we men did not know before about the gods and about the demigods, [5] when you caught him up and brought him from Libya to Helicon, bringing him among the Muses. And in answer to him asking about the origins (*Aetia*) of the primeval heroes, they spoke about the origins of the gods.

d See also T 65 on Cydippe below.

Hecale

28 Crinagoras

This burnished poem is by Callimachus, and on it the man shook out all the sails of the Muses. He sings of the hovel of hospitable Hecale and the labors that Marathon imposed upon Theseus. [5] May it be yours to have the strength of his young hands, Marcellus, and equal praise for a life of renown.

29 Ovid, *The Remedies for Love*

Why is there no man who has taken Hecale, no woman who has taken Irus? Because one was a beggar and the other was poor, of course.

30 *Priapea* 12.1, 3–5

Quaedam . . .
aequalis tibi, quam domum revertens
Theseus repperit in rogo iacentem,
5 infirmo solet huc gradu venire.

31 Petron. *Sat*. 135.8–10

qualis in Actaea quondam fuit hospita terra
digna sacris Hecale, quam Musa †loquentibus annis
†Baccineas veteres mirando† tradidit aevo.

32 Stat. *Theb*. 12.581–82

Si patriam Marathona metu, si tecta levasti
Cresia, nec fudit vanos anus hospita fletus.

33 Apul. *Met*. 1.23

si contentus lare parvulo Thesei . . . virtutes aemulaveris,
qui non est aspernatus Hecales anus hospitium tenue.

34 [Julian.] *Epist*. 186 Bidez-Cumont (41 Hertlein)

πάντως οὐδὲ τῆς Ἑκάλης ὁ Θησεὺς τοῦ δείπνου τὸ
λιτὸν ἀπηξίωσεν, ἀλλ' ᾔδει καὶ μικροῖς ἐς τὸ ἀνα-
γκαῖον ἀρκεῖσθαι.

30 *Priapea*

A certain woman . . . the same age as you, whom Theseus found lying on a funeral pile when he was returning home, [5] was accustomed to come here with a feeble step.

31 Petronius, *Satyricon*

Such a hostess as once there was in the land of Attica, Hecale worthy of rites, whose [fame] the Muse handed down throughout the years.

32 Statius, *Thebaid*

If ever you relieved from fear the homes of your native Marathon and of Crete, the hospitable old woman did not shed tears in vain.

33 Apuleius, *Metamorphoses*

If content with a small hearth you emulate . . . the virtues of Theseus, who did not reject the modest hospitality of the old woman Hecale.

34 Pseudo-Julian, *Epistles*

Not at all did Theseus disrespect the frugal meal of Hecale, but he knew how to make do even with small things as necessary.

CALLIMACHUS

35 Michael Choniates, *Theano* 337–42 (vol. 2, p. 386 Lambros)

εἰ δὲ γρηὶ πενιχρῇ, τὴν Ἑκάλην καλέεσκον,
Θησεὺς ὤφελε χάριν ξενίης ὀλίγης τε μιῆς τε
καί ἑ θανοῦσαν ἐνὶ μνήμῃ θέτο οὐ θνησκούσῃ—
340 οὐ γὰρ ἔην νήκουστα ἐτήσια δεῖπν᾽ Ἑκάλεια—
φεῦ δύστηνος ἐγὼ τόσ᾽ ὀφείλων πῶς ἀποτείσω
νήσῳ τῇδε . . . ;

36 Michael Choniates, *Dem.* 1.1 (vol. 1, pp. 157–59 Lambros)

Τὸν Θησέα τοίνυν ἐκεῖνον βαδίζοντά ποτε Μαραθῶ-
νάδε κατὰ ὑβριστοῦ ταύρου, μυρία παρεχομένου τοῖς
ἐκεῖ που Τετραπολίταις πράγματα, καταλῦσαι φασι
καὶ ἐπιξενωθῆναι παρά τινι γυναικί (Ἑκάλη τῇ γυ-
ναικὶ τὸ ὄνομα ἦν), γραῖ μὲν πεμπέλῳ καὶ πενιχρᾷ,
ξενοδόχῳ δ᾽ ἄλλως καὶ τοῖς παροδεύουσιν ἄκλειστον
ἀεὶ προβαλλομένη τὸ οἴκημα, καὶ οὕτω τι φιλοφρο-
νηθῆναι ἥδιον, ὡς ἀεὶ μεμνῆσθαι τῆς ὀλίγης τρα-
πέζης ἐκείνης καὶ αὐχμηρᾶς καὶ μὴ ἂν ἄλλην οὕτω
ποτὲ τερπνοτέραν λογίσασθαι. . . . ὅτε καὶ Θησεὺς ὡς
ὁ λόγος ἀρχόμενος ἀνεβάλετο τὸ πτωχικὸν καὶ ‹. . .›
φιλοξένημα τῆς Ἑκάλης τῆς Ἀττικῆς ἥδιστον ἐλο-
γίσατο.

35 Michael Choniates, *Theano*

If to the impoverished old woman they used to call Hecale, Theseus owed gratitude for her one, modest entertainment, and he memorialized her after she died, not while she was dying [340]—for the annual dinners of the Hecaleia were not unknown—alas, wretch that I am owing so much, how will I make recompense to Egypt . . . ?

36 Michael Choniates, *Address to Demetrius*

And so they say that Theseus traveling once to Marathon against the bull, which was doing much violence to the cities of the Tetrapolis there, lodged with and was entertained by a certain woman (Hecale was her name), a very old and poor woman, but hospitable and otherwise good (*Hec.* 2), always offering her home unlocked to those passing by, and so he was welcomed sweetly, so that always he recalled the table of that woman, though meager and squalid, and did not think that any other was ever more enjoyable. . . . And Theseus, as the story begins, put off the impoverished . . . thought the hospitality of Attic Hecale was the sweetest.

37 Schol. ad *Hymn* 2.106

ἐγκαλεῖ διὰ τούτων τοὺς σκώπτοντας αὐτὸν μὴ δύνα-
σθαι ποιῆσαι μέγα ποίημα, ὅθεν ἠναγκάσθη ποιῆσαι
τὴν Ἑκάην.

[**38**] Dubia

a Mnaseas [Patar.?] ap. Zenob. 3 (in cod. Atheniensi
1083)

Βουλίας γὰρ Ἀθηναῖος ἐγένετο, ὥς φησι Μνασέας,
Ἑκάλης υἱός.

b Ptolem. Chenn. *Kaine hist.* 3.3 ap. Phot. *Bibl.* 190
(p. 148.29b Bekker)

Περὶ Ἑκάλης, καὶ πόσαις γέγονεν ἐπώνυμον τοὔνομα.

Ibis

39 Ov. *Ib*. 45–46, 53–62, 643–44

45   prima quidem coepto committam proelia versu,
        non soleant quamvis hoc pede bella geri

. . .

postmodo, si perges, in te mihi liber iambus
        tincta Lycambeo sanguine tela dabit.
55   nunc quo Battiades inimicum devovet Ibin,
        hoc ego devoveo teque tuosque modo,
utque ille historiis involvam carmina caecis,
        non soleam quamvis hoc genus ipse sequi.

37 Scholia to Callimachus, *Hymn to Apollo*

He makes this charge on account of those blaming him because he was not able to write a long poem, and from this he was forced to write the *Hecale*.

[38] Dubia

a Mnaseas [Patrensis?] (in Zenobius)

For Bulias the Athenian was born, as Mnaseas says, the son of Hecale.

b Ptolemy Chennus, *Strange History* (in Photius, *Library*)

On Hecale, and how it got its name.

Ibis

39 Ovid, *Ibis*

I will engage in the first battles in the meter with which I began, although wars are not usually waged in elegy.
. . .

Later, if you continue, my book of iambs will send darts against you tinged with the blood of Lycambes. [55] Now in the same the way that the son of Battus curses his enemy Ibis, I execrate you and yours. And like that man I will wrap my songs in obscure stories, although I myself am not accustomed to pursue this style. It will be said that I

illius ambages imitatus in Ibide dicar
60   oblitus moris iudiciique mei,
et quoniam, qui sis, nondum quaerentibus edo,
    Ibidis interea tu quoque nomen habe.

. . .

643 postmodo plura leges et nomen habentia verum
    et pede, quo debent acria bella geri.

40 Ov. *Ib*. 447–50

et quae †Pentides† fecit de fratre Medusae,
    eveniant capiti vota sinistra tuo
et quibus exiguo volucris devota libello,
    corpora proiecta quae sua purgat aqua.

Epigrammata

41 Ath. 15.669c

διὰ τί δὲ λέγονται, τῶν ἐστεφανωμένων ἐὰν λύωνται
οἱ στέφανοι, ὅτι ἐρῶσιν; τοῦτο γὰρ ἐν παισὶ τὰ Καλ-
λιμάχου ἀναγιγνώσκων ἐπιγράμματα, ὧν ἐστι καὶ
τοῦτο, ἐπεζήτουν μαθεῖν, εἰπόντος τοῦ Κυρηναίου . . .

imitated his riddling, [60] forgetful of my custom and my taste, and since I do not yet announce your identity to those who ask, for the time being you too take the name of Ibis.

. . .

[643] Afterward you will read many verses that have your true name, and in a meter in which fierce wars ought to be waged.

40 Ovid, *Ibis*

And may the unlucky curses that Pittheus made concerning Medusa's brother fall on your head, and those with which the bird that cleans its own body with piss is vilified in a slender little book.

Epigrams

41 Athenaeus, *The Learned Banqueters*

Why do they say of those wearing wreaths that they are in love if the wreaths are unbound? For I was eager to learn this when I was a boy reading the epigrams of Callimachus, of which this is one. The Cyrenean says (*Epig.* 43.3–4).

COMMENTARII IN CALLIMACHI
CARMINA SCRIPTA

42 *Suda* α 4259

Ἀστυάγης· γραμματικός. Τέχνην γραμματικὴν . . .
καὶ εἰς Καλλίμαχον τὸν ποιητὴν ὑπόμνημα.

43 Suda ν 375

Νικάνωρ· ὁ Ἑρμείου, Ἀλεξανδρεύς, γραμματικός, γε-
γονὼς ἐπὶ Ἀδριανοῦ τοῦ Καίσαρος . . . Περὶ στιγμῆς
τῆς παρὰ Καλλιμάχῳ.

44 *Suda* α 4105

Ἀρχίβιος· Ἀπολλωνίου, γραμματικός. τῶν Καλλιμά-
χου ἐπιγραμμάτων ἐξήγησιν.

45 *Etym. Gen.* B s.v. ἀλυτάρχης

ἀλυτάρχης· ὁ τῆς ἐν τῷ Ὀλυμπιακῷ ἀγῶνι εὐκοσμίας
ἄρχων. Ἠλεῖοι γὰρ τοὺς ῥαβδοφόρους . . . παρὰ τοῖς
ἄλλοις καλουμένους ἀλύτας καλοῦσι . . . Ἡδύλος δὲ
εἰς τὰ ἐπιγράμματα Καλλιμάχου διὰ δύο λλ ὀνομάζει
τοὺς ἀλύτας ἀλλύτας. Μεθόδιος.

46 De Theonis in *Aetia* commentario v. *Aet.* 42, 53b.

COMMENTARIES ON THE POETRY
OF CALLIMACHUS

42 *Suda*

Astyages: a grammarian. [He wrote] the *Art of Grammar*
. . . and a treatise on the poet Callimachus.

43 *Suda*

Nicanor: the son of Hermeius, Alexandrian, grammarian;
lived in the time of the emperor Hadrian . . . *On Punctuation in Callimachus*.

44 *Suda*

Archibius: son of Apollonius, grammarian. [He wrote] a
commentary on the *Epigrams* of Callimachus.

45 *Etymologicum Genuinum*

Alytarch: the one governing the orderly conduct of the
Olympic games. The Eleans call rod carriers . . . the ones
who are called *alytas* by others . . . Hedylus in The *Epigrams* of *Callimachus* calls the *alytas* (thanks to the double lambdas) *allytas*. Methodius.

46 On the commentary of Theon, see *Aetia* 42, 53b.

47 De Epaphroditi in *Aetia* commentario v. *Aet.* 53–53a.

48 De Iamborum hypomnemate v. *Fr. Inc. Sed.* 555.

49 De Salusti commentario v. *Fr. Inc. Auct.* 741.

CETERA TESTIMONIA
MEMORIAE CALLIMACHEAE

50

a Apollod. νεῶν καταλ. (*BNJ* 244 F 157d) ap. Strabo 1.2.37

Ἀπολλόδωρος δὲ ἐπιτιμᾷ Καλλιμάχῳ συνηγορῶν τοῖς περὶ τὸν Ἐρατοσθένη, διότι, καίπερ γραμματικὸς ὤν, παρὰ τὴν Ὁμηρικὴν ὑπόθεσιν καὶ τὸν ἐξωκεανισμὸν τῶν τόπων, περὶ οὓς τὴν πλάνην φράζει, Γαῦδον καὶ Κόρκυραν ὀνομάζει.

b Strabo 7.3.6

καὶ τοῖς μὲν ἄλλοις συγγνώμην εἶναι Καλλιμάχῳ δὲ μὴ πάνυ, μεταποιουμένῳ γε γραμματικῆς· ὃς τὴν μὲν Γαῦδον Καλυψοῦς νῆσόν φησι, τὴν δὲ Κόρκυραν Σχερίαν.

47 On the commentary of Epaphroditus, see *Aetia* 53–53a.

48 On a treatise on the *Iambi*, see *Fragments of Uncertain Location* 555.

49 On the commentary of Salustius, see *Unattributed Fragments* 741.

REMINISCENCES OF CALLIMACHUS IN LATER AUTHORS

50

a Apollodorus of Athens, *Catalogue of Ships* (in Strabo, *Geography*)

Apollodorus, in agreement with the pupils of Eratosthenes, blames Callimachus because although he is a scholar he names Gaudus and Corcyra as scenes of Odysseus' wandering against the plan of Homer, who located the wanderings in the Ocean.

b Strabo, *Geography*

For the others there is an excuse, but not for Callimachus who claims to be a scholar. He says that the island of Calypso is Gaudos and that Corcyra is Scheria.[1]

[1] Cf. *Aet.* 13b.

51 Mel. *Anth. Pal.* 4.1.21–22

ἡδύ τε μύρτον Καλλιμάχου, στυφελοῦ ἀεὶ μέλιτος.

52 Catull. 65.15–16

sed tamen in tantis maeroribus, Ortale, mitto
    haec expressa tibi carmina Battiadae.

53 Catull. 116.1–2, 6

Saepe tibi studioso animo venante requirens
    carmina uti possem mittere Battiadae
. . .
    Gelli.

54 Cic. *De or.* 3.132

num geometriam Euclide aut Archimede, num musicam
Damone aut Aristoxeno, num ipsas litteras Aristophane
aut Callimacho tractante tam discerptas fuisse, ut nemo
genus universum complecteretur atque ut alius aliam sibi
partem, in qua elaboraret, seponeret?

55 [Verg.] *Catal.* 9.61–64

             si adire Cyrenas,
   si patrio Graios carmine adire sales
possumus . . .
         pingui nil mihi cum populo.

51 Meleager, Proem to the *Garland*

[and he inserted] the sweet myrtle berry of Callimachus, always with astringent honey.

52 Catullus

But nevertheless in such great griefs, Hortalus, I send you these translations of Callimachus.

53 Catullus

Often casting about (with my mind studiously on the hunt) for some means to send you, Gellius, the poems of Callimachus . . .

54 Cicero, *On the Orator*

It cannot be true, can it, that with Euclid or Archimedes practicing geometry, Damon or Aristoxenus music, or Aristophanes or Callimachus literature itself, that these were so separate that no one embraced the universal genre and that each separated off a part for himself in which to work, and another, another part?

55 Pseudo-Virgil, *Catalepton*

If we are able to approach Cyrene, to approach Greek wit in a Latin poem . . . I have nothing to do with the unsophisticated populace.

56 Hor. *Epist*. 2.2.91–92, 99–101

carmina compono, hic elegos: "mirabile visu
caelatumque novem Musis opus!"
. . .
discedo Alcaeus puncto illius; ille meo quis?
100 quis nisi Callimachus? si plus adposcere visus,
fit Mimnermus et optivo cognomine crescit.

57 Prop. 2.1.39–40

sed neque Phlegraeos Iovis Enceladique tumultus
    intonet angusto pectore Callimachus

58 Prop. 3.1.1–2, 5–6

Callimachi manes et Coi sacra Philitae,
    in vestrum, quaeso, me sinite ire nemus.
. . .
5 dicite, quo pariter carmen tenuastis in antro?
    quove pede ingressi? Quamve bibistis aquam?

59 Prop. 3.9.43–44

inter Callimachi sat erit placuisse libellos
    et cecinisse modis, †dure poeta, tuis.

60 Prop. 4.1.63–64

ut nostris tumefacta superbiat Umbria libris,
    Umbria Romani patria Callimachi.

56 Horace, *Epistles*

[Let's say] I compose lyrics, this man elegies: "wondrous to behold, a work engraved by the nine Muses!" . . . by his vote I come off as Alcaeus, and who is he by mine? [100] Who except Callimachus? If he seems to call for more, he becomes Mimnermus and is glorified by his chosen title.

57 Propertius, *Elegies*

But neither could Callimachus intone in his narrow breast the battle at Phlegra between Jupiter and Enceladus

58 Propertius, *Elegies*

Shades of Callimachus and sacred rites of Coan Philitas, allow me, I ask, to enter your grove . . . [5] Say in what cave did you both rarefy your song? With what foot did you enter? What water did you drink?

59 Propertius, *Elegies*

It will be enough to have been welcome among the little books of Callimachus and to have sung in your meters, hard poet.

60 Propertius, *Elegies*

So that Umbria will swell with pride at my books, Umbria the homeland of the Roman Callimachus.

345

61 Prop. 4.6.3–4

cera Philitaeis certet Romana corymbis
  et Cyrenaeas urna ministret aquas.

62 Ov. *Am.* 1.15.13–14

Battiades semper toto cantabitur orbe;
  quamvis ingenio non valet, arte valet.

63 Ov. *Am.* 2.4.19–20

est, quae Callimachi prae nostris rustica dicat
  carmina: cui placeo, protinus ipsa placet.

64 Ov. *Ars am.* 3.329–30

sit tibi Callimachi, sit Coi nota poetae,
  sit quoque vinosi Teia Musa senis.

65 Ov. *Rem. am.* 381–82

Callimachi numeris non est dicendus Achilles,
  Cydippe non est oris, Homere, tui.

66 Ov. *Rem. am.* 759–60

Callimachum fugito: non est inimicus Amori;
  et cum Callimacho tu quoque, Coe, noces.

61 Propertius, *Elegies*

Let Roman tablets contend with the ivy of Philitas, and let the urn supply Cyrenean waters.

62 Ovid, *Amores*

Callimachus will always be sung throughout the world; although he is not strong in talent, he is strong in art.

63 Ovid, *Amores*

There is a woman who says that the poems of Callimachus are rustic compared with mine: she whom I please, at once she pleases me.

64 Ovid, *The Art of Love*

May the Muse of Callimachus be known to you, the Muse of the Coan poet, and also the Teian Muse of the drunken old man.[1]

  [1] Anacreon.

65 Ovid, *The Remedies for Love*

Achilles should not be spoken of in the meters of Callimachus, nor is Cydippe suited to your mouth, Homer.

66 Ovid, *The Remedies for Love*

Flee from Callimachus. He is not an enemy of love; and with Callimachus you also, Coan,[1] do harm.

  [1] Philitas of Cos (4th c. BC), elegiac poet.

67 Ov. *Tr.* 2.367–68

nec tibi, Battiade, nocuit, quod saepe legenti
  delicias versu fassus es ipse tuas.

67a Ov. *Pont.* 4.16.32

Callimachi Proculus molle teneret iter

68 Strabo 9.5.17

[Καλλίμαχος] καὶ μὴν πολυίστωρ, εἴ τις ἄλλος, καὶ
πάντα τὸν βίον, ὡς αὐτὸς εἴρηκεν, ὁ ταῦτα μυθεῖσθαι
βουλόμενος.

69 Phil. Thess. *Anth. Pal.* 11.321

Γραμματικοὶ Μώμου στυγίου τέκνα, σῆτες ἀκανθῶν,
  τελχῖνες βίβλων, Ζηνοδότου σκύλακες,
Καλλιμάχου στρατιῶται, ὃν ὡς ὅπλον ἐκτανύσαντες,
  οὐδ' αὐτοῦ κείνου γλῶσσαν ἀποστρέφετε,
5 συνδέσμων λυγρῶν θηρήτορες, οἷς τὸ "μὶν" ἢ
    "σφὶν"
  εὔαδε καὶ ζητεῖν, εἰ κύνας εἶχε Κύκλωψ,
τρίβοισθ' εἰς αἰῶνα κατατρύζοντες ἀλιτροὶ
  ἄλλων· ἐς δ' ἡμᾶς ἰὸν ἀποσβέσατε.

67 Ovid, *Tristia*

Nor did it harm you, son of Battus, that often to the reader you yourself confessed your pleasures in verse.

67a Ovid, *Ex Ponto*

Proculus followed the soft path of Callimachus.

68 Strabo, *Geography*

[Callimachus] was very wise, if anyone was, and throughout his whole life, as he himself says, he wished to tell these tales.[1]

 [1] Cf. *Aet.* 178.30.

69 Philip of Thessalonica

Grammarians, children of infernal Momus,[1] diggers of thorns, wizards of books, cubs of Zenodotus,[2] soldiers of Callimachus, whom even as you hold him out as a shield you do not turn aside your tongue from that man; [5] hunters of lugubrious conjunctions, to whom *min* or *sphin* is a delight, and who inquire whether the Cyclops had dogs, may you wear yourselves away for eternity, sinners grumbling against others: extinguish your poison against me.

 [1] Personification of blame (Hes. *Theog.* 213–14).
 [2] Grammarian and editor of Homer; first head of the Library at Alexandria.

70 Phil. Thess. *Anth. Pal.* 11.347.5–6

γινώσκοιμ', ὅσα λευκὸν ἔχει στίχον· ἡ δὲ μέλαινα
  ἱστορίη τήκοι τοὺς Περικαλλιμάχους.

71 Antiph. *Anth. Pal.* 11.322

Γραμματικῶν περίεργα γένη, ῥιζώρυχα μούσης
  ἀλλοτρίης, ἀτυχεῖς σῆτες ἀκανθοβάται,
τῶν μεγάλων κηλῖδες, ἐπ' Ἠρίννη δὲ κομῶντες,
  πικροὶ καὶ ξηροὶ Καλλιμάχου πρόκυνες,
5 ποιητῶν λῶβαι, παισὶ σκότος ἀρχομένοισιν,
  ἔρροιτ', εὐφώνων λαθροδάκναι κόριες.

72 Pollian. *Anth. Pal.* 11.130

Τοὺς κυκλίους τούτους τοὺς "αὐτὰρ ἔπειτα" λέγοντας
  μισῶ, λωποδύτας ἀλλοτρίων ἐπέων.
καὶ διὰ τοῦτ' ἐλέγοις προσέχω πλέον· οὐδὲν ἔχω
  γὰρ
  Παρθενίου κλέπτειν ἢ πάλι Καλλιμάχου.
"θηρὶ μὲν οὐατόεντι" γενοίμην, εἴ ποτε γράψω
  εἴκελος, "ἐκ ποταμῶν χλωρὰ χελιδόνια."
οἱ δ' οὕτως τὸν Ὅμηρον ἀναιδῶς λωποδυτοῦσιν,
  ὥστε γράφειν ἤδη "μῆνιν ἄειδε, θεά."

73 Stat. *Silv.* 1.2.252–54

  Hunc ipse Coo plaudente Philitas
Callimachusque senex Umbroque Propertius antro
ambissent laudare diem.

70 Philip of Thessalonica

Let us recognize whatever verse has a clear meaning: may an obscure narrative waste away the Super-Callimachuses.

71 Antiphanes

Busybody race of grammarians, root grubbers of others' poetry, ill-fated bookworms who walk on thorns, defilers of the great, revelers in Erinna,[1] shrill and dry dogs of Callimachus, [5] outrage of poets, a mystery to beginning students, away with you, vermin secretly biting the eloquent!

[1] Author of the *Distaff* in hexameters, and epigrams (early 4th c. BC).

72 Pollianus

I hate cyclic poets who say "moreover hereafter," thieves of others' words. I devote myself more to elegies for I have nothing to steal from Parthenius[1] or Callimachus. May I become like a "long-eared beast"[2] if ever I write "from the rivers yellow celadine." But the cyclic poets steal shamelessly from Homer so that they even write "Sing, Goddess, the wrath."

[1] Parthenius of Nicaea (1st c. BC), grammarian and poet.
[2] Cf. *Aet.* 1.31.

73 Statius, *Silvae*

Philitas himself with Cos applauding and old man Callimachus, and Propertius in his Umbrian cave would have enlisted their supporters to praise this day.

351

74 Statius *Silvae* 5.3.156–57

       tu pandere doctus carmina
Battiadae latebrasque Lycophronis atri.

74a Plin. *HN* 1.4 (de nominibus insularum)

. . . Callimacho . . .

75 Mart. 4.23.1–5

Dum tu lenta nimis diuque quaeris
quis primus tibi quisve sit secundus
Graium quos epigramma comparavit;
palmam Callimachus, Thalia, de se
5   facundo dedit ipse Bruttiano.

76 Quint. *Inst*. 10.1.58

tunc et elegiam vacabit in manus sumere, cuius princeps habetur Callimachus, secundas confessione plurimorum Philitas occupavit.

77 Plin. *Ep*. 4.3.3 (ad Antoninum)

Nam et loquenti tibi illa Homerici senis mella profluere et, quae scribis, complere apes floribus et innectere videntur. Ita certe sum affectus ipse, cum Graeca epigrammata

74 Statius, *Silvae*

You were skilled in expounding the songs of Callimachus and the hidden places of the obscure Lycophron.[1]

[1] Contemporary of Callimachus and author of the riddling *Alexandra*.

74a Pliny the Elder, *Natural History*

. . . Callimachus . . .[1]

[1] Cf. *Fr. Inc. Sed.* 580.

75 Martial, *Epigrams*

While you, Thalia, are considering too leisurely and too long which of the Greeks who contest in epigram you should put in first place and which in second, Callimachus himself [5] has conceded the palm to eloquent Bruttianus.[1]

[1] Lustricus Bruttianus (Plin. *Ep.* 6.22).

76 Quintilian, *The Orator's Education*

Then there will be leisure to take in hand elegy, the chief of which is held to be Callimachus; and Philitas occupied second place by the judgment of most.

77 Pliny the Younger, *Letters* (to Arrius Antoninus)

When you speak, the honey of Homer's old man[1] seems to flow forth and bees seem to fill what you write with interwoven flowers. I was certainly so affected when lately I

[1] Nestor.

tua, cum mimiambos proxime legerem. Quantum ibi humanitatis venustatis, quam dulcia illa quam amantia quam arguta quam recta. Callimachum me vel Heroden, vel si quid his melius tenere credebam.

78 Lucian, *Hist. cons.* 57

Ὅμηρος . . . παραθεῖ τὸν Τάνταλον καὶ τὸν Ἰξίονα καὶ τὸν Τιτυὸν καὶ τοὺς ἄλλους. εἰ δὲ Παρθένιος ἢ Εὐφορίων ἢ Καλλίμαχος ἔλεγε, πόσοις ἂν οἴει ἔπεσι τὸ ὕδωρ ἄχρι πρὸς τὸ χεῖλος τοῦ Ταντάλου ἤγαγεν; εἶτα πόσοις ἂν Ἰξίονα ἐκύλισεν;

79 [Achill. Tat.] *Vit. Arat.* 1 (Martin 1974, 6)

Καλλιμάχου πολυΐστορος ἀνδρὸς καὶ ἀξιοπίστου Σολέα αὐτὸν γεγονέναι διὰ τούτων.

80 Origen, *C. Cels.* 3.43

ὁ Κυρηναῖος Καλλίμαχος πλεῖστα ὅσα ἀναγνοὺς ποιήματα καὶ ἱστορίαν σχεδὸν πᾶσαν ἀναλεξάμενος Ἑλληνικήν.

read your epigrams and your mimiambs. How much charm of human nature there was, how sweet they were, how antique, how subtle, how excellent. I thought I was holding Callimachus or Herodas,[2] or perhaps something even better than these.

[2] Contemporary of Callimachus who wrote *Mimiambi* in choliambic meter using Ionic dialect forms.

78 Lucian, *How to Write History*

Homer . . . runs by Tantalus and Ixion and Tityus[1] and the others. If Parthenius or Euphorion or Callimachus were writing, with how many words do you think they would have brought water to the lip of Tantalus? Then with how many would they have rolled along Ixion?

[1] Famous mythical sinners later consigned to Tartarus.

79 Pseudo-Achilles Tatius, *Life of Aratus*

[We learn] from Callimachus, a very learned and trustworthy man, that [Aratus] lived in Soli, through these [words].[1]

[1] *Epig.* 27.3.

80 Origen, *Against Celsus*

Callimachus the Cyrenean knew well as much poetry as possible and read through nearly all Greek history.

81 Porph. *Quaest. Hom.* in Schol. B ad *Il.* 23.422

ἀγνοήσας δὲ ταῦτα ὁ Καλλίμαχος φησίν· "ἀλλὰ—
ἁματροχιάς"· βούλεται μὲν γὰρ εἰπεῖν ὡς οὐδεὶς εἶδεν
ἴχνος διὰ τὸ θεῖν ὡς ἀνέμους. ἁματροχιαὶ δὲ οὐ δη-
λοῦσι τὰ ἴχνη τῶν θεόντων ἁρμάτων, ἀλλ᾽ αἱ μετὰ
τοῦ ρ λεγόμεναι ἁρματροχιαί.

82 Pallad. *Anth. Pal.* 9.175.1–2

Καλλίμαχον πωλῶ καὶ Πίνδαρον, ἠδὲ καὶ αὐτὰς
    πτώεις γραμματικῆς, πτῶσιν ἔχων πενίης.

83 Epigr. adesp. *Anth. Pal.* 7.41

Ἆ μάκαρ, ἀμβροσίῃσι συνέστιε φίλτατε Μούσαις
    χαῖρε καὶ εἰν Ἀΐδεω δώμασι, Καλλίμαχε.

84 Eunap. *VS* (p. 94 Boissonade)

ἡ δὲ αὐτὴ δόξα τῶν ἀνθρώπων Προαιρεσίῳ κἀκεῖνον
ἀντήγειρεν, ὡς εἰ Καλλίμαχον Ὁμήρῳ τις ἀναστή-
σειεν.

85 Suda σ 180

Σεβηριανός· ἀπὸ Δαμασκοῦ . . . τὰ μὲν οὖν τῶν ἄλ-
λων ποιητῶν ἀπεδέχετο μετρίως, τὸν δὲ Καλλίμαχον
εἰς χεῖρας λαβών, οὐκ ἔστιν ὅτε οὐ κατέσκωπτε τὸν
Λίβυν ποιητήν· ἀνιώμενος δὲ ἐπὶ μᾶλλον, ἤδη πολλα-
χοῦ καὶ τῷ βιβλίῳ προσέπτυε.

81 Porphyry, *Homeric Questions*

Not knowing these things Callimachus says *"alla . . . (h)amatrochias."* He wishes to say that no one saw the track (of the chariot) because it was running like the wind. But ⟨*h*⟩*amatrochiai* does not mean the tracks of running chariots, rather ⟨*h*⟩*armatrochiai* with a rho.[1]

[1] Cf. *Aet.* 54.10.

82 Palladas

I sell Callimachus and Pindar, and the very modes of grammar, I who am in the mode of poverty.

83 Anonymous epigram

Hail Callimachus, even in the house of Hades, happy, beloved companion to the immortal Muses.

84 Eunapius, *Lives of the Sophists*

The judgment of men compared even that one to Proaeresius,[1] just as if someone set Callimachus against Homer.

[1] Sophist teaching in Athens (3rd c. BC).

85 *Suda*

Severianus: from Damascus . . . accepted the works of the other poets with moderation, but when he took Callimachus into his hands he always jeered at the Libyan poet; and growing ever more vexed he spat in the book in many places.

86 Procl. *In Tim.* 1 ad 21c (vol. 1, p. 90.25 Diehl)

μάτην οὖν φληναφῶσι Καλλίμαχος καὶ Δοῦρις ὡς
Πλάτωνος οὐκ ὄντος ἱκανοῦ κρίνειν ποιητάς.

87 Procl. *Chrest.* ap. Phot. *Bibl.* (p. 319.14b Bekker)

λέγει δὲ καὶ ἀριστεῦσαι τῷ μέτρῳ Καλλῖνόν τε Ἐφέ-
σιον καὶ Μίμνερμον τὸν Κολοφώνιον, ἀλλὰ καὶ τὸν
Τηλέφου Φιλίταν τὸν Κῷον καὶ Καλλίμαχον τὸν Βάτ-
του· Κυρηναῖος δ᾽ οὗτος ἦν.

88 Diom. (*Gramm. Lat.* vol. 1, p. 484.21 Keil)

elegia: . . . quod genus carminis praecipue scripserunt
apud Romanos Propertius et Tibullus et Gallus, imitati
Graecos Callimachum et Euforiona.

89 Schol. (R) ad Ar. *Thesm.* 80

ἐπεὶ τρίτη ᾽στι· . . . τοῦτο δὲ αἰνιγματῶδες κατὰ Καλ-
λίμαχον ἄν τις φαίη.

90 Phot. *Quaest. ad Amphiloch.* 93.24 (*PG* 101, 599) ad
2 Cor. 8:23 εἴτε ὑπὲρ Τίτου κτλ.

. . . καὶ οἶδα ὅτι οὐκ ἄν σοι δόξῃ παράδοξον εἶναι τὸ
τοιοῦτον τῆς ἐλλείψεως εἶδος· πολλὰ γὰρ τοιαῦτα καὶ
παρ᾽ Ὁμήρῳ καὶ Ἀντιμάχῳ καὶ Ἀριστοφάνει Θουκυ-

86 Proclus, *Commentary on Plato's Timaeus*

Falsely, therefore, Callimachus and Duris[1] jabber about how Plato is not competent to judge poets.[2]

[1] Duris of Samos (4th c. BC), historian, critic of art and literature.　[2] Cf. *Fr. Inc. Sed.* 589.

87 Proclus, *Chrestomathy* (in Photius, *Library*)

He says that the best in this meter is Callinus of Ephesus and Mimnermus of Colophon,[1] but also Philitas the son of Telephus from Cos and Callimachus the son of Battus. This one was from Cyrene.

[1] Elegiac poets (7th c. BC).

88 Diomedes

Elegy: . . . a genre which among the Romans Propertius and Tibullus and Gallus wrote especially well in imitation of the Greeks Callimachus and Euphorion.

89 Scholia to Aristophanes, *Women at the Thesmophoria*

Since it is the third day: . . . Someone might say this is a riddle in the manner of Callimachus.

90 Photius, *Questions for Amphilochius* on Paul, *Second Letter to the Corinthians* (or concerning Titus, etc.)

. . . I do not think that such a style of ellipsis should seem to you to be surprising. There are many such things in Homer and Antimachus and Aristophanes and Thucydi-

δίδῃ τε καὶ Πλάτωνι καὶ Δημοσθένει, καὶ σχεδόν τι
τοῖς ἄλλοις ποιηταῖς τε καὶ λογογράφοις· εἰ καί τινες,
ὧν καὶ Καλλίμαχος ὁ Λίβυς, τά τε ἄλλα πολλῶν ἡτ-
τώμενοι καὶ οὐκ εἰς κόρον μόνον, ἀλλὰ καὶ εἰς ἐκτο-
πωτάτην τομὴν τοῦ συνήθους καὶ παρατροπὴν καὶ
ἀφαίρεσιν τὸ τοιοῦτον εἶδος βιασάμενοι, οὐκ ἀναι-
τίως ὑπὸ τῶν ἐπιστήμην ἐχόντων κρίνειν τὰ τοιαῦτα
(κριτικοὶ δὲ οὗτοι) ὑπὸ ἐπιτίμησιν ἔπεσον.

91 (T 9 Harder) Synesius Περὶ ἐνυπνίων 4 (p. 150.19
Terzaghi)

ὥστε εἰ μέν τῳ γέγονε θησαυρὸς ὕπνου δῶρον, οὐκ ἐν
θαυμαστοῖς ἄγω· οὐδ' εἴ τις, καταδαρθὼν ἄμουσος,
ἔπειτα ἐντυχὼν ὄναρ ταῖς Μούσαις καὶ τὰ μὲν εἰπών,
τὰ δὲ ἀκούσας, ποιητής ἐστι δεξιός, ὥσπερ ὁ καθ'
ἡμᾶς χρόνος ἤνεγκεν, οὐδὲ τοῦτο τῶν λίαν ἐστὶ παρα-
δόξων.

92 (T 10 Harder) P.Vindob. Gr. inv. 39966

Καλ‹λ›ιμά‹χου›
Αἰτίω(ν) α . [.] Ὕμ(νοι) [Ἐπιγράμ[ματα]
Ἑκάλη

des and Plato and Demosthenes and something close to it in other poets and prose authors, and if some (including Callimachus the Libyan) who are inferior to many in other respects are forced into such a style (not only to the point of excess, but even to a very strange deviation from the norm and error and abstraction), not without reason have they fallen under censure by these critics who have the knowledge to judge such things.

91 (T 9 Harder) Synesius, *On Dreams*

And so, if the gift of sleep is a treasure house for someone, I do not consider it amazing. Not even if some unpoetic person falls asleep and happens upon the Muses in a dream, and after saying some things and hearing others, is a skillful poet, as the one that time has brought us, not even this is too marvelous.

92 (T 10 Harder) List of Callimachus' Works (Vienna papyrus)

Of Callimachus
Aetia Book 1 . . . *Hymns*, *Epigrams*
Hecale.

CONCORDANCES

AETIA

a

Harder/LCL	Pfeiffer
1	1
1e + 2g	1a
2	2
2f	2a
2h	2b
2i	2c
2j	2d
3	3
4	4
5	5
6	6
7 + 7c	7
8	8
9	9
10	10
11	11
12	12
13	13
14	14
15	15
16	16

CONCORDANCES

Harder/LCL	Pfeiffer
17	17
18	18
19	19
20	20
21	21
22	22
23	23
24	24
25	25
25e	27
25f	28
26	26
29	29
30	30
30a	31a
31	31
31a	26–31a *Dieg.*
31c	31b
31d	31c
31e	31d
31f	31e
31g	31 b–e *Dieg.*
31h	31f *Dieg.*
31i	31g *Dieg.*
32	32
33	33
34	34
35	35
36	36
37	37

Harder/LCL	Pfeiffer
38	38
39	39
40	40
41	41
42	42
43 + 43b	43
44	44
45	45
46	46
47	47
48	48
49	49
50	50
51	51
52	52
53	53
54, 1–19	383
54b, 21–34	176
54c	177
54e, 2	557
54e, 9	333
54h	57
54i	59
55	55
56	56
58	58
60a	677
60b	597
60c	54
61	61

CONCORDANCES

Harder/LCL	Pfeiffer
62	62
62a	60
62c	665
63	63
64	64
65	65
66	66
67	67
68	68
69	69
70	70
71	71
72	72
73	73
74	74
75	75
76	76
77a	77a
78	78
79	79
80,1–22	80
80,19–24	82
81	81
83	83
84	84
85	85
86	86
87	87
88	88
89	89

AETIA

Harder/LCL	Pfeiffer
90	90
91	91
92	92
93	93
94	94
95	95
96	96
97	97
98	98
99	99
100	100
101	101
102	102
103	103
104	104
105	105
106	106
107	107
108	108
109	109
110	110
111	111
112	112
113	113
113d, 4	601
113e	115
113f + 114 + 114a	114
116	116
117	117
118	118

CONCORDANCES

Harder/LCL	Pfeiffer
119	119
120–37	120–37
138–74	138–74
175	175
178	178
179	179
180	180
181	181
182	182
183	183
184	184
185	185
186	186
187	187
188	188
189	189
190	190
190c	667
190d	725a recto
190e	725a verso

b

Harder/LCL	Supplementum Hellenisticum
7, 9–11	249A verso
7d	249A recto
17, 8–10	250
21c	251
46, 2–11	252
137a	238
137b	239
137c	240
137d	241
137e	242
137f	243
137g	244
137h	245
137i	246
137j	247
137k	248
137l	249

CONCORDANCES

c

Harder/LCL	Massimilla
1	1
1e, 12–19	2
2	4
2h	—
2i	—
2j	—
3	5
4	6
5	7
6	8
7 + 7c	9.1–34
8	10
9	11
10	12
11	13
12	17
13	14
14	15
15	16
16	18
17	19
18	20
19	21
20	22
21	23
22	24
23	25

Harder/LCL	Massimilla
24	26
25	27
25e	28
25f	29
26	30
29	31
30	32
30a	34
31	33
31a	—
31c	35
31d	36
31e	37
31f	38
31g	—
31h	—
31i	—
32	39
33	40
34	41
35	42
36	43
37	44
38	45
39	46
40	47
41	48
42	49
43 + 43b	50
44	51

CONCORDANCES

Harder/LCL	Massimilla
45	52
46	53.1a–1
47	54
48	56
49	57
50	59
51	60
52	61
53	62
54, 1–19	143
54b, 21–34	148.21–34
54c	149
54e, 2	151.2
54e, 9	151.9
54h	154
54i	156
55	146
56	147
58	155
60a	274
60b	264
60c	145
61	157
62	158
62a	160
62c	159
63	162
64	163
65	164
66	165

Harder/LCL	Massimilla
67	166
68	167
69	168
70	169
71	170
72	171
73	172
74	173
75	174
76	175.76b = 178
77a	180
78	181
79	182
80, 1–22	184.1–22
80, 19–24	184.19–24
81	183
83	185
84	186
85	187
86	188
87	189
88	190
89	191
90	192
91	193
92	195
93	196
94	197
95	198
96	199

CONCORDANCES

Harder/LCL	Massimilla
97	200
98	201
99	202
100	203
101	204
102	205
103	206
104	207
105	208
106	209
107	210
108	211
109	212
110	213
111	214
112	215
113	63
113d	119
113e	65
113f + 114 + 114a	64
116	66
117	67
118	68
119	69
120	70
121	71
122	72
123	73
124	74
125	75

Harder/LCL	Massimilla
126	76
127	77
128	78
129	79
130	80
131	81
132	82
133	83
134	84
134a	85
135	86
136	87
137	88
138	216
139	217
139a	218
140	219
141	220
142	221
143	222
144	223
145	224
146	225
147	226
148	227
149	228
150	229
151	230
152	231
153	232

CONCORDANCES

Harder/LCL	Massimilla
154	233.2–7
156	233.1
159	235
160	236
161	237
162	238
163	239
164	240
165	241
166	242
167	243
168	244
169	245
170	246
171	247
172	248
173	249
174	250
175	251
178	89
179	90
180	91
181	92
182	93
183	94
184	95
185	96
186	97
187	111

Harder/LCL	Massimilla
188	112
189	113
190	114
190c	110
190d	Schol. 163
190e	Schol. 162

HECALE

a

Hollis/LCL	Pfeiffer	*Supplementum Hellenisticum*
1	230	—
2	231	—
3	364	—
4	232	—
5	230 + v. 1, p. 506	—
6	230 + v. 1, p. 507	—
7	233	—
8	234	—
9	235	—
10	236.1–2	—
11	236.3	—
12	237	—
13	345	—
14	361	—
15	281	—
16	283	—
17	238.1–14	281
18	238.15–32	—
19	319	—
20	238a	—

CONCORDANCES

Hollis/LCL	Pfeiffer	Supplementum Hellenisticum
21	238b	—
22	238c	—
23	238d	—
24	311	—
25	269	—
26	525	—
27	—	282
28	239	—
29	240	—
30	241	—
31	242	—
32	243	—
33	244	—
34	246	—
35	251	—
36	248	283
37	334	—
38	249	—
39	250	—
40	253.1–6	285.1–6
41	254	—
42	253.7–12; 255	285.7–12
43	293	—
44	376	—
45	274	—
46	304	—
47	639, 327, 629	286
48	337, 366, 247, 284	287.1–10
49	350, 294, 368	287.11–30

Hollis/LCL	Pfeiffer	*Supplementum Hellenisticum*
50	367	—
51	300	—
52	272	—
53	275	—
54	329	—
55	290	—
56	365	—
57	313	—
58	310	—
59	296	—
60	245	—
61	306	—
62	328	—
63	256	—
64	257	—
65	292	—
66	355	—
67	258	—
68	259	—
69	260.1–15	288.1–15
70	260.16–29	288.16–29
71	261	289
72	374	—
73	260.30–43	288.30–43A
74	346; 260.44–69; 351	288.43B–69
75	267	—
76	271	—
77	326	—
78	371	—

Hollis/LCL	Pfeiffer	Supplementum Hellenisticum
79	262	—
80	263	—
81	342	—
82	252	284
83	264	—
84	266	—
85	305	—
86	321	—
87	338	—
88	308	—
89	349	—
90	288	—
91	297	—
92	341	—
93	268	—
94	344	—
95	307	—
96	279	290
97	—	291
98	280	—
99	278	—
100	285	—
101	339	—
102	277	—
103	302	—
104	273	—
105	265	—
106	270	—
107	276	—

Hollis/LCL	Pfeiffer	*Supplementum Hellenisticum*
108	343	—
109	282	—
110	286	—
111	287	—
112	289	—
113	291	—
114	295	—
115	298	—
116	299	—
117	301	—
118	303	—
119	309	—
120	312	—
121	314	—
122	315	—
123	316	—
124	317	—
125	318	—
126	320	—
127	322	—
128	323	—
129	324	—
130	330	—
131	325	—
132	331	—
133	332	—
134	333	—
135	335	—
136	336	—

CONCORDANCES

Hollis/LCL	Pfeiffer	Supplementum Hellenisticum
137	340	—
138	347	—
139	348	—
140	352	—
141	353	—
142	354	—
143	356	—
144	357	—
145	358	—
146	359	—
147	360	—
148	362	—
149	363	—
150	369	—
151	372	—
152	373	—
153	375	—
154	377	—
155	245	—
156	495	—
157	585	—
158	682	—
159	619	—
160	370	—
161	591	—
162	721	—
163	489	—
164	513	—
165	732	—

Hollis/LCL	Pfeiffer	Supplementum Hellenisticum
166	756	—
167	519	—
168	608	—
169	552	—
170	704	—
171	680	—
172	611	—
173	490	—
174	705	—
175	684	—
176	687	—
177	527a	—
178	725	—
179	741	—

b

Pfeiffer	Hollis/LCL
230	1
231	2
232	4
233	7
234	8
235	9
236.1–2	10
236.3	11
237	12
238.1–14	17
238.15–32	18
238a	20
238b	21
238c	22
238d	23
239	28
240	29
241	30
242	31
243	32
244	33
245	60
246	34
247	48
248	36
249	38
250	39

Pfeiffer	Hollis/LCL
251	35
252	82
253.1–6	40
253.7–12	42
254	41
255	42
256	63
257	64
258	67
259	68
260.1–15	69
260.16–29	70
260.30–43	73
260.44–69	74
261	71
262	79
263	80
264	83
265	105
266	84
267	75
268	93
269	25
270	106
271	76
272	52
273	104
274	45
275	53
276	107

CONCORDANCES

Pfeiffer	Hollis/LCL
277	102
278	99
279	96
280	98
281	15
282	109
283	16
284	48
285	100
286	110
287	111
288	90
289	112
290	55
291	113
292	65
293	43
294	49
295	114
296	59
297	91
298	115
299	116
300	51
301	117
302	103
303	118
304	46
305	85
306	61

HECALE

Pfeiffer	Hollis/LCL
307	95
308	88
309	119
310	58
311	24
312	120
313	57
314	121
315	122
316	123
317	124
318	125
319	19
320	126
321	86
322	127
323	128
324	129
325	131
326	77
327	47
328	62
329	54
330	130
331	132
332	133
333	134
334	37
335	135
336	136

CONCORDANCES

Pfeiffer	Hollis/LCL
337	48
338	87
339	101
340	137
341	92
342	81
343	108
344	94
345	13
346	74
347	138
348	139
349	89
350	49
351	74
352	140
353	141
354	142
355	66
356	143
357	144
358	145
359	146
360	147
361	14
362	148
363	149
364	3
365	56
366	48

HECALE

Pfeiffer	Hollis/LCL
367	50
368	49
369	150
370	160
371	78
372	151
373	152
374	72
375	153
376	44
377	154
489	163
490	173
495	156
513	164
519	167
525	26
527a	177
552	169
585	157
591	161
608	168
611	172
619	159
629	47
639	47
680	171
682	158
684	175
687	176

CONCORDANCES

Pfeiffer	Hollis/LCL
704	170
705	174
721	162
725	178
732	165
741	179
756	166

c

Supplementum Hellenisticum	Hollis/LCL
280	4
281	17
282	27
283	36
284	82
285.1–6	40
285.7–12	42
286	47
287.1–10	48
287.11–30	49
288.1–15	69
288.16–29	70
288.30–43A	73
288.43B–69	74
289	71
290	96
291	97

EPIGRAMS

a

Pfeiffer/LCL	Gow-Page	Source
1	54	*Anth. Pal.* 7.89
2	34	*Anth. Pal.* 7.80
3	52	*Anth. Pal.* 7.318
4	51	*Anth. Pal.* 7.317
5	14	Ath. 7.318b
6	55	Strabo 14.638
7	57	*Anth. Pal.* 9.565
8	58	*Anth. Pal.* 9.566
9	41	*Anth. Pal.* 7.451
10	33	*Anth. Pal.* 7.520
11	35	*Anth. Pal.* 7.447
12	43	*Anth. Pal.* 7.521
13	31	*Anth. Pal.* 7.524
14	44	*Anth. Pal.* 7.519
15	40	*Anth. Pal.* 7.522
16	37	*Anth. Pal.* 7.459
17	45	*Anth. Pal.* 7.271
18	38	*Anth. Pal.* 7.272
19	46	*Anth. Pal.* 7.453
20	32	*Anth. Pal.* 7.517
21	29	*Anth. Pal.* 7.525

CONCORDANCES

Pfeiffer/LCL	Gow-Page	Source
22	36	*Anth. Pal.* 7.518
23	53	*Anth. Pal.* 7.471
24	60	*Anth. Pal.* 9.336
25	11	*Anth. Pal.* 5.6
26	47	*Anth. Pal.* 7.460
27	56	*Anth. Pal.* 9.507
28	2	*Anth. Pal.* 12.43
29	5	*Anth. Pal.* 12.51
30	12	*Anth. Pal.* 12.71
31	1	*Anth. Pal.* 12.102
32	7	*Anth. Pal.* 12.148
33	21	*Anth. Pal.* 6.347
34	22	*Anth. Pal.* 6.351
35	30	*Anth. Pal.* 7.415
36	62	*Anth. Pal.* 7.454
37	17	*Anth. Pal.* 13.7
38	20	*Anth. Pal.* 13.24
39	19	*Anth. Pal.* 13.25
40	48	*Anth. Pal.* 7.728
41	4	*Anth. Pal.* 12.73
42	8	*Anth. Pal.* 12.118
43	13	*Anth. Pal.* 12.134
44	9	*Anth. Pal.* 12.139
45	10	*Anth. Pal.* 12.149
46	3	*Anth. Pal.* 12.150
47	28	*Anth. Pal.* 6.301
48	26	*Anth. Pal.* 6.310
49	27	*Anth. Pal.* 6.311
50	49	*Anth. Pal.* 7.458
51	15	*Anth. Pal.* 5.146

Pfeiffer/LCL	Gow-Page	Source
52	6	*Anth. Pal.* 12.230
53	23	*Anth. Pal.* 6.146
54	24	*Anth. Pal.* 6.147
55	16	*Anth. Pal.* 6.148
56	25	*Anth. Pal.* 6.149
57	18	*Anth. Pal.* 6.150
58	50	*Anth. Pal.* 7.277
59	59	*Anth. Pal.* 11.362
60	39	*Anth. Pal.* 7.523
61	42	*Anth. Pal.* 7.725
62	61	*Anth. Pal.* 6.121
63	63	*Anth. Pal.* 5.23
393/1	64	Diog. Laert. 211; SE *M.* 1.309
394/2	65	Ath. 7.284c, 7.327a
395/3	66	Steph. Byz. Δύμη
396/4	—	Schol. ad Ov. *Ib.* 591
397/5	—	Eustr. in Arist. EN 6.7.1
398/6	67	Schol. ad Dionys. Per. 3
399/7	68	*Anth. Pal.* 13.9
400/8	69	*Anth. Pal.* 13.10
401/9	70	Hephaest. 64.4 Cons.
402/10	—	Caes. Bass. *Gramm. Lat.* 6.255

b

Gow-Page	Pfeiffer/LCL	Source
1	31	*Anth. Pal.* 12.102
2	28	*Anth. Pal.* 12.43
3	46	*Anth. Pal.* 12.150
4	41	*Anth. Pal.* 12.73
5	29	*Anth. Pal.* 12.51
6	52	*Anth. Pal.* 12.230
7	32	*Anth. Pal.* 12.148
8	42	*Anth. Pal.* 12.118
9	44	*Anth. Pal.* 12.139
10	45	*Anth. Pal.* 12.149
11	25	*Anth. Pal.* 5.6
12	30	*Anth. Pal.* 12.71
13	43	*Anth. Pal.* 12.13
14	5	Ath. 7.318b
15	51	*Anth. Pal.* 5.146
16	55	*Anth. Pal.* 6.148
17	37	*Anth. Pal.* 13.7
18	57	*Anth. Pal.* 6.150
19	39	*Anth. Pal.* 13.25
20	38	*Anth. Pal.* 13.24
21	33	*Anth. Pal.* 6.347
22	34	*Anth. Pal.* 6.351
23	53	*Anth. Pal.* 6.146
24	54	*Anth. Pal.* 6.147
25	56	*Anth. Pal.* 6.149
26	48	*Anth. Pal.* 6.310
27	49	*Anth. Pal.* 6.311

Gow-Page	Pfeiffer/LCL	Source
28	47	*Anth. Pal.* 6.301
29	21	*Anth. Pal.* 7.525
30	35	*Anth. Pal.* 7.415
31	13	*Anth. Pal.* 7.524
32	20	*Anth. Pal.* 7.517
33	10	*Anth. Pal.* 7.520
34	2	*Anth. Pal.* 7.80
35	11	*Anth. Pal.* 7.447
36	22	*Anth. Pal.* 7.518
37	16	*Anth. Pal.* 7.459
38	18	*Anth. Pal.* 7.272
39	60	*Anth. Pal.* 7.523
40	15	*Anth. Pal.* 7.522
41	9	*Anth. Pal.* 7.451
42	61	*Anth. Pal.* 7.725
43	12	*Anth. Pal.* 7.521
44	14	*Anth. Pal.* 7.519
45	17	*Anth. Pal.* 7.271
46	19	*Anth. Pal.* 7.453
47	26	*Anth. Pal.* 7.460
48	40	*Anth. Pal.* 7.728
49	50	*Anth. Pal.* 7.458
50	58	*Anth. Pal.* 7.277
51	4	*Anth. Pal.* 7.317
52	3	*Anth. Pal.* 7.318
53	23	*Anth. Pal.* 7.471
54	1	*Anth. Pal.* 7.89
55	6	Strabo 14.638
56	27	*Anth. Pal.* 9.507
57	7	*Anth. Pal.* 9.565

CONCORDANCES

Gow-Page	Pfeiffer/LCL	Source
58	8	*Anth. Pal.* 9.566
59	59	*Anth. Pal.* 11.362
60	24	*Anth. Pal.* 9.336
61	62	*Anth. Pal.* 6.121
62	36	*Anth. Pal.* 7.454
63	63	*Anth. Pal.* 5.23
64	393/1	Diog. Laert. 211; SE *M.* 1.309
65	394/2	Ath. 7.284c, 7.327a
66	395/3	Steph. Byz. Δύμη
67	398/6	Schol. ad Dionys. Per. 3
68	399/7	*Anth. Pal.* 13.9
69	400/8	*Anth. Pal.* 13.10
70	401/9	Hephaest. 64.4 Cons.

c

Source	Gow-Page	Pfeiffer/LCL
Anth. Pal. 5.6	11	25
Anth. Pal. 5.23	63	63
Anth. Pal. 5.146	15	51
Anth. Pal. 6.121	61	62
Anth. Pal. 6.146	23	53
Anth. Pal. 6.147	24	54
Anth. Pal. 6.148	16	55
Anth. Pal. 6.149	25	56
Anth. Pal. 6.150	18	57
Anth. Pal. 6.301	28	47
Anth. Pal. 6.310	26	48
Anth. Pal. 6.311	27	49
Anth. Pal. 6.347	21	33
Anth. Pal. 6.351	22	34
Anth. Pal. 7.80	34	2
Anth. Pal. 7.89	54	1
Anth. Pal. 7.271	45	17
Anth. Pal. 7.272	38	18
Anth. Pal. 7.277	50	58
Anth. Pal. 7.317	51	4
Anth. Pal. 7.318	52	3
Anth. Pal. 7.415	30	35
Anth. Pal. 7.447	35	11
Anth. Pal. 7.451	41	9
Anth. Pal. 7.453	46	19
Anth. Pal. 7.454	62	36
Anth. Pal. 7.458	49	50

Source	Gow-Page	Pfeiffer/LCL
Anth. Pal. 7.459	37	16
Anth. Pal. 7.460	47	26
Anth. Pal. 7.471	53	23
Anth. Pal. 7.517	32	20
Anth. Pal. 7.518	36	22
Anth. Pal. 7.519	44	14
Anth. Pal. 7.520	33	10
Anth. Pal. 7.521	43	12
Anth. Pal. 7.522	40	15
Anth. Pal. 7.523	39	60
Anth. Pal. 7.524	31	13
Anth. Pal. 7.525	29	21
Anth. Pal. 7.725	42	61
Anth. Pal. 7.728	48	40
Anth. Pal. 9.336	60	24
Anth. Pal. 9.507	56	27
Anth. Pal. 9.565	57	7
Anth. Pal. 9.566	58	8
Anth. Pal. 11.362	59	59
Anth. Pal. 12.43	2	28
Anth. Pal. 12.51	5	29
Anth. Pal. 12.71	12	30
Anth. Pal. 12.73	4	41
Anth. Pal. 12.102	1	31
Anth. Pal. 12.118	8	42
Anth. Pal. 12.134	13	43
Anth. Pal. 12.139	9	44
Anth. Pal. 12.148	7	32
Anth. Pal. 12.149	10	45
Anth. Pal. 12.150	3	46

Source	Gow-Page	Pfeiffer/LCL
Anth. Pal. 12.230	6	52
Anth. Pal. 13.7	17	37
Anth. Pal. 13.9	68	399/7
Anth. Pal. 13.10	69	400/8
Anth. Pal. 13.24	20	38
Anth. Pal. 13.25	19	39
Ath. 7.284c, 7.327a	65	394/2
Ath. 7.318b	14	5
Diog. Laert. 211; SE *M.* 1.309	64	393/1
Hephaest. 64.4 Cons.	70	401/9
Schol. Dionys. Per. 3	67	398/6
Steph. Byz. Δύμη	66	395/3
Strabo 14.638	55	6

INDEX

Combinations of Roman and Arabic numerals indicate references to volume and page numbers, respectively (e.g., III.4 refers to vol. III, p. 4). All other references follow conventions appropriate to each work.

INDEX

INDEX

411

INDEX

412

INDEX

INDEX

INDEX

434

INDEX

438

INDEX

441

INDEX